The Little Dictators

The Little Dictators

The History of Eastern Europe since 1918

Antony Polonsky

Department of International History
London School of Economics

Routledge & Kegan Paul
London and Boston

First published in 1975
by Routledge & Kegan Paul Ltd
Broadway House, 68–74 Carter Lane,
London EC4V 5EL and
9 Park Street,
Boston, Mass. 02108, USA
Set in Monotype Walbaum
and printed in Great Britain by
Unwin Brothers Limited
The Gresham Press, Old Woking, Surrey
A member of the Staples Printing Group
© Antony Polonsky 1975

ISBN 0 7100 8095 6

For my parents,
in love and gratitude

Contents

Maps

Preface

What I have tried to do in this book is to give a short account of how and why democratic political institutions broke down in Eastern Europe after 1918 and to describe the character of the regimes which replaced them. Eastern Europe was one of the first places where the belief was applied that western-style democracy could be transplanted to areas which had vastly different histories and social structures from those of Western Europe and North America where this political system had grown up. The experience of Eastern Europe in the interwar years thus seems to me to have considerable relevance to an understanding of the world today. The regimes which emerged in the wake of the democratic collapse have many parallels to what has occurred in the third world since 1945. In particular, though fascism has been entirely discredited as a result of the German débâcle, the combination of social radicalism and nationalism, which one finds in such movements as the Hungarian Arrow Cross or the Rumanian Iron Guard, has been frequently repeated in Africa and Asia. I hope this book will enable those not particularly familiar with Eastern Europe to become aware of these parallels. I have therefore tried to keep my narrative as simple as possible. There is a widespread belief that the politics of Eastern Europe, with its multiplicity of national groups and political orientations, is highly complex. This I do not believe to be the case, and I have tried to show, as clearly as I can, how politics operated in the principal countries of the area.

I would like to thank Macmillan International, Ltd, for

permission to reproduce maps from *Independent Eastern Europe* by C. A. Macartney and A. W. Palmer.

I owe too many debts of gratitude to the large number of people who have helped me to mention them all here. But I should like here to record my gratitude to Professor James Joll, who first interested me in Eastern Europe, to Esmonde Roberson and George Schöpflin who read and criticized my manuscript and to my wife, without whom, the cliché phrase for once true, this book could never have appeared.

Introduction

Eastern Europe is often seen as a homogeneous entity. Yet if we define the area as that between Russia and Germany and include the peripheral areas of Greece, Austria and the Baltic states, it comprised twelve countries (thirteen with Finland) in the period between the two wars. They differed greatly in size from Poland, the sixth largest state in Europe with a population of 30 million, to Albania with barely a million. Eastern Europe had no religious unity, for while Poland, Czechoslovakia, Hungary, Lithuania and Austria were predominantly Catholic, Estonia, Latvia and Finland were Lutheran, Bulgaria, Rumania, Greece and, for the most part, Yugoslavia were Orthodox, and Albania was predominantly Moslem. Neither did the area possess any geographic unity; there is a strong contrast between the flat open plains of north-eastern Europe, the Danube basin ringed on the north and east by the Carpathians, and the rugged mountainous terrain of the Balkans.

The countries of Eastern Europe also differed in their level of economic development, highest in the Czech lands of Bohemia and Moravia, one of the main industrial centres of the Austro-Hungarian monarchy, and lowest in Bulgaria, Greece and Albania. They had been on opposing sides during the First World War: Bulgaria and Hungary had fought with the Central Powers, while Serbia and, at times, Rumania and Greece had been on the side of the Allies. The Czechs had been committed to the Allies while Polish forces had fought on both sides. The political organization of the different countries was also dissimilar: Rumania, Yugoslavia, Bulgaria, Albania and Greece were monarchies in which the prerogatives of the king were a constant and usually disruptive factor in politics, while Czechoslovakia, Poland and the Baltic states were republics. Hungary was an anomaly: a monarchy without a king because of the impossibility of a Habsburg restoration. In the Austrian republic, too, there remained a fair measure of support for the Habsburgs.

The Hungarians, the Poles and the Croats were 'historic' nationalities. Their traditional aristocracies had survived the loss of independence, a factor which considerably affected the political and social framework. In these areas, the attitudes of the gentry had been adopted by the rest of society, in particular their disdain for trade and industry and their belief that service to the state, primarily through the civil service, was the only career, apart from agriculture, worthy of a gentleman. It was a characteristic feature of these countries that liberal capitalism was introduced to a significant extent by non-native groups, primarily Germans and Jews. The patriarchal way of life of the country squire on his estate still enjoyed great prestige, and almost all Polish and Hungarian industrialists, like their English counterparts, bought land and tried to make themselves over as gentry.

The Czechs and Slovaks, the nations of the Balkans and somewhat questionably the Rumanians, were 'non-historic' nationalities. Their native aristocracies had been destroyed as a result of the different foreign conquests they had suffered, and their national revivals had been inspired and led by the sons of peasants who had moved to the towns. The political culture of these areas had a markedly different character from that of Poland and Hungary. In the Czech lands, the struggle against the economically dominant German landowners and industrialists had created a resourceful and efficient, if somewhat *petit bourgeois* and philistine, Czech society. In both Serbia and Bulgaria, the links between the ruling élite, almost entirely of peasant origin, and the mass of the population were much closer than elsewhere in the area. Rumania is slightly more complicated a case. The traditional aristocracy in Regatine Rumania (the area which had become independent in 1862), though largely Greek in origin, had been closely linked with the struggle for national independence and played a large part in national life before 1914. In Transylvania, however, the landowners were almost entirely Hungarian and the Rumanian population was overwhelmingly peasant.

Yet, in spite of these marked differences, the countries of Eastern Europe did have an enormous amount in common. In the first place, they all lie to the east of what is perhaps the most fundamental frontier in European history, the line running roughly along the Elbe and then down to the Mediterranean at Trieste, which divides those areas in which serfdom disappeared as a result mainly of economic forces in the fifteenth and sixteenth centuries, from those in which it survived until the nineteenth century. Serfdom was only abolished in Austria-Hungary in 1848, in Prussia in the 1850s and in Russia in 1861. In all cases the abolition came from above, as an act of government and it tended for the most part to favour the landowners. In Prussia, the peasant in the majority of cases received no title to the land he cultivated, and tended increasingly to become a landless agricultural labourer – although a class of prosperous peasants also emerged. It is true that in Russian Poland (the Congress Kingdom) the abolition of the *corvée* was seen as a means for undercutting the power of the Polish gentry, who were regarded by the Russian authorities as the main instigators of the nationalist uprisings of 1831 and 1863. Thus the peasants received the freehold of their land under fairly favourable conditions. But elsewhere in Russia, as in Austria-Hungary, substantial areas of conflict between peasants and landowners remained.

The situation was somewhat more complex in the areas which had been formerly ruled by Turkey (Serbia, Bulgaria, Greece, Albania and Regatine Rumania). Moldavia and Wallachia, the constituent parts of the Regat, had enjoyed wide-ranging autonomy and the boyars were left to settle their accounts with their peasants as they wished – as indeed they did. After the achievement of independence in 1862, Alexandru Cuza, who had been elected prince in both Moldavia and Wallachia, attempted to improve the position of the peasants by ending serfdom. The law he enacted in 1864 freed them of all restrictions on their movements and abolished all labour dues and contributions in kind. The peasants were to receive holdings and for this purpose up to two-thirds of the boyars' land could be subdivided. In practice, however, the local landowners were able to frustrate his intentions, and though the peasants were no longer bound, most land remained in the hands of the boyars. A divergent development took place in Bulgaria, Serbia and Greece, which had been more directly administered by the Turks. The position of the peasants in these areas had improved as a result of the Ottoman conquest, though serfdom remained the rule. But as the central government's authority weakened, the power of the local beys over their peasants increased continuously. The growing rights of the landowners in relation to their peasants were given legal recognition by the new land law of 1858, which ended serfdom, but at the same time confirmed the property rights of landlords, including leaseholders and tax-farmers. The actual cultivators found their rights and status much diminished and became 'sharecroppers or hired labourers at the mercy of a reinforced landlord class'.[1] With independence, however, the power of the beys, who were to a considerable extent Moslem and identified with Turkish rule, was broken. Land passed into the hands of the peasantry, and as a result, the proportion of large landholdings in Serbia and Bulgaria was the lowest in Eastern Europe.

The long persistence of serfdom had a deep and lasting effect on economic, social and political life. Without exaggeration, this effect can be compared to the impact of slavery in the West Indies, in the Southern States of America or in Brazil. Even today, more than 100 years after the abolition of serfdom, some of the attitudes which resulted from it are still visible. Serfdom had meant that for several hundred years these societies had been divided into landlords and serfs. As a result a native intermediary class had not arisen. At the same time, the enormous gap between landlords and peasants meant that there was no mobility from one group to the other. In eighteenth-century Poland for instance, it had been an aristocratic commonplace that the peasant was a completely different type of being from the noble. He was descended from Ham, whereas the gentry took their origin from Japhet and the Jews from Shem. These attitudes were slow in dying, and this resulted in an almost caste-like division within the society. Harold Nicolson has described his encounter at the Versailles Peace Conference with the Polish diplomat Count Potocki. When the name of Paderewski, the prime minister of the new state, was mentioned, Potocki described him as 'a very remarkable man'. 'Do you realize that he was born in one of my villages? And yet when I speak to him,

I have absolutely the impression of conversing with an equal.'[2]
The division of society into landlords and serfs had important consequences. It meant that the intermediary occupations of trading and money-lending were everywhere performed by groups which differed in language and religion from the majority: Jews and Germans in Poland, Slovakia and Hungary, Germans in the Czech lands, Greeks and Jews in Rumania and to a lesser extent Bulgaria and Serbia. This had the further effect of hindering the emergence of a native middle class, and with the rise of new nationalist ideas the Jews, in particular, became the object of resentment which trading communities have everywhere provoked. Moreover, even when a native middle class did begin to develop, it remained weak everywhere, except in the Czech lands. The dominant urban group was rather the intelligentsia, which embraced a far wider group than it would have in the West and, in fact, included all people with secondary education as well as those who had adopted the manners and language of the educated classes. The intelligentsia differed somewhat in character in the 'historic' and 'non-historic' nations. In the former it tended to take over many of the values of the gentry, their belief that they embodied the conscience of the nation and had a special responsibility for its survival and future development. In Poland, for instance, in the words of the journalist Leon Wasilewski, 'the intelligentsia was the élite which kindled the national spirit from a spark among ashes and carried its flame to the reborn Polish state'.[3] In addition, the intelligentsia shared with the aristocracy a general disdain for trade and commerce, which were regarded as careers unsuitable for a gentleman. When the lesser gentry in Poland and Hungary found their economic livelihood undermined in the 1870s and 1880s by the importation of cheap wheat from the Ukraine and the USA, they flocked into the towns. But there they were only prepared to consider careers in the liberal professions or, more important, in the civil service. Hungary was thus burdened with a large class of officials of gentry origin, who were not only fervent Magyarizers, but who also left the development of trade and industry to the Jewish and German minorities. A parallel development took place in both Russian and Austrian Poland, though in the former area it was somewhat inhibited by the hostility of the Russian government to Polish national aspirations. According to the Polish politician Roman Dmowski, a

severe critic of the aristocratic prejudices of the Polish gentry, writing in 1904, 'the new forms of national production were initiated by foreign elements, free of the traditions of Polish passivity, particularly Jews and Germans, and the declassed *petit-noble* intelligentsia made use of them only to obtain ready-made jobs'.[4]

The feeling of special mission was also felt by the intelligentsia of countries where the native aristocracy had been destroyed, such as Serbia or Bulgaria. Yet paradoxically the intelligentsia even in these countries, where it was largely of peasant origin, was divided by a great gulf from the illiterate and poverty-stricken peasantry. This gap between the intelligentsia and the masses often led to disdain and even disgust for the primitive peasantry on the part of townspeople, a feeling which was particularly strong among officials and at its worst in the Balkans. It is very well described by Hugh Seton-Watson:[5]

> The Balkan official regards himself as immeasurably superior to the peasants, among whom he lives and from whose ranks he has sprung. To be an official is the fondest dream of every able young son of a peasant. The Balkan official does not like to work. He considers himself so fine a fellow that the state should be proud to support him for life and should not ask him to make efforts that will tax his intellect or character. A visitor to a Balkan Ministry or Police Headquarters in the middle of the morning will find the rooms filled with good-natured fellows comfortably enjoying a cup of Turkish coffee and a chat with their friends. The papers lie on their desks. Outside stand, sit and squat patient queues of peasants awaiting their various permits and receipts. Foreigners and citizens with *protekcja* obtain swift and prompt attention, but the people can wait. They have waited many hundreds of years already for justice and a few more hours will not make much difference.

Yet at the same time, the intelligentsia all over Eastern Europe was almost neurotically obsessed with the desire to re-establish its lost links with the mass of the population. This led everywhere in the area to movements among the intelligentsia which sought, like the Russian *narodniki* of the nineteenth century, to find the true soul of their country in the villages.

These movements were of the most varied character politically. In Hungary in the 1930s the 'village explorers' sought a third, agrarian, path for their country which would be neither communist nor fascist, and basically upheld western democratic values. In Rumania, a similar attempt to seek out peasant traditions and redress the grievances of the rural population led to the fascist mysticism of the Iron Guard, with its anti-western populism and its exploitation of peasant superstitions and rituals. According to the leaders of the Iron Guard, western liberal ideas were fundamentally alien to the deepest aspirations of the Rumanian people. As a Legionary paper wrote in 1933: 'The imported state, the state of today was invented for us by the economic and political interests of the European powers. . . . The invention-state continued as their state, the state of the foreign protectors . . . and of their tools.'[6]

A further consequence of the way in which serfdom was abolished was the persistence, outside Serbia and Bulgaria, of a substantial degree of large landholding. In Regatine Rumania before the great peasant *jacquerie* of 1907, 48·6 per cent of the land had been in estates of more than 100 hectares, while in Poland in 1921, 47·3 per cent had been in holdings of over 50 hectares. In Hungary, as late as 1935, 48·1 per cent had been in estates of over 100 acres. Here the degree of concentration had been particularly marked, and 30 per cent had been in estates of more than 1,000 acres. In the Czech lands, before 1914, 26 per cent of the total state area had been in the hands of about 1,000 families. The extent to which large estates had disappeared in Bulgaria can be judged from the fact that in 1934 only 6 per cent of all arable land was held in estates of more than thirty hectares.[7]

The large estates were generally efficient and well-run, though there were cases of gross neglect both in Hungary and Rumania. But they constituted everywhere a great source of social bitterness, which was exacerbated by the fact that in many regions the landowners differed in nationality from their peasants and were in many cases connected with the pre-independence regimes. The most far-reaching land reforms thus took place in Czechoslovakia, where the landowners were German in the Czech lands and Hungarian in Slovakia, and in Yugoslavia, where the landowners in Bosnia were largely Moslem, and those in Vojvodina mainly Hungarian. The

Croatian gentry, somewhat compromised by their close links with Hungary, also lost much of their land.

In Rumania, a combination of factors led to the adoption of a radical land reform. In Transylvania the landowners were mainly Hungarian, and in Bessarabia they were largely Russian. In the Regat, as we have seen, they were mostly Rumanian. Pre-war Rumanian politics had been characterized by its division into two broad groupings, the Conservatives, mostly large landowners who favoured close relations with the Central Powers, and the Liberals, both more nationalistic and more urban, led by the leading Rumanian statesman and successful creator of Greater Rumania, Ionel Brâtianu. The political power of the Conservatives was undermined by the introduction of universal suffrage in 1919. Brâtianu's radical reform was intended to do the same to their economic power, which indeed it did. The Conservatives were a negligible force in Rumania in the interwar period.

A fairly radical land reform was enacted in Poland, after much political strife, but its application was considerably impeded by pressures from the landowners and the impact of the great depression. In Hungary, only 271,000 hectares were redistributed in the interwar period, a derisory figure.

Nowhere did land reform provide an adequate solution of the problem of peasant poverty. This greatly affected political life, since in virtually all of Eastern Europe the peasantry was by far the largest social group. In Rumania, 78 per cent of the population was rural, in Bulgaria 80 per cent, in Yugoslavia 75 per cent, in Poland 63 per cent, in Hungary 55 per cent. Only in Czechoslovakia (where the rural population was 34 per cent of the total) and in Austria did peasants not constitute a majority of the population.[8] Before 1914, their position had everywhere been improving. The percentage of land in large estates had declined as landowners had sold off land to rationalize and improve their estates, and the amount of land in peasant hands had thus increased. Peasant holdings also tended to increase in size as the poorer peasants sold up their holdings and either moved to the rapidly developing industrial areas of Bohemia, central Poland and Budapest, or emigrated to the golden land of America. From the New World, a stream of remittances furthered the improvement of peasant plots. After 1918, these favourable conditions came to an end. Industry ceased to expand as rapidly as it had done before 1914 and the towns showed little absorptive capacity. Emigration became more and more difficult, particularly after the Americans passed legislation establishing a quota system for immigrants in 1921 and 1924, and when the French started curtailing immigration in the 1930s.[9] Finally, after 1929, the world suffered the most severe agricultural depression for eighty years and this further undermined the prosperity of the village, for even the poorest and most backward areas in Eastern Europe were now linked with the market.[10] Nostalgia for the pre-war period, increasingly idealized, became common among the peasantry. Many found independence a hollow disappointment and remembered the conditions of foreign rule with some regret.

The most fundamental problem of the peasantry was the pressure of numbers on the land. The overwhelming majority of them possessed holdings barely adequate or even inadequate to support them. In Poland in 1921, 64·8 per cent of all holdings were smaller than 5 hectares and comprised 14·8 per cent of the arable land. Similar figures could be produced for every other country. Even in Czechoslovakia, which possessed the healthiest social structure in the area, 44 per cent of holdings were of less than 2 hectares and comprised 7 per cent of agricultural land.[11] This pressure was exacerbated by the extremely rapid rise of population over the whole area,[12] and by the disappearance of opportunities for emigration. The superfluity of labour also significantly impeded the introduction of modern technology in the East European countryside. The number of tractors and the amount of fertilizer used were markedly lower than in Western Europe.[13] Bulgaria and Yugoslavia were still almost entirely without industry, and Rumania had little industrial development apart from the petroleum complex at Ploesti. In Hungary there was some heavy industry around Budapest, while Poland had some developed industries, notably textiles in Łódź, coal and steel in the Dąbrowa basin and the highly developed coal, steel and chemical industries in that part of Upper Silesia assigned to the new state by the League in 1921.[14] However, all these industries had been closely linked with the economies of Germany and Russia and their adaptation to the new framework created by independence was to prove a long and difficult task. In Eastern Europe, only the Czech lands possessed a many-sided and balanced industrial base. Yet the two other constituent elements

of Czechoslovakia, Slovakia and Ruthenia, were both overwhelmingly rural and closely linked economically with the
Magyar plain, from which they were now cut off by the high
tariffs that followed Czech independence, and even more by the
Czech-Hungarian tariff war of 1930.

Some attempts were made to foster industrial development in
Eastern Europe between the wars. However, the native
bourgeoisie for the most part lacked the capital and initiative to
carry out industrialization on its own, and the new industries
created were either foreign-owned,[15] and thus a target for
nationalist resentments, or in state hands and thus adversely
affected by the overweighted bureaucracy which characterized
all these countries. Moreover, the devastation of the war and the
new tariff barriers created by national independence hampered
industrial development. Many factories were cut off from their
traditional markets and sources of supply. The Polish textile
industry of Łódź and Białystock had produced for the whole of
Russia. The Slovak saw-mills had, to a great extent, sent their
finished timber down the rivers to Hungary. This list could be
prolonged indefinitely.

All of the countries of Eastern Europe did enjoy a fair amount
of prosperity in the 1920s and in a number a significant advance
in industrialization was achieved. But the great depression
cruelly exposed the area's economic weakness.[16] In the first
place, all the countries of Eastern Europe, except for Austria
and Czechoslovakia, were overwhelmingly exporters of primary
products and they were hard hit by the rapid fall in the price of
agricultural goods relative to industrial goods. They had, moreover, based their hopes for industrialization on the belief that, as
was the case before 1914, the international financial system would
make possible large-scale foreign investment in their economies.
But even in the 1920s this system was no longer working as
well as it had done before 1914. The political instability of the
area and the belief that its new frontiers would prove fragile in
the face of the inevitable revival of Russia and Germany meant
that foreign capital was hard to come by. The states of Eastern
Europe were thus forced to borrow at high rates of interest and
found themselves increasingly heavily burdened by this indebtedness as the result of the falling agricultural prices brought
about by the great depression. In 1930, for instance, the service
on foreign debts amounted to nearly 50 per cent of Hungarian

imports.[17] The states of the area also hesitated, for a long time, to repudiate their debts, still vainly hoping that foreign lending would revive. This meant that almost every country adopted rigid deflationary measures in the face of the depression to preserve the stability and convertibility of its currency and thus prove attractive to foreign investors. This needlessly prolonged the depression and had much to do with the radicalization of politics in Poland, Hungary, Rumania and the German-areas of Czechoslovakia. Moreover, as the level of international trade failed to recover with the rise of international production in the 1930s, the states of Eastern Europe, whose currencies were now in many cases not convertible, had great difficulty in selling their agricultural produce. Their easiest and most obvious market thus proved to be Germany, whose currency was also not convertible and whose rulers were keen to barter their surplus industrial production for primary products. The late 1930s saw an enormous increase in German economic penetration everywhere in Eastern Europe, except for Poland and Czechoslovakia, which were more wary of the political implications of this development.[18]

One final feature of political life specific to Eastern Europe, and resulting from its largely agricultural character, was the existence of peasant parties. These claimed to represent the peasants' interests and demanded for them, as the largest and most significant group in society, a dominant say in government. In the words of Wincenty Witos, a Polish peasant leader:[19]

> Poland fell as a state of the nobility. . . . Poland rises again as a state of the peasantry, and as such can and must survive. The peasant masses must assume responsibility for the future of the state, and if they are to bear this heavy burden, they must acquire political influence, the possibility of ruling the state.

Agrarianism is not, of course, confined to Eastern Europe. Peasant parties have emerged in Latin America and parts of Asia, while the Western United States has had its farmer parties. But it was in Eastern Europe that the movement developed most fully. One of its characteristic features here was its hostility to the towns, which particularly in the pre-independence period had been sources of foreign influence and had often had a population which differed in nationality from that of the majority

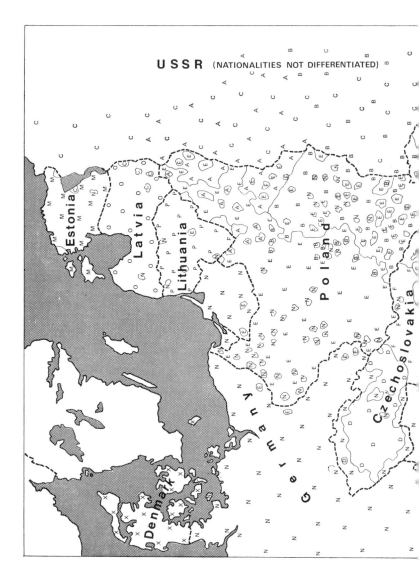

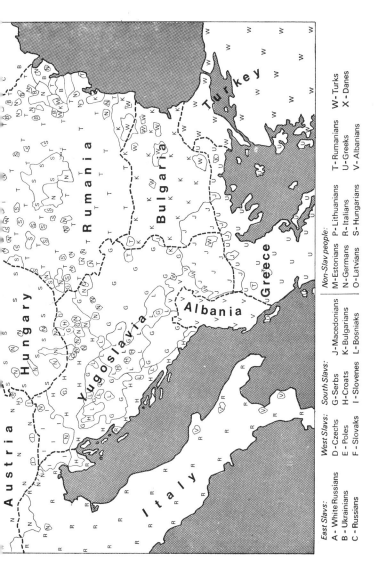

East Slavs:
A - White Russians
B - Ukrainians
C - Russians

West Slavs:
D - Czechs
E - Poles
F - Slovaks

South Slavs:
G - Serbs
H - Croats
I - Slovenes
J - Macedonians
K - Bulgarians
L - Bosniaks

Non-Slav people:
M - Estonians
N - Germans
O - Latvians
P - Lithuanians
R - Italians
S - Hungarians
T - Rumanians
U - Greeks
V - Albanians
W - Turks
X - Danes

Map 1 Nationalities in Eastern Europe

of the country. This antagonism not only survived independence, but was in some respects intensified by it. According to the Bulgarian writer Marksimov in 1892:[20]

> The peasant has but the vaguest idea of the transition
> from servitude to independent life; for him it matters little
> whether he pays tax to Akhmed or Ivan. In fact, Ivan is
> often more distasteful to him than Akhmed, for Akhmed
> could be more easily fooled or bribed; Akhmed was naive
> and spoke Turkish, while Ivan is to all appearances a
> Christian like him, speaks Bulgarian, yet exacts more from
> him than did Akhmed. The meaning of the state of rights
> and duties for the peasant adds up to tax payment and
> sending his son off as a soldier. His attitude to nature, life
> and livelihood are still those of fifty years ago.

Eastern Europe also differed from Western Europe in the presence there of a very large number of states and nationalities.[21] We have already noted the existence of twelve states (thirteen with Finland) between Germany and Russia. The list of nationalities is even larger, including Poles, Ukrainians, Byelorussians, Finns, Swedes, Lithuanians, Latvians, Estonians, Czechs, Germans, Slovaks, Hungarians, Rumanians, Bulgarians, Turks, Serbs, Croats, Slovenes, Albanians, Macedonians, Vlachs, Jews and Greeks. Moreover, in many cases the landowners in an area were of one nationality, and the peasantry of another. Thus in East Galicia the peasantry was Ukrainian, the landowners Polish; in Western Poland, the landowners were largely German, the peasants Polish; in Slovakia the landowners were Hungarian, the peasants Slovak, and in Transylvania the landowners were Hungarian and the peasants Rumanian. In addition, as we have seen, the predominant nationality in the towns was often different from that of the surrounding countryside, though this phenomenon tended to disappear as more and more peasants moved to the towns. There were, as well, territorially compact groups of a single nationality surrounded by another nationality. In East Galicia, in the area around Lvov, the peasantry was for the most part Polish-speaking, or considered itself Polish. Yet between this part of the country and West Galicia, with its clear Polish majority, there was a band of settlement in which Ukrainians constituted a majority. In Transylvania, the area in which the Magyar Szeklers constituted a majority was divided from the rest of ethnic Hungary by a band of Rumanian settlement. Finally there were areas, such as Bessarabia, Macedonia and perhaps East Galicia which were so mixed that it was difficult to say which was the dominant nationality.

Two minorities fall into a special category, the Germans and the Jews. There were over 12 million Germans in Eastern and Central Europe outside the boundaries of Germany. They were divided into two groups: those who lived in areas contiguous to the Reich in Czechoslovakia, Austria and Western Poland, and the long-established German settler communities in Central Poland, Hungary, Rumania and Yugoslavia. The former group tended to be more nationalistic and less satisfied with their situation than the latter, since in the case of Austria they had mostly hoped to be allowed to join the Reich, while in Bohemia and Western Poland they deeply resented the imposition of Polish and Czech rule. With the advent of Hitler, National Socialist ideas found willing listeners in all the German communities and fear that they might prove a fifth column intensified suspicion of Germans and created a vicious circle, making them even more eager to obtain Nazi support. During the Second World War *Volksdeutsche* communities everywhere in Eastern Europe proved willing tools of the Nazis.

The 6 million Jews, concentrated mainly in Poland, Hungary, Rumania and Slovakia were an even more difficult problem.[22] In all these countries they played a large role in the intermediary occupations of trading and money-lending and attracted to themselves the hostility which such groups have everywhere always aroused. In this sense, the Jewish problem was no different from that of the Chinese in Malaysia, Indonesia and the Philippines or the Indians in Burma and East Africa. But what made their situation much worse was that with the diminution of opportunities to emigrate, above all to the USA, the widespread demand in the 1930s for them to leave and settle elsewhere coincided with a situation in which it was virtually impossible for them to find anywhere to go. They were truly 'superfluous people', 'waiting for death' in the words of one of their spokesmen.[23] Moreover, the 'Jew' was widely seen in Eastern Europe as a demonic force, the embodiment of both international communism and capitalism, whose mere existence posed a threat to national existence. As Zelea Codreanu, leader of the Rumanian Iron Guard put it, 'Every Jew, whether he is a trader, intellectual or banker is . . . an agent of Communist ideas aimed at the Rumanian people.'[24]

A final distinctive feature of Eastern Europe was that it had been ruled from the early modern period by four dynastic empires hostile to the idea of the national state: Austria, Russia, Prussia and Turkey. From the late eighteenth century, Turkey had gradually been dislodged from Europe, a process which had virtually come to an end by 1912. Austria too had grown progressively weaker in the later nineteenth century and had tended to become more and more dependent on Germany. But both Germany and Russia had continued to pursue active policies in Eastern Europe, which both regarded as a vital sphere of influence. Each, moreover, had seen in the First World War the opportunity to consolidate its position there. The post-war settlement in Eastern Europe rested on the elimination of both Germany and Russia from the area, an elimination unlikely to prove lasting. Indeed from the very beginning the post-war settlement in Eastern Europe was strongly challenged by both these powers. German objectives can be fairly clearly stated, since they are embodied in the Treaty of Brest-Litovsk of March 1918. This 'forgotten peace' involved the setting up of a number of German client states in the Baltic area, Poland and the Ukraine, and the limitation of Russia to her narrow ethnic frontiers. At the same time the Germans sought, through Austria-Hungary, to maintain their dominance in the Balkans. The importance of the Treaty of Brest-Litovsk in the interwar period cannot be overrated. Though the Germans had been defeated in the west, they had won the war in the east. Implicit in many of their demands for the return of Germany's 1914 frontiers was the re-establishment of the Brest-Litovsk system.

Russian aims are somewhat more difficult to document, both because they were not embodied in a peace treaty, and because of the great changes caused by the February and Bolshevik revolutions. Though Tsarist diplomats had wavered somewhat in their objectives, a fairly clear pattern emerges. The empire would have extended westward to include all the ethnically Polish areas in Germany, as well as East Prussia. Galicia too had to be annexed. No decision was reached before the revolution as to whether Czech independence, and thus the effective dismemberment of Austria-Hungary, was desirable. In the

Map 2   Europe at the outbreak of the First World War

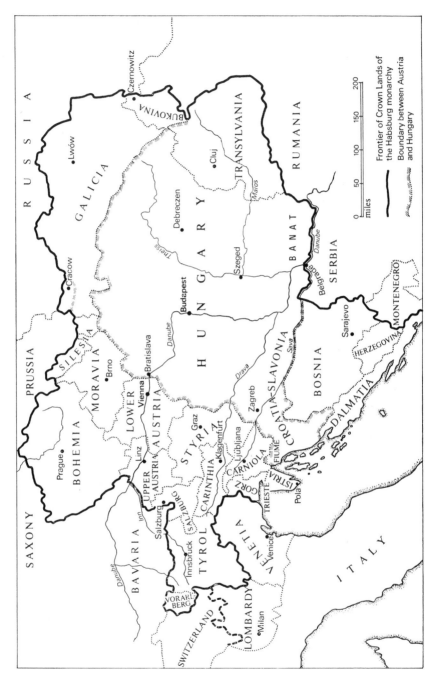

Map 3   Austria-Hungary

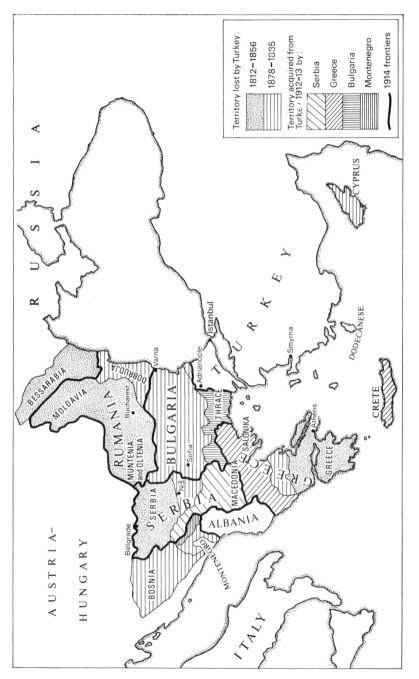

Map 4　The decline of Turkey in Europe, 1812–1914

Balkans, Russian dominance would have been assured. Constantinople would have been annexed, and Austria's South Slav lands linked with Russia's ally Serbia. The Bolsheviks renounced all 'imperialist' plans for the creation of 'spheres of influence'. They believed that revolution in Germany was imminent, and that this would spark off a world revolution. But at the same time, they bitterly resented the territorial concessions which they had been forced to make, particularly Bessarabia and Eastern Poland. They were thus very hostile to the 'imperialist' Versailles settlement, and up to 1933 co-operated closely with Germany, the leading revisionist power. The basic question posed by the post-war settlement in Eastern Europe was how far it would be able to maintain itself in the face of the inevitable recovery of the two great powers on its flanks.

What was the nature of this post-war settlement? In the first place, it rested on the assumption that a reorganization based on the creation of national states would be juster and more lasting than the division of the area between the dynastic empires which had ruled before 1914. It was recognized that the complicated human geography of the area made impossible the creation of truly national states. In the new Poland, Poles were only 69·2 per cent of the population, in Rumania, Rumanians constituted 71·9 per cent, in Czechoslovakia, Czechs and Slovaks were 65·5 per cent of the population, in Yugoslavia, Serbs, Croats and Slovenes made up 82·8 per cent of the population. Even in Bulgaria and Hungary, defeated in the First World War and thus reduced to their narrowest ethnic frontiers, national minorities constituted 10 per cent of the population.

The peacemakers were aware of the impossibility of drawing boundaries which would do justice to all national claims, and which would also do the least harm economically. In addition they regarded as undesirable the excessive Balkanization of the area. They thus had recourse to two expedients. In the first place, they acquiesced in the creation of states in which it was hoped a ruling nation would emerge. There was no Czechoslovak nation in 1918, though one could still hope that one would come into being, as an Italian nation had followed the creation of a united Italy. There was certainly no Yugoslav nation, and though a certain amount of feeling for South Slav unity existed in Croatia, the unitary nature of the new state did not bode well for its future. Secondly, the rights of minorities were to be

Within the map:

Territory lost by:
Germany
Russia
Bulgaria
Turkey
1920-1923
Austria and Hungary
FRONTIERS new
old

FINLAND
Helsinki
Leningrad
Tallinn
SWEDEN
Stockholm
ESTONIA
Riga
LATVIA
U S S R
DENMARK
Copenhagen
Memel
LITHUANIA
Vilna
Minsk
Hamburg
Danzig
EAST PRUSSIA
Berlin
Warsaw
Leipzig
P O L A N D
Breslau
Kiev
GERMAN REPUBLIC
Prague
UPPER SILESIA
Cracow
GALICIA
Czernowitz
Munich
C Z E C H O S L O V A K I A
Vienna
BUKOVINA
BESSARABIA
AUSTRIA
Budapest
Innsbrück
H U N G A R Y
R U M A N I A
S.TYROL
SLOVENIA
TRANSYLVANIA
Milan
ISTRIA
Fiume
SLAVONIA
VOIVODINA
Bucharest
CROATIA
Y U G O S L A V I A
Belgrade
Zadar
BOSNIA
I T A L Y
HERZE-GOVINA
DOBRUDJA
Varna
MONTE-NEGRO
SERBIA
Sofia
Rome
ALBANIA
B U L G A R I A
Istanbul
TURKEY
Naples
MACEDONIA
GREECE
Smyrna
Athens
Sicily
Dodecanese

Map 5   The Peace Settlement, 1919–23

safeguarded by treaties concluded by the Allies with the new states. The minorities were to be given the right of appealing to the League of Nations if they felt their rights were being abused. This system of minority protection did not work well: the states on whom minority treaties were imposed resented them as limiting their sovereignty and giving them a second-class status in Europe. Poland, for instance, was bitter that the League of Nations allowed Germans in her territory to enjoy its protection while the rights of the Polish minority in Germany were in no way safeguarded. Some tension was inevitable, and it was often difficult to decide whether the expropriation of German landowners in Western Poland or Hungarian land-owners in Slovakia was the result of a much-needed land reform or of an unjustified abrogation of the rights of minorities. Furthermore, in many cases the minorities, notably the Hungarians in Slovakia and Transylvania, did not wish to reconcile themselves to their new rulers and hoped for reunion with the country from which they had been divided.

A second feature of the system established in Eastern Europe after the war was that the new states were all endowed with extremely democratic constitutions, mostly modelled on that of the Third French Republic, with a dominant legislature and a relatively weak executive. This was the pattern in Austria, Poland, the Baltic states and, to a lesser extent, Czechoslovakia. In Rumania, Yugoslavia, Greece and Bulgaria, the Crown retained important prerogatives, but the political centre of gravity shifted increasingly to parliament, elected by universal suffrage. Hungary too, for a brief period between November 1918 and March 1919, adopted a democratic constitution. From today's perspective, it is easy to see that highly democratic constitutions were unlikely to work well in an area characterized by deep national and social divisions, where most of the politicians had little practical experience of government and where the majority of the population was ignorant and, in many cases, illiterate. But in 1918, the Wilsonian heresy, the idea that liberal democracy was the only desirable form of government, was widespread. The victory of the Allies contributed to its prestige, since the war was seen as a victory of democracy over autocracy. Indeed, though the *naiveté* of the constitution builders in Eastern Europe is obvious today, surely what was at fault was not their commitment to democracy, but their adoption of the French model, since a strong executive was vitally necessary in all the countries of the areas. At the same time, excessive centralization made it difficult to deal fairly with the minorities, particularly those which were territorially compact.

A final feature of the Versailles settlement in Eastern Europe was its reliance on international guarantees. The new states had emerged as a result of the temporary eclipse of Russia and Germany, and sought to guarantee their new independence against German, Hungarian and Bulgarian demands for revision by close links with France. To France, her East European allies were to provide a substitute for Russia in forcing Germany to fight a war on two fronts. They were also to form a *cordon sanitaire* against Bolshevism. (The fear of 'communism' was one of the major political factors in interwar Eastern Europe and had much to do with the fragility of democratic institutions.) The French guarantee of the East European settlement took the form of a number of alliances. Treaties of alliance were concluded with Poland in 1921 and with Czechoslovakia in 1924, treaties of friendship were concluded with both Yugoslavia and Rumania in 1927. In addition the French sponsored the creation in 1922 of the Little Entente of Czechoslovakia, Rumania and Yugoslavia, directed primarily against Hungarian revisionism. A Polish-Rumanian treaty of 1921 further buttressed the framework.

The French system of alliances was never as strong as it appeared. To the French, the Eastern European allies were to provide the manpower to diminish the force of a German attack in the west. French strategy remained strongly dominated by defensive preoccupations and by the idea that the 'infantry is the queen of the battlefield'. France was not interested in intervening actively in Eastern Europe to maintain the system established there. In addition, her two principal allies, Poland and Czechoslovakia, remained at odds for almost the entire period. The Poles resented what they regarded as the unjust frontier settlement in Austrian Silesia, the Czechs' failure to allow the transit of military material to Poland during the Polish-Soviet war, and their willingness to support Stresemann, the German Chancellor, in his anti-Polish foreign policy. The Czechs regarded the Polish eastern border as unstable, and believed that it would be overturned when the Whites regained power in Russia. They also resented Polish support for Slovak separatism. This antagonism was never really overcome in the interwar period and gravely weakened the French system of alliances. In addition, the states of the Little Entente were primarily concerned with Hungarian revisionism, and both Yugoslavia and Rumania had reservations about committing themselves too strongly to an anti-German course.

The history of Eastern Europe between the wars is the story of the collapse of the political system established in 1918. We shall be concerned above all to show why the democratic constitutions adopted with such high hopes after the war worked so badly. At the same time, it is important to see the close connection between the failure of liberal democracy and the breakdown of the French system of alliances. The challenge to the French system, first from Italy and then, in the 1930s, much more effectively from Germany, went along with an ideological offensive against liberal and democratic values. As more countries moved into the German sphere of influence, the tendency to adopt fascist or Nazi political models grew steadily stronger. Indeed, fascism seemed to many the philosophy of the future – an efficient and orderly means of modernizing a backward country. Nevertheless a general sympathy for Right-radical views did not succeed in eliminating the many conflicts of interest in the region. The German-Italian rivalry in Eastern Europe was not fully reconciled even by the creation of the Axis. When war finally broke out it was for the maintenance of the independence of Poland, a state with a semi-autocratic constitution in which democracy had broken down already in the 1920s.

Notes

1 B. Lewis, *A History of Modern Turkey* (London, 1960), p. 119.
2 H. Nicolson, *Peacemaking 1919* (London, 1945), p. 176.
3 L. Wasilewski, 'Na widowni', *Myśl Narodowa*, no. 16, 15 April 1934.
4 R. Dmowski, *Myśli nowoczesnego Polaka* (Lwów, 1904), p. 88.
5 H. Seton-Watson, *Eastern Europe between the Wars* (Cambridge, 1945), pp. 146–7.
6 *Axa*, 5 February 1933, quoted in E. Weber, '*Romania*' in E. Weber and H. Rogger (eds), *The European Right* (London, 1965).
7 For some figures on the percentage of land in large estates, see the Statistical appendix, Tables 14–20, pp. 166–9.

8 For figures on the percentage of the population engaged in agriculture, see the Statistical appendix, Table 11, p. 164.

9 Some statistics on emigration are provided in the Statistical appendix, Tables 25–30, pp. 117–24.

10 For the impact of the depression, see the Statistical appendix, Tables 35–41, pp. 178–81.

11 For more detailed figures, see the Statistical appendix, Tables 14–20, pp. 166–9.

12 Figures on population growth are provided in the Statistical appendix, Table 25, p. 172.

13 Table 12 (p. 165) in the Statistical appendix gives some figures on the use of tractors.

14 Tables 31–4 (pp. 175–7) of the Statistical appendix provide some statistical detail on industry in Eastern Europe.

15 See the Statistical appendix, Table 34 p. 177.

16 See the Statistical appendix, Tables 35–41, pp. 178–81.

17 See the Statistical appendix, Table 36 (p. 179) for similar figures for other countries.

18 On this, see the Statistical appendix, Tables 39–41, pp. 180–1.

19 Quoted in A. Beciłkowska, *Stronnictwa i związki polityczne w Polsce* (Warsaw, 1925), pp. 167–8.

20 Quoted in L. Stavrianos, *The Balkans since 1453* (New York, 1965), p. 423.

21 See the Statistical appendix, Tables 1–10, pp. 158–63.

22 For figures on the Jews, see the Statistical appendix, Tables 42–60, pp. 182–91.

23 A communal leader in Lwów, as reported by O. Janowsky in *People at Bay: The Jewish Problem in East Central Europe* (London, 1938), pp. 92–3.

24 Quoted in F. L. Carsten, *The Rise of Fascism* (London, 1970), p. 182.

Chapter 1

Poland

The re-emergence of the Polish state after 130 years of foreign rule was the most obvious example of the triumph of the principle of nationality in the post-First World War settlement. The new state, with a population of nearly 30 million, was the largest and most powerful in East-Central Europe, and the feeling was widespread that the shedding of foreign rule would make it possible quickly to dispel Polish backwardness, and would soon enable Poland to take her place as a highly developed European country. The euphoria which followed the achievement of independence masked, if only briefly, the extent of the divisions which were to mar Poland's political life. For the country's partition before 1914 between the three great dynastic empires of Eastern Europe, Russia, Germany and Austria-Hungary, had created political groupings which differed not only in ideology but also in their view of how the Polish cause could best be advanced, and which of the partitioning powers should be sought as an ally.

The National Democrats, led by Roman Dmowski, a man of great political intelligence but lacking any real warmth, had been the pro-Russian party. They argued that Germany was Poland's main enemy. Prussia had played the principal role in the partition of Poland, and the territories she had gained, unlike those acquired by Austria and Russia, were held to be indispensable to her national existence. Germany, moreover, was bound to oppose the re-creation of a Polish state, since it would call into question her hold on her Polish lands. In

Dmowski's words, 'Prussia grew up from the fall of Poland; the revival of Poland . . . would be a brake on German eastward expansion and would undermine the leading role which Prussia plays in the German *Reich*.'[1] He believed that the German desire for dominance in East-Central Europe would inevitably lead to a clash with Russia, and the National Democrats thus hoped to achieve a compromise with the Tsarist state on an anti-German basis.

Before the First World War, the National Democrats had had little success in obtaining concessions from the authorities, though they had made some headway in convincing Russian public opinion and some officials that Polish aspirations were not necessarily hostile to the interests of the Russian state. But by 1914 they had become the strongest political force both in the Congress Kingdom (that part of Russian Poland which had been given autonomy, subsequently almost entirely done away with, at the Congress of Vienna) and Prussian Poland.

Already before the outbreak of war, a secret National Democrat congress attended by delegates from all three parts of Poland had decided that in the event of war the party would support the Entente powers. Thus in August 1914 the party had enthusiastically accepted the Manifesto to the Poles, issued by the Grand Duke Nicholas, which promised the Poles national unification under the sceptre of the Romanovs. In November a pro-Entente Polish National Committee was established, which recruited Polish units to fight beside the Russian forces. Yet once again little was achieved, and the self-government promised to the Congress Kingdom had still not been granted when the Russians were forced to withdraw.

The situation changed somewhat after the February revolution. The Provisional Government of Prince Lvov issued a manifesto on 30 March 1917 promising to set up a Polish state composed of the Congress Kingdom, Galicia (Austrian Poland) and Prussian Poland linked to Russia in a military union. However, it was clear that Russia was by now a less significant part of the Allied coalition, and in August 1917 the Polish National Committee moved to Western Europe, where its main office in Paris was headed by Dmowski himself. During 1918, the Allies committed themselves to the establishment of a Polish state and in November recognized the Polish National Committee as the future government. This new state, in

National Democrat eyes, was to be unitary and national, closely allied with France, which would serve as a barrier to the revival of the German *Drang nach Osten*.

The National Democrats' main political opponent was Józef Piłsudski, a man of commanding presence, a fine speaker and a person who embodied the Poles' image of themselves as reckless patriots who would sacrifice all for the sake of their beloved country. The 'noble socialist', as the National Democrats' leader called him, was almost the exact opposite of Dmowski, who was unemotional and *petit bourgeois* in his origins. Born on a large estate near Wilno, Piłsudski was in many ways the direct descendant of the romantic Polish revolutionaries of the nineteenth century. Whereas Dmowski had seen the uprising of 1863 as criminal folly, to Piłsudski it was a glorious and heroic event. He had first become active in politics in one of the later offshoots of the Russian terrorist organization, Narodnaya Volya. Sentenced in 1887 to five years in Siberia for his involvement in a plot against the life of Alexander III (the same plot for which Lenin's elder brother was executed), he quickly came to the conclusion that Tsarist Russia, that 'Asiatic monster covered with European veneer',[2] was Poland's main enemy and that he had overestimated the strength and significance of the Russian revolutionary movement. What was now needed was a new uprising on the lines of 1863, in which the Poles along with the other oppressed nationalities of Russia would destroy the Tsarist state. On his return to Poland he assumed a leading role in the Polish Socialist Party, which unlike its rival, led by Rosa Luxemburg, the Social Democracy of the Congress Kingdom and Lithuania, argued that national liberation was as important a goal as social revolution. Piłsudski's socialism was never very deep, however, and was above all the reflection of his belief that now that both the landowners and the bourgeoisie, under National Democrat leadership, had decided on collaboration with the Russians, only the industrial working class was interested in national liberation. During the Russo-Japanese war, he tried, unsuccessfully, to persuade the Japanese to sponsor a rising in Poland. In the 1905 revolution he took control of the fighting organization of the PPS (the Polish Socialist Party) and led a series of terrorist attacks on Russian government outposts. His devotion to terrorism and his belief in the precedence of national liberation over social revolution led to a split within the PPS and though it culminated in an attack on the railway station at Bezdany (north of Wilno) in September 1908, it did not spark off a national uprising.

Piłsudski himself was increasingly dissatisfied with the results of terrorism and became more and more convinced that only war between the partitioning powers, which by now seemed increasingly likely, would change Poland's position. But he saw that if Polish desires were to be given any consideration, a Polish military force, capable of playing an independent role in such a conflict, would have to be created. Already in June 1908 he had participated in the formation of the League of Active Struggle to organize and train military units. Soon afterwards he moved to Galicia where political conditions were least restrictive and where the Austrian government was not un-sympathetic to his anti-Russian aims. By 1914, in spite of some internal disputes, he was in a position to put nearly 7,000 Polish Legionaries into the field.

On the outbreak of war, Piłsudski attempted again to foment a national uprising in Russian Poland. On 6 August 1914, he crossed the Austro-Russian border near Cracow with his troops, hoping in this way to gain a certain freedom of manoeuvre in relation to the Central Powers, whom he had not consulted before acting. His plans failed utterly. The Poles in the Congress Kingdom, for the most part sympathetic to the National Demo-crats and even to the Russian war effort, greeted his troops with a mixture of hostility and indifference. He was thus faced with the alternative of disbanding his Legion or co-operating with the Austrian government. He decided to co-operate, and grew still firmer in his resolve when the Central Powers' successful offensive in the summer of 1915 led to the Russian evacuation of the Congress Kingdom. He was probably sincere when he wrote in August 1915,[3]

> The political aim of the War . . . was and is the incorpora-
> tion of Galicia and the Congress Kingdom into the frame-
> work of the Austro-Hungarian monarchy. I did not, and
> do not, believe that it is possible to obtain better conditions
> for Poland in this war.

He remained true to the policy of turning to Austria until mid-1916, when the increasing weakness of Austria, and the hostility of the Hungarians, the Germans and the Austrian

Army to the 'Austro-Polish' solution became evident. Already in August 1916 Bethmann Hollweg, the German Chancellor, had forced the Austrians to agree to the setting up of an 'independent' Polish state. Piłsudski now became convinced that a satisfactory resolution of the 'Polish question' depended on an agreement with Germany. When the Germans established a rump Polish state on 5 November 1916, Piłsudski supported their action; however, he demanded the setting up of a civilian government before he would help in the creation of an army. When this condition was met in January 1917, by the formation of a Provisional Council of State, he went ahead. This co-operation did not prove lasting, for Piłsudski soon realized that the Germans were not seriously interested in Polish independence. When he counselled his troops to refuse to swear allegiance to the German Empire in July 1917, he was imprisoned by the Germans in Magdeburg for the duration of the war. Piłsudski's internment proved to be a blessing in disguise. It enabled him to return to Poland following the collapse of Germany in 1918 with the aura of a martyr and the reputation of an indomitable fighter for independence, unsullied by compromise. He quickly assumed a pre-eminent position in the new state, holding the offices of supreme commander and head of state. Though he had no single political group supporting him, he had adherents in most of the major political parties, apart from the National Democrats, and enjoyed wide support on the Left. He wanted the new state to be, not a unitary national state, but a federation of Poland, Lithuania, Byelorussia and the Ukraine. The Poles were to hold the dominant position in the federation but the rights of the other nations were to be recognized and respected. Only a powerful state of this type could maintain its independence against Germany and Russia. 'Poland will be great', asserted Piłsudski, 'or she will not exist.'

The clash between the National Democrats and the supporters of Piłsudski had been extremely bitter before 1914. Dmowski had attacked Piłsudski and his followers as pathetic and dangerous imitators of the nineteenth-century gentry revolutionaries, men with no practical sense of politics who preached insurrection for its own sake and who were likely to bring new disasters on their unfortunate country. Piłsudski's supporters saw the National Democrats as subservient, lacking any real desire for Polish independence, and prepared to go to any lengths to appease the Russians. In the immediate aftermath of independence, attempts were made to bring the two groups together, but the dispute broke out with new bitterness as a result of the Polish-Soviet war of 1920, which was precipitated by Piłsudski, at this time both head of state and commander-in-chief, in an attempt to foster his federalist schemes by exploiting the weakness of the Soviet Union after the civil war. He aimed at dislodging the Ukraine and Byelorussia and linking them federally with Poland, and his plans were denounced by the National Democrats as rash, indeed even as criminal folly. The catastrophe they feared very nearly materialized and was only averted by the Polish victory in the Battle of Warsaw in August 1920. In spite of this, recriminations continued and the question of how far the victory in this 'miracle on the Vistula' was Piłsudski's own achievement was much disputed.

The quarrel between the National Democrats and the Piłsudski faction affected every aspect of political life. The National Democrats dominated the constituent Assembly, and were determined that Piłsudski should never again exercise the influence he had enjoyed between 1918 and 1922 as head of state. It was with the specific aim of curbing Piłsudski's influence that the powers of the presidency as established by the new constitution were so limited, and the marshal, realizing this, refused to stand for election to the new office. The constitution as a whole was never accepted by his followers as a legitimate political framework.

The conflict also spilled over into the army. The officer corps derived from a variety of sources. Some officers were veterans of Piłsudski's wartime Legions. They were generally without formal military training, but because of their past as the first Polish army, which had acknowledged the need for 'active struggle against Russia',[4] they felt that they were entitled to special consideration. In the words of one of their spokesmen,[5]

The Legions, through the genius of their creator and leader, were not only the inheritors of the national chivalric spirit, but also the inheritors of the great historic mission of Poland – the Jagiellonian tradition based on modern methods of realization.

They were continually at odds with the officers who had

formerly served with the Austrian Imperial Army, whom they reproached for their long servility to the Austrians, as well as with the officers from the Tsarist army and the Polish corps of General Józef Haller, which had gone over to the Allies from the Austrian side in protest against the Treaty of Brest-Litovsk. On the surface, this conflict took the form of a dispute over the method of organizing the army, but what was really at issue was the question of who should control the military. Throughout the conflict, the National Democrats were aggressively hostile to Piłsudski.

The deep chasm between the followers of Dmowski and Piłsudski was not the only problem facing the state. The constitution adopted in March 1921 was highly democratic in character, in accordance with the general belief that the war had shown the superiority of democratic over autocratic systems. It was modelled on that of the Third French Republic, with an all-powerful Lower House (the Sejm) and a weak presidency and Upper House. The president had no power of veto over legislation and the senate could only delay laws by demanding they be passed by an 11/20 majority in the Lower House. This sophisticated system did not work well in Poland. The long years of partition had created very different political traditions among those who had lived in areas administered by semi-constitutional Germany and Austria and those who had been ruled by autocratic Russia. In no sphere more than politics, claimed Stanisław Thugutt, a peasant leader, was it so important,[6]

> whether one became active under the Russians or under
> the Austrians, with the tradition of armed uprisings and
> mole-like conspiratorial work in the blood or with the
> habit of small struggles for the achievement of very
> limited aims.

The different political traditions, together with the introduction of proportional representation and the exuberant individualism of the Polish intelligentsia, which played a leading role in all political groupings, led to far-reaching fragmentation. In 1925, for example, there were 92 registered political parties in Poland of which 32 were represented in the Sejm, organized into 18 parliamentary clubs. This extreme political atomization made it most difficult to create a stable and lasting government: between the achievement of independence in November 1918 and Piłsudski's coup of May 1926 there were 14 different regimes. Political inexperience was one of the principal causes of this instability. The Polish clubs in the Austrian, Russian and Prussian parliaments had been small, minority pressure groups, concerned almost exclusively with Polish problems and with attempts to gain redress for political grievances. This background did not adapt easily to the demands of parliamentary government in independent Poland. As Thugutt wrote, 'everyone wants to be in opposition; on no account will anyone accept responsibility'.[7]

Moreover, in spite of the failure of Piłsudski's federal schemes, the new state was multi-national in character. Germans, Jews Ukrainians and Byelorussians made up a third of the population and were all to some degree dissatisfied with their position. The highly centralized constitution gave no scope for self-government to the territorially compact Ukrainians and Byelorussians, who were also embittered by the failure to introduce a significant measure of land reform. The Germans resented the attempts to undo the policies of Germanization which had been pursued in Prussian Poland, while the large Jewish population was subject to a fair measure of discrimination and harassment.

The failure to deal fairly with the national minorities was partly due to the pervasive air of national insecurity. Poland had re-emerged not so much as a result of its own efforts as because of the simultaneous collapse of Russia, Germany and Austria-Hungary. Both Germany and Russia were dissatisfied with the 1921 frontiers of Poland and, as their strength revived, the validity of the state was often questioned in the west.

The country's economic problems were also daunting. Partition had made her different areas integral parts of Russia, Germany and Austria, and it proved a long and difficult task to create a single economic unit from them. Communications, for example, had been constructed with the interests of the partitioning powers in mind: more than 50 Austrian and German railway lines led to the Russian frontier; only 10 continued on the other side.[8] There were, as well, sharp contrasts in the level of economic development in the different territories. Industry was highly developed only in Upper Silesia, and in isolated areas in the Congress Kingdom such as the textile centre of Łódź or the Dąbrowa basin with its coal mines and metallurgical industries.

In fact, despite comparatively rapid industrial development in the fifty years before 1914, the new Polish state was still overwhelmingly rural, with 74 per cent of its population on the land, and in agriculture too it proved difficult to achieve integration of the different areas. Whereas the agriculture of the former Prussian partition was highly capitalized and efficient, its development encouraged by the rapidly growing needs of Germany, that of Russian and Austrian Poland was characterized by overpopulation and inefficiency outside the large estates, which in 1921 constituted 47·3 per cent of the arable land, but only 0·9 per cent of all holdings.[9]

The rapid industrial development necessary if the pressing social problems of the country were to be alleviated was impeded by wartime destruction. By 1920, 55 per cent of the bridges, 63 per cent of the railway stations, 48 per cent of the locomotives and 18 per cent of the buildings in the country had been destroyed.[10] Industry had also been adversely affected by Russian and German requisitions. In addition the new state was plagued by inflation almost from its inception. The military operations between 1918 and 1921, culminating in the Polish-Soviet War, had increased the demand for all kinds of goods while imposing a strain on their supply. With the ceasing of hostilities the necessities of reconstruction became a continual financial strain, the more so since many of the taxes of the partitioning powers were allowed to lapse after the war. Finally, the euphoria created by independence, the feeling that everything must now improve, increased the already difficult problem of exercising some control over wages and prices. Whereas in December 1918 the exchange rate for the Polish mark was 9·8 to the dollar, by the end of 1922 it had reached 17,808. In 1923 the inflation assumed gigantic proportions: by the end of November one dollar was worth 2,300,000 marks.[11] The effects of this inflation on the political situation were enormous. As the members of the intelligentsia saw their savings wiped out, their political attitudes grew more and more extreme; confidence in the parliamentary system was undermined and the temptation to adopt extra-parliamentary solutions grew stronger both on the Right and on the Left.

The breakdown of the democracy

Given these conditions it is not surprising that the democratic constitution functioned badly. The internal history of the Republic between March 1921 when it was enacted and May 1926 was exceedingly stormy, and civil war was very near on a number of occasions. The first of these followed immediately the elections called for by the new constitution which were held in November 1922. No political group obtained a clear majority, although the National Democrats and their allies emerged as the strongest single bloc with 125 seats of the 444 in the Sejm. The Right-Centre parties won 44 seats, the Centre 88, the Left 98 and the National Minorities, who had formed a joint bloc, 89. A crisis arose when Gabriel Narutowicz, who had the support of the Left, the National Minorities and some of the Centre, was elected president by a simple majority vote in the national assembly. The right, regarding themselves as cheated of their electoral victory, unleashed a violent and demagogic campaign against the new president whom they accused of being the pawn of the minorities, in particular the Jews. Deputies were attacked outside parliament by right-wing mobs, and on 16 December Narutowicz was assassinated by a nationalist fanatic while speaking to the British ambassador at an art exhibition. Civil war seemed imminent, especially since some of Piłsudski's associates saw this as the right moment for achieving a final reckoning with the National Democrats. However, the leadership of the PPS refused to go along with these plans, and the crisis was resolved by the formation of a non-parliamentary 'cabinet of pacification' by General Sikorski, a former Legionary officer who had clashed with Piłsudski, but was still on relatively good terms with him. Narutowicz was succeeded as President by Stanisław Wojciechowski, a former Socialist.

Violence again came to the surface late in 1923. Although the Piast Peasant Party was disgusted by the National Democrats' complicity in the Narutowicz assassination, it was won over to a coalition with them by the promise of land reform. The new government set up in May 1923 under the remarkable peasant leader Wincenty Witos eased the leading Piłsudski men out of the army, but failed to control the inflation, which got completely out of hand later in the year. Since wages lagged behind the rise in prices, working-class discontent grew, and the country was hit by a wave of strikes. These culminated in riots in Cracow in November when the workers, led by the PPS, took over the town. Again on this occasion the Piłsudski faction wished to act against the Right, but when the government reached a compromise with the strikers, Piłsudski became convinced that he could no longer really rely on his old Socialist allies.

In any case, Witos's government fell soon afterwards, to be followed by two years of successful non-parliamentary rule by Władysław Grabski, who was granted special powers by the Sejm. His government, the longest-lasting before the coup, fell at the threat of a new inflation caused by the Polish-German tariff war which began late in 1925. It was replaced by a broad coalition led by Count Skrzyński which included all parties from the National Democrats to the PPS. This government, in an attempt to conciliate Piłsudski, made possible the return of many of his followers to prominent positions in the army. However, it collapsed when its deflationary economic policy led to the resignation of its Socialist ministers at the end of April 1926.

It now proved extremely difficult to form a new government and eventually, on 9 May, the president called upon Witos to head a cabinet of the Centre and Right. This was a disastrous miscalculation, raising the spectre of the Centre-Right government of 1923 which had provoked so much opposition on the Left. It outraged Piłsudski, whose influence in the army had been steadily increasing, and who, in retreat at his house in Sulejówek, near Warsaw, seemed to many Poles the one man, untainted by the incompetence and corruption of the politicians, who could restore the state to equilibrium. On 12 May 1926 he called an armed demonstration in an attempt to induce his old friend President Wojciechowski to prevent the formation of a new Witos government. However when Wojciechowski refused to submit to the marshal's demands, fighting broke out between government and rebel troops. The PPS supported Piłsudski, although it had not been informed in advance of his plans, by calling a general strike of railway workers, thus preventing the transfer of government troops to the capital. After three days of conflict Piłsudski was master of Warsaw and, in effect, of Poland.

The reluctant dictator

The Piłsudski regime was an exception among the dictatorships of the interwar years. Piłsudski, whose main interests lay in foreign policy and army affairs, had no well-defined political ideas. It was only with extreme reluctance that he had brought himself to order the armed demonstration which led to his assuming power, and indeed, it had been his hesitation and indecisiveness in the years before 1926 which had encouraged the politicians of the Right to create another Centre-Right coalition. Even after his victory the marshal was completely cast down by the realization that his actions had provoked civil war. In his first public pronouncement after the coup, the Army Order of the Day for 22 May, he appealed for reconciliation:[12]

> Our blood has sunk into one common earth, an earth
> equally dear to, equally loved by both sides. May this warm
> blood, this soldiers' blood, the most precious in Poland, be
> the new seed of brotherhood beneath our feet, may it
> proclaim a common truth for brothers.

Piłsudski's whole political past had lain with the Left, and his bitterest political disputes had been with the Right. He continued to think of himself as a democrat, stressing to one of his associates in August 1926 his 'intention of still maintaining what is called parliamentarianism. It is the basis of democracy, for which there is always place in Poland, even directly in governing.'[13] Piłsudski never spelled out his political beliefs. Attempts have been made to claim for him some conscious design for a new political system; this seems exaggerated, since he generally worked from day to day in politics. But in so far as he did have a conception of the most valid political framework for Poland, it was one in which parliament could criticize and even to some extent modify the actions of the government, though the government could not be overthrown by a vote of no confidence as under the 1921 constitution. He was, in fact, a curious combination of an old-fashioned military dictator and a political manager along the lines of Giolitti in Italy before 1914 or Taaffe in Austria-Hungary.

It was because of these views that Piłsudski, to the surprise of some of his supporters, did not establish a dictatorship after the coup. He refused to accept the presidency of the republic, claiming that the powers of this office were too circumscribed, and preferred to exercise his influence from behind the scenes. From 1926 until his death in May 1935, the only office he held continuously was that of minister of war. Although he was twice prime minister, from October 1926 until June 1928, and from August until December 1930, his tenure of the post was largely formal. He attended few cabinet meetings and as a rule delegated his official duties. In the aftermath of the coup it was his immediate intention to maintain the 1921 constitution; however, he introduced a number of modifications, among which the most important provided that the government's financial proposals be enacted automatically if the legislature should fail to approve a budget within a specified time, and conferred upon the president the right to dissolve parliament.

Piłsudski had the insight to realize that, irascible and moody as he was, he was not the man to co-operate successfully with parliament. Therefore, in his desire to retain some semblance of parliamentary democracy in Poland, he entrusted the day-to-day running of his government to Kazimierz Bartel, a former radical politician, who was prime minister from May to September 1926 and again from June 1928 to April 1929 (between October 1926 and June 1928 he was vice-premier). Yet although Piłsudski's political past was largely linked with the Left, particularly the PPS, with whose help he had come to power, he refused to comply with the party's demands for new elections and for radical social reforms. On the contrary, he made approaches to the Conservatives (the large landowners), hoping in this way to win over some of the National Democrats' support and to provide a broad underpinning, from Right to Left, for his policies. He had little sympathy for, or understanding of, party politics, and apparently hoped to unite the different groupings in a vague national consensus under his leadership. He even hesitated to create a political organization to support his government, and when he finally did so, for the elections of March 1928, it bore the characteristic title of the 'Non-party Bloc for Co-operation with the Government' (BBWR) and had no well-defined programme beyond what its name suggests.

Under Polish conditions there was much to be said for this semi-autocratic system. It allowed a fair degree of personal and political freedom: parties, apart from Communist organizations, were not banned, few people were arrested and the press was relatively free. At the same time, it provided a strong government with continuity of policy, indispensable if any consistent plan concerning the national minorities, economic problems or foreign policy was to be pursued. And indeed, in the early years, the regime did enjoy a number of successes. The economic situation improved considerably, the result mainly of the general upturn in world trade and the opportunities created for Polish coal exports by the protracted British coal strike of 1926. But the increased stability and effectiveness of the government also played a part. In relation to the minorities, some success was achieved in winning their co-operation, particularly among the Jews and some of the Ukrainians. In foreign policy some fairly successful attempts were made to bring about a relaxation in Poland's extremely tense relations with Germany.

Nevertheless, in the long run, the 'Piłsudski system' proved scarcely more successful than its predecessors, the much maligned 'sejmocracy'. Although Piłsudski had come to power, as we have seen, with the support of the parties of the Left (the PPS and the two radical peasant groups, the Liberation and the Peasant Party), he came into increasing conflict with them. At the root of this clash lay the desire of the Left to exercise more influence over government policy; when at length its leaders, after repeated rebuffs, came to the conclusion that Piłsudski was no longer on their side, they began to call more and more insistently for a return to a fully democratic system. The conflict came to a head following the elections of March 1928. The voting was relatively free, and the results were seen by the government as a victory, since its electoral grouping, the BBWR, emerged as the largest bloc in parliament, although it did not win an over-all majority. However, the methods the government had employed in its campaign, notably the use of the local administration to put pressure on voters and the misappropriation of government funds for its electoral expenses, were keenly resented by the parties of the Left. As a result, in April 1929 they impeached the minister of finance, Gabriel Czechowicz, for failing to submit for ratification to parliament the government's supplementary credits for 1927–8 (those not already provided for in the budget). This failure was almost certainly dictated by Piłsudski's reluctance to reveal that he had authorized the appropriation of public funds for the government's electoral campaign. Although the verdict on Czechowicz was inconclusive, it was generally interpreted as a defeat for the government. For the following eighteen months the parliamentary conflict dominated political life, growing more and more acrimonious after the onset of the great depression, which was to prove exceedingly severe in Poland. The clash led six parties of the Centre and Left, the Piast, the Christian Democrats, the National Workers' Party, the Liberation, the Peasant Party and the PPS, to ally themselves in a Centre-Left bloc. When the government decided to resolve the dispute by dissolving parliament in August 1930, the Centre-Left, which refused all along to consider extra-parliamentary action, believed it could force Piłsudski to resign by defeating him in the coming elections. However, by arresting a large number of the Opposition's supporters and by strong administrative pressure, the government won a resounding victory in November 1930.

After 1930 the *Sanacja*, as the Piłsudski regime was called, was securely in power. It became increasingly autocratic, though still not totalitarian, and increasingly isolated from society as Piłsudski came more and more to rely on the views of his inner group of advisers, the so-called 'Colonels', mostly veterans from his Legion. It lost, too, such dynamism as it had once possessed, for Piłsudski, old, sick and somewhat demoralized by his clash with parliament, failed to provide effective leadership and there was no one among his associates who could do so in his place. To them he remained, not a political leader but the commander of Legionary days, to whom unquestioning obedience was due. Within the government, the interchange of opinion and the discussion of possible alternative policies atrophied almost completely.

Partly for this reason the government was markedly less successful in its later years. Its orthodox deflationary policy prolonged the depression in Poland until early 1936, and caused enormous hardship. In foreign affairs, Piłsudski continued to see Russia as Poland's main enemy and failed to appreciate the danger created by the rise of Hitler. He did not believe that Nazism posed a serious threat to Poland, since its aggressive tendencies would be directed first towards Austria and Czechoslovakia and subsequently towards the Soviet Union, and he continued, after Hitler's seizure of power, to seek friendly relations with Germany, concluding a non-aggression agreement in January 1934. Claims that he proposed a preventive war

against the Nazis to the French in 1933 have little basis. Moreover, although the Marshal, as Piłsudski was generally referred
to by his followers, had claimed that the interests of the army
had been neglected by the politicians before 1926, his old-
fashioned views on strategy and tactics hindered any real
attempt at modernization and meant that Poland's weakness in
relation to Germany and the Soviet Union grew steadily more
pronounced.

Poland without Piłsudski

After Piłsudski's death in May 1935 the negative features of the
regime he had established became even more evident. Though
the Marshal in his later years had taken little actual part in the
running of the government, his mere presence had provided an
ultimate authority which could settle all disputes over the
direction of policy and which could unite the somewhat disparate
elements which made up the *Sanacja*. After his death there was
no one among his successors who could assume his authority and
exercise his control, for his chosen successor, Sławek, meant
well, but was quite incapable of performing such a role, while
Rydz-Śmigły's attempt to use the vast powers he enjoyed as
supreme commander of the army to achieve such a position was
also a failure. As a result, the government was riven by deep
division of personality and policy. Indeed, the open conflict
between those like President Mościcki, who favoured a return
to a constitutional system, and those like Rydz, who wished to
introduce more open totalitarianism, had still not been resolved
by 1939, and a decisive confrontation was prevented only by the
increasingly threatening nature of the international situation.

The regime also became more autocratic. The new constitution, enacted by a very dubious legal procedure in April
1935, just before Piłsudski's death, reduced still further the
powers of parliament and increased those of the president and
the supreme commander. The new electoral law passed after the
marshal's death considerably impeded the participation in
elections of political parties, and led the opposition to boycott
the elections of 1935 and 1938. At the same time, the 1930s
had seen a strong growth in Poland of Right-radical and anti-
Semitic organizations, fuelled by the incapacity of the government to deal with the economic crisis. In an attempt to diminish

its unpopularity, the regime increasingly adopted nationalist slogans, and the government Camp of National Unity created in May 1936 after the dissolution of the BBWR was openly anti-Jewish in character. Though the government still discouraged anti-Jewish violence, it now increasingly claimed that the solution of the Jewish problem could only lie in the emigration of the overwhelming majority of the country's 3 million Jews. It is probable that only the outbreak of war prevented the adoption of anti-Jewish legislation.

In foreign affairs, the unimaginative application by Józef Beck, the foreign minister, of the Piłsudski formula that Poland should pursue a policy of balance between her two powerful neighbours, meant closely aligning the country with Nazi Germany, particularly in 1938. This policy derived from the belief that Nazi Germany was fundamentally anti-Soviet and anti-Russian and could never reach an accommodation with the Soviet Union. As a result, it was held good relations should be maintained with Germany, though an alliance was ruled out. This policy saw no danger in Hitler's destruction of the Versailles system, and its effect was to place Poland in an increasingly exposed position in relation to Nazi Germany. It rested on the assumption that Poland was a great power, and hence the failure effectively to reorganize the Polish army meant that it was based to a considerable extent on bluff, as was cruelly revealed in September 1939. Beck's policy was finally abandoned early in 1939, but the change came too late to save Poland's independence.

Yet it would be wrong to see the history of Poland between the wars largely in negative terms. The twenty years of independence witnessed the integration of the different parts of the country after over a century of foreign rule. National consciousness became far more widely extended, particularly among the peasantry, while much progress was made in training a class of administrators and civil servants. Considerable advance was achieved in the economic sphere, with the development of the port of Gdynia and the creation of a single railway network in the 1920s and the development of the Central Industrial Region in the 1930s. Much was also done in the field of education, particularly in the reduction of the level of illiteracy.

One of the striking features of the late 1930s was the growing maturity and political skill of the parties of the Centre and Left. Their victory, a brief and inconclusive one, it is true, came after the catastrophic defeat of Poland by Germany in the three-week campaign of September 1939, which exposed the emptiness of the Piłsudski followers' pretentious insistence that they had created a 'Great Power Poland'. The government formed in France under General Sikorski was composed of the successors of the Centre-Left bloc and the liberal elements among the National Democrats. Its politics were unquestionably democratic in the western sense. On this new government fell the heavy task of continuing the war with Germany and defending the Polish cause. But its establishment did not end the political conflicts among the *émigrés*, which became particularly bitter after the death of Sikorski in July 1943. Moreover, as it turned out, it was unable to reach an accord with the Russians. As a result, with the victory of the Soviet Union in Eastern Europe, the Poles were not given a second chance to see if they could make democracy work.

Notes

1 R. Dmowski, *Niemcy, Rosja i kwestja polska* (Warsaw, 1908), p. 30.
2. J. Piłsudski, 'Jak stałem się socjalista', *Pisma zbiorowe* (Warsaw, 1937–8), vol. II, p. 52.
3 Quoted in J. Hupka, *Z czasów wielkiej wojny* (Niwiska, 1936), p. 116.
4 A. Uziembło, 'Przegrupowanie', *Głos Prawdy*, 6 September 1924.
5 W. Stpiczyński, 'Po dziesięciu latach', *Głos Prawdy*, 9 August 1924.
6 S. Thugutt, *Wybór pism i autobiografia* (Glasgow, 1943), p. 109.
7 S. Thugutt, *Wyzwolenie*, 27 July 1924.
8 Z. Landau and J. Tomaszewski, *Zarys historii gospodarczej Polski* (Warsaw, 1962), p. 51.
9 See the Statistical appendix, Table 14, p. 166.
10 A. Ajnenkiel, *Od 'Rządów ludowych' do prewrotu majowego* (Warsaw, 1964), p. 18.
11 *Ibid.*, p. 234.
12 J. Piłsudski, *Pisma zbiorowe*, IX, p. 10.
13 W. Baranowski, *Rozmowy z Pilsudskim 1916r–1931r* (Warsaw, 1938), pp. 205–6.

Chapter 2

Hungary

Hungarian political life throughout the entire interwar period, and indeed until 1945, was completely dominated by revisionism – the desire to regain for Hungary the territory lost by the Treaty of Trianon of June 1920. The treaty had certainly dealt Hungary some cruel blows. By the Compromise of 1867, the Hungarians had gained control of the whole of historic Hungary, an area in which the Magyars constituted in 1910 barely $48 \cdot 1$ per cent of the total population (or $54 \cdot 5$ per cent if one excluded Croatia-Slavonia),[1] and in which there were substantial Slovak, Rumanian, Serb and Croat minorities. It is true that the Croats were granted wide-ranging autonomy, and that by the nationalities law of 1868 the other groups were assured their national rights, above all the right to education in the mother tongue. But in practice the Hungarian authorities continually attempted to encroach on the rights of Croatia, while the other nationalities were subjected to an increasing and unrelenting campaign of Magyarization. The result was the opposite of what was intended. The Magyars had considerable success in assimilating their German and Jewish minorities. They were also able to give the towns throughout Hungary a Magyar character. However all the other minorities, Rumanians, Serbs and, to a lesser extent, Slovaks, proved resistant to Magyar pressure, and by 1914 all were seriously alienated from the state. In Croatia, too, the pro-Hungarian orientation continually lost ground, while the Croat nationalist and pan-Yugoslav groupings gained in strength. The discontent of the nationalities was easily controlled before 1914, but it became far more difficult to deal with when Hungary went to war, together with Austria, in alliance with Germany. Ranged on the other side among the Allied powers were Serbia, from August 1916 Rumania, and the 'Czechoslovaks', whose national aspirations were recognized as an Allied war aim in January 1918. From July 1917, when Serbian objectives had come to involve the establishment of a Yugoslav state incorporating Croats and Slovenes, as well as the Serbs of Austria-Hungary, these belligerents all made far-reaching claims on Hungarian territory. Their claims were fully met after the defeat of the Central Powers. By the Treaty of Trianon, Hungary lost 67 per cent of its prewar area (71·5 per cent if one includes Croatia) and 58·3 per cent of its population (63·5 per cent if one includes Croatia).[2]

These losses were painfully felt, the more so since pre-war Hungary had formed an admirable economic unit, the raw-material-producing mountainous regions complementing the industries of the plains, while the whole communications system had been concentrated on Budapest. Moreover, the Magyars had certain valid grievances against the way they had been treated. It had proved impossible to draw boundaries which coincided with national divisions. In Slovakia, for instance, the area in which Slovaks constituted the majority ended approximately where the mountain valleys met the plain. Yet, if the frontier had been drawn along this line, the different Slovak valleys would have had no means of communicating with each other, and thus a strip of Magyar plain was also included. There were, moreover, a number of large pockets of Magyar settlement, for instance in Transylvania, which were divided by a belt of Rumanian settlement from Hungary proper. The result was that nearly 3½ million Magyars were left outside Hungary.

The belief that Hungary had been done a grave injustice at Trianon and the desire to modify the treaty was almost universal. It is true that there were differences of emphasis. Some called for the return to Hungary's prewar frontiers, while others demanded only those areas in which Hungarians constituted a majority or a significant minority. There were also differences as to how revision could best be achieved, whether alliance with Italy or Germany was necessary, or whether one could trust to the sense of justice of the western powers, in particular

Great Britain. Nevertheless the history of Hungary from 1920 to 1945 can be written almost entirely in terms of Hungarian revisionism.

The Hungarian governments of the interwar period were not only revisionist but also counter-revolutionary, in that they all aimed at returning to and maintaining the political system which had been operating before 1914. This had been a tightly knit oligarchy, in which serious differences had existed on the nature of the relationship between Hungary and Austria, but in which there were no other major political divisions. The land-owning class and its offshoots in the towns, to which many gentry had migrated from the 1880s onwards to find employ-ment in the civil service, had been at one on most significant issues. They agreed that political power should remain in their own hands (as late as 1914 only 8 per cent of the population had the vote), that the political and social demands of the large class of small peasants and agricultural labourers and the growing class of industrial workers should be held in check, and that no significant concessions should be made to the nationalities. The handful of men like Count Mihály Károlyi and Oszkár Jászi, who had prophesied the disasters which these policies in the end produced, were entirely disregarded before 1914.

The system came under strong attack as a result of the First World War, which ended disastrously for Hungary and which also greatly exacerbated social tensions. In this situation Károlyi, who before the war had called for Hungary to break her ties with Austria and Germany and pursue a more equitable policy towards Hungary's minorities, was able to emerge as a major political force. The prewar ruling class was widely held responsible for Hungary's catastrophic defeat, and the time seemed ripe for the long-overdue reform of Hungary's political and social system.

Károlyi believed that his political record before and during the war would induce the Allies to deal generously with Hungary. He was grievously mistaken, for the Allies were determined to reduce Hungary to her narrowest ethnic frontiers. The ulti-matum presented to Károlyi in March 1919 by Colonel Vyx, the French Chief of the Allied Mission in Budapest, even demanded that a neutral zone be created in the eastern part of ethnic Hungary to facilitate Rumanian intervention in the Russian civil war, and implied that this area too would have to be ceded. In this situation the only alternative seemed to be to link the fate of Hungary to that of the revolution in Russia. Károlyi resigned and transferred power to the Social Democrats. Although the Social Democrats were anything but revolutionary (they had suppressed in February Communist-inspired riots against Károlyi and had arrested Béla Kun and most of the Communist leadership), they saw no alternative to a Soviet-Russian orientation. As one of their leaders, Sándor Garbai, put it: 'We must take a new direction and obtain from the East what has been refused to us by the West.'[3] The Communists were released, a union between the Socialist and Communist parties negotiated and a Soviet republic established. This soon alienated most of its support by refusing to distribute land to the peasantry, by its wholesale nationalization of virtually everything, including barbers' shops, and by its anti-church campaign. Its only hope of success rested on Russian help, and the Soviets, hard pressed at this critical stage of the civil war, were never able to provide significant aid. The desperate attempts made by the Communist Police Commissar, Tibor Szamuely, to keep the regime in power, and the attendant executions, only further undermined the regime, and at the end of July it was easily overthrown by Hungarian counter-revolutionaries and Rumanian troops.

The 133-day Soviet republic had an enormous impact on Hungarian politics throughout the interwar period. It caused a widespread distaste among virtually the entire political class not only for communism and socialism, but also for liberal democracy. Anti-Semitism also became much more widespread because of the large role played by the Jews in the revolution (the majority of the Soviet's commissars had been Jews). Before the First World War the Hungarian oligarchy had encouraged the assimilation of the Jews, and the large majority of the Jews had become enthusiastic Magyars. In 1907, for instance, seven of the thirteen members of the highest appeal court had been Jewish, while Jews played a prominent role both in the world of business and finance and in the liberal professions. Attempts to exploit political anti-Semitism had been as ruthlessly suppressed as the separatist aspirations of the nationalities. Now, however, anti-Semitism had gained a new respectability, and was to acquire a new force, particularly with the impact of the great depression.

The crushing of the revolution had been primarily the result of its own weakness and of the intervention of the Rumanian army. But the revolution had also given rise to a Hungarian counter-revolution, whose adherents assembled in Vienna, where an 'Anti-Bolshevik' committee had been established in April 1919, and still more in Szeged, where a counter-revolutionary government was formed under the former admiral of the Austro-Hungarian fleet and *aide-de-camp* to the Emperor Franz Josef, Miklós Horthy. The counter-revolutionaries included, of course, a large number of representatives of the oligarchy that had governed Hungary before 1914. It also brought a new feature to Hungarian political life, that Right-radicalism which was soon to become such an unlovely feature of the political life of much of Eastern Europe. The Right-radicals were very hostile to the pre-war system, which they rejected not only because of its frustration of the more extreme Hungarian national demands (as for instance, the claims for a separate Hungarian army with Hungarian as the language of command), but also because of its repression of the claims of the socially oppressed classes. Its largely middle-class adherents were, however, equally strongly opposed to Marxist socialism, which they saw as an anti-national and Jewish conspiracy. Their anti-Semitism was further buttressed by the belief that the prewar political system had been merely a front behind which the dominance of Jewish finance capitalism had been achieved. Right-radicals of this type, of whom the prominent was the former army officer, Captain Gyula Gömbös, were the strongest element in the counter-revolutionary army established at Szeged, and also in the independent armed formations such as the 'Ragged Guard' which had been responsible for the worst excesses of the counter-revolution. They drew a good deal of their strength from the more than 300,000 refugees who fled to Hungary from Czechoslovakia, Rumania and Yugoslavia after 1918 and who had great difficulty in establishing new lives for themselves. Their strongholds were the numerous secret and semi-secret patriotic societies which proliferated in the fertile soil of post-war Hungary. Of these the most important was the Hungarian Association of National Defence, founded and dominated by Gömbös, and its two secret subgroups, the Hungarian Scientific Race Protecting Society and the Society of the Double Cross (so named after the Cross of Lorraine, which was part of the Hungarian royal insignia).

Another of the sources of Right-radical support was the

Hungarian army. The army of Austria-Hungary had been one of the common institutions of the monarchy and, in spite of Hungarian agitation for a separate army, German had remained its language of command right up to 1918 (though the Hungarians had been promised their own army after victory). The only military force in which Hungarian was the language of command was the second-line militia, the Honvéd. Because of this, the Imperial Army was always regarded by Hungarian patriots as a slightly suspect and anti-national force, and Imperial Army officers were looked on with a mixture of suspicion and contempt. Few members of the Hungarian oligarchy felt a career in the army to be compatible with the maintenance of their national identity. The army did, however, prove a highly attractive career to the able sons of the German (Swabian) peasantry in central Hungary, who were at the same time enthusiastically Magyarizing themselves.

As a result, the large majority of the officers in the small Hungarian army of 35,000 permitted by the Treaty of Trianon were Swabians. They were eager Magyar patriots, but their German ancestry affected them in two ways. First, they were much more prepared than other Hungarians to believe in the invincible might of the German Reich. At the same time, coming from outside the traditional oligarchy, they were extremely susceptible to Right-radical views, and also imbibed from their Austrian military schooling a strong belief in the special responsibilities which fell on the army as the embodiment of the national interest. They were thus regarded with considerable suspicion by the more moderate conservative politicians.

The Regent Miklós Horthy and Count István Bethlen

The Right-radicals did not, for the moment, take power. This was partly because the Entente, professing a belief in liberal democracy, was prepared to use its influence to prevent the counter-revolution getting too far out of hand. However, it was far more the result of a successful reassertion of their political strength by the prewar oligarchy. It is true that its members were deeply divided on the question of a Habsburg restoration, a problem brought into the open by the two attempts of the former King Charles to regain his throne in 1921. This division had a social basis in that the larger aristocrats and the Catholics

tended to favour the Habsburgs, whereas the gentry and the
Calvinists, while not republican, took the view that the Habsburgs
had forfeited the throne, and that the nation had the right to
elect any one it wished as sovereign. Nevertheless this question,
which had aroused strong passions, ceased to be actual with the
death of King Charles in 1922. His successor was a minor,
Otto, and, deeply under the influence of his unpopular mother,
Zita, did not possess the same attractions as his father. On all
other matters, the vast majority of the oligarchy were at one.
They won their first victory with the election in March 1920 of
Miklós Horthy to the vital office of Regent. The Regent's
powers were indeed vast. He was not only head of the armed
forces, the members of which swore an oath of loyalty to him
personally, but he had the right to dissolve parliament and
appoint and dismiss the prime minister. He had a suspensive
veto over legislation and was, for all practical purposes, irre-
movable. Horthy had some close links with the Right-radicals
and remained on extremely close terms with the most prominent of them, Gyula Gömbös, until the latter's death in 1936,
but he was hostile to most of their views and became more so
as the period wore on. A conservative of the old school, he
disliked their demagogy and virulent anti-Semitism (though he
was not himself particularly friendly to the Jews). He was
deeply suspicious of their calls for land reform, which he
regarded as totally unwarranted and also disliked their attempts
to interfere with the army, over which he regarded himself as
possessing proprietary rights. He disliked, too, the plebeian
origins of many of the Right-radicals, whom he did not regard
as 'gentlemen'. An admirer of Great Britain, he also did not
share the Right-radicals' belief that the democracies of the
west were decadent. He had, moreover, been deeply influenced
by his years in Franz Josef's service, and in a difficult situation
he would, he claimed, always ask himself how his old master
would have acted. At the same time, he became even more hostile
to a Habsburg restoration with the perils it would inevitably
have brought for Hungary.

As the years passed, he became more and more opposed to the
attempts of the Right-radicals to introduce a fascist system into
Hungary. This is not to suggest that he was a particularly wise or
percipient politician. Never an especially intelligent man, he
was continually exposed to the most extreme flattery and grew

to trust implicitly his own judgment, which was not always particularly sound. He was also not well informed: never aware, for instance, of the extent to which the army officers, who he believed were devoted to his person, were committed to Right-radical views, as was to become painfully obvious when he tried to take Hungary out of the war in October 1944.

The main architect of the re-establishment of the position of the 'historic classes' was Count István Bethlen, who became prime minister in April 1921. Bethlen, a Transylvanian Calvinist nobleman from a family which had played a distinguished part in Hungarian history, was a deeply conservative man. He was as fully committed to the revision of the Treaty of Trianon as the most rabid of the Right-radicals, but he had a longer view than most of his contemporaries and realized that before an active foreign policy could be pursued, the country would need to achieve a certain degree of political and economic consolidation. Given the lack of resources in Hungary, he saw that the only source of the finance necessary for economic reconstruction must come from abroad. In order to obtain foreign capital he was prepared to make far-reaching verbal concessions. Before he obtained the loan of 250 million gold crowns in March 1924, which he used to stabilize the Hungarian currency and end the runaway inflation, he signed a protocol with Britain, France, Italy and the Little Entente by which Hungary undertook 'strictly and loyally to fulfil the obligations contained in the . . . Treaty [of Trianon], and in particular the military clauses'.[4] He also made considerable concessions to the domestic capitalists, many of whom were Jews.

Bethlen's rigorous financial orthodoxy had a good deal of success. The inflation ceased, and behind a high tariff new factories developed to make good the losses the country had sustained. Between 1921 and 1930 the number of workers employed in factories rose markedly, while the index of industrial production increased from 50 to 112·5.[5] Foreign trade also grew rapidly. Moreover, though little was done to implement the rather meagre land reform of 1921, and the second instalment promised when the Smallholders merged with the Government Party was not introduced, nevertheless the decline in the rural birth rate and the high price of agricultural produce meant that the countryside in Hungary was relatively prosperous.

Bethlen's stabilization rested on rather shaky foundations. In spite of the development of industry, for most of the 1920s over three-quarters of Hungary's exports consisted of agricultural produce, above all wheat. The country was dependent on these exports to finance the import of the raw materials used in its factories and was thus desperately vulnerable to a fall in international wheat prices. Moreover, throughout the 1920s the Hungarian trade balance had been negative, and the gap had been met by borrowing abroad. By 1931–2 the service of Hungary's external debts amounted to 48 per cent of her total foreign trade.[6]

Bethlen's foreign policy was also not unsuccessful. In the 1920s, the Hungarians were relatively inactive in this field. In the first place, the Treaty of Trianon had restricted the Hungarian army to 35,000 men, and had laid down that its armaments were not to exceed 105 light guns and 140 trench mortars. These stipulations were by and large enforced by the Allied control commissioners and were moreover rather difficult to evade because of the concentration of Hungarian arms production in three or four large factories. Both Germany and Russia, the principal opponents of the Versailles settlement, were little involved in South-Eastern Europe and thus the French-sponsored Little Entente of Czechoslovakia, Rumania and Yugoslovia was able to hold Hungarian revisionist aims in check with relative ease. The Hungarians did make some attempts to break out of the ring round them. In spite of the bitterness engendered by the loss of the Burgenland, they were able to establish fairly satisfactory relations with Austria, particularly when the Christian Socials, who were much less hostile to the counter-revolutionary character of the Hungarian regime, increasingly displaced the Socialists as the dominant party. More important, in April 1927 a treaty of friendship and alliance was signed with the Italians, who had also established close relations with Bulgaria, the other main revisionist country in the Balkans and who had, by this stage, achieved a virtual protectorate over Albania. However, Italian commitment to Hungarian revisionism was at this stage never more than half-hearted, for Mussolini was not at all enamoured of the 'feudal' character of Bethlen's regime. In addition, the Italian revisionist group of states was still far too weak to challenge effectively the rival French grouping.

In the political sphere, Bethlen's aim was, as far as possible, to return to the situation as it had existed before 1914. In this he had a surprising degree of success. He was aided by the widespread revulsion against socialist and even democratic ideas which was the legacy of the Soviet republic, and also by his own opposition to a Habsburg restoration, which won him a good deal of support from people who might otherwise have been chary of his conservative views. He reached an agreement with the Socialists by which, in return for legalizing the party and granting a political amnesty, its leaders agreed not to agitate among agricultural labourers and to regard 'the general interests of the country and the nation'[7] as identical with their own. More important, he was able to induce the more radical of the two parties which had emerged after the war, the Smallholders, to merge with the conservative Christian Nationals in February 1922, an alliance in which Bethlen held the dominant position. At the same time, he was able to do away with the post-war franchise which had given some 40 per cent of the population the vote and had introduced the secret ballot, and to return to the franchise enacted in 1913 but never implemented, under which only 27·5 per cent of the population had the vote, and voting was open, except in a small number of towns.

The result of these changes was effectively to end any control by the electorate over the government. The United Party had no fixed principles except to maintain the government in power, and the patronage dispensed by the prime minister was more than sufficient to keep its members under control. Indeed the party generally came to be known as the 'Government Party'. As the semi-official newspaper, *Pester Lloyd*, put it, 'this Party has the natural calling of showing itself a serviceable and willing instrument of the Government'.[8] Moreover, the system of open voting and the government's control over local-government officials ensured that an election could never be lost. There might be revolts from within the Government Party, but these could usually be contained. There was certainly no real prospect of the government's being overthrown.

This oligarchical system had some relatively liberal features. Bethlen was hostile to the Right-radicals, and the power of the paramilitary groupings was diminished. At the same time, radical criticism of the government was allowed, provided it kept within certain bounds, and the press preserved a modicum of freedom.

Nevertheless, though out of power, the Right-radicals remained a significant force. Bethlen had succeeded in neutralizing their influence by employing a fair number of refugees in the civil service. But the precarious character of Hungary's economic recovery and the need to balance the budget forced him to dismiss 25,000 civil servants, who had great difficulty in finding alternative employment and who constituted a strong repository for Right-radical views. The army officers too remained highly suspicious of Bethlen's policy of fulfilment of the Treaty of Trianon. Near-fascist views also made important progress among the younger generation, who were repelled by the reactionary and socially repressive features of Bethlen's regime. Hostile to socialism and communism because of the experience of the Soviet republic, they adopted with alacrity the view that his government was merely the tool of international Jewish capitalism. Moreover, the policy of expanding university places in order to produce the administrators who would carry through the Magyarization of Hungary's lost provinces when these were regained created a large number of people who had great difficulty in finding suitable employment and who bitterly resented the Jewish near-monopoly of trade and industry and the strong Jewish position in the free professions. In 1914 the total number of students graduating in the whole of Hungary had been 11,000. By 1925, in the new, greatly reduced state, 12,000 graduated annually.[9] The Right-radicals also enjoyed a fair amount of support in government circles. In 1929, for instance, the most important of them, Gyula Gömbös, the advocate of a revisionist axis of Italy, Germany and Hungary, who had been closely associated with Hitler's activities in Munich in 1923, became minister of defence.

Gömbös, the unsuccessful fascist

The Bethlen system was destroyed by the great depression. From 1929 the world price for wheat began to fall catastrophically, and it became increasingly difficult to find markets, particularly when the Czechs denounced their commercial treaty with Hungary in December 1930. The failure in 1931 of the Austrian Creditanstalt, with which the main Hungarian banks were closely connected, and the spread of the crisis to Germany, precipitated a financial panic in Hungary. Unemployment rose rapidly and the condition of the countryside deteriorated disastrously.

Faced with mounting opposition in the Government Party and increasingly out of favour with Horthy, Bethlen resigned in August 1931. As he told a friend, he did not feel himself 'possessed of sufficient energy to carry through to the end, a second time, the distasteful task of *Sanierung*'.[10] With his fall Hungarian politics entered a state of flux from which it was not to emerge until the defeat of Germany and the occupation of Hungary by the Red Army. There were two elements in this crisis. In the first place, the issue was how far the relatively liberal character of the Bethlen regime should be maintained and to what extent a totalitarian system on Italian and German lines should be introduced. Second was how far should Hungary look to fascist Italy and Nazi Germany for help in achieving her revisionist goals. These two questions were closely connected, in that those who favoured the introduction of a fascist regime were also strong supporters of an Italian and German orientation. The effect was to divide the politically active classes in Hungary into two major groupings, rather confusingly called the Left and the Right. The Left included the Regent himself, conservatives of the Bethlen stamp, the great Catholic and legitimist magnates, the democratic and socialist opposition, and the Jews. The Right was supported by a section within the Government Party, the Right-radicals and the fascist groups, which had mushroomed during the depression, and the army officers, who became steadily more extreme as the power of Nazi Germany grew. As will be evident, both the Right and the Left had supporters in the government and in the opposition, and this gave to the political conflicts from 1931 to 1945 a curious air of unreality, with socialists implicitly supporting Horthy and being opposed by Right-radicals calling for far-reaching land reforms. On the face of it the Left, with the support of most of the 'historic' classes, seemed well placed to uphold its position. Yet the increasing dynamism of Nazi Germany and the ease with which Hitler was able to destroy the Versailles system played into the hands of the Right, and their views increasingly dominated policy, although it was not until the eve of the German collapse that they were actually able to take power.

Bethlen was succeeded by another aristocratic conservative, Count Gyula Károlyi, but he too was unable to deal with the situation, and in September 1932 power was handed over to Gyula Gömbös. Gömbös, an army officer of German origin, had been the organizer of the military forces of the counter-revolutionaries at Szeged and was a convinced Right-radical and admirer of Hilter and Mussolini. He had been involved in Hilter's abortive Munich plot in 1923 and in 1927 had founded a short-lived 'Party of Racial Defence'. He was on good terms with the Regent, with whom he had co-operated closely at Szeged and, though he entered the cabinet in 1929, he did not abandon his Right-radical views. His appointment was the result of strong dissatisfaction within the Government Party at the methods which had been employed by Bethlen and Károlyi to deal with the depression. It owed a good deal to the rival of Right-radical agitation among the lower civil servants and junior army officers, who were bearing the brunt of the government's deflationary measures, and among the university students whose opportunities had been even more severely restricted by the depression.

It was widely believed that his appointment would result in the introduction of a fascist system in Hungary. These fears were given substance by his first actions after taking office. An enormous procession of patriotic societies paraded throughout Budapest chanting 'Long live our Leader' and were duly addressed by him in Mussolini style from a balcony. Gömbös, however, was not the stuff of which fascist dictators are made. He tamely accepted the far-reaching limitations imposed on him by the Regent, agreeing not to dissolve parliament, in which Bethlen's influence remained predominant, and undertaking not to introduce a radical land reform or anti-Semitic legislation. His choice of ministers was severely circumscribed, and of these only one shared his Right-radical views. Even before taking office, Gömbös had assured a number of leading industrialists that he would not introduce a policy hostile to their interests. He subsequently reached an agreement with the Jews, as a result of which he 'revised his views on the Jewish question'[11] and specifically repudiated any intention of pursuing an anti-Semitic policy. Furthermore he was quite unwilling to break with orthodox financial doctrine, since he believed that only by pursuing a policy of rigid deflation could he obtain from international financial circles the loans he regarded as necessary for Hungary's recovery from the economic crisis. This policy had the same effect as in Poland, in that it delayed the end of the depression in Hungary until 1934–5.

However, though Gömbös did not fulfil the fears and hopes of those who saw him as a Hungarian Mussolini, his three-year premiership was a significant stage in the process by which Hungary became far more authoritarian and far more committed to the Axis powers. He brought this about above all by his initiatives in foreign affairs. Immediately after taking office, he visited Mussolini in Rome and was able to induce the Duce to give much greater substance to the Italo-Hungarian friendship treaty of 1927. Mussolini now became a far more convinced supporter of Hungarian revisionism, condemning the Treaty of Trianon as 'inspired by political calculations which time and experience had already condemned'.[12] This went much further than any of his earlier statements and made it virtually impossible for any of Gömbös's successors to abandon the Italian orientation, with its necessary internal consequences, one of which was a constant stressing of the similarity between the political systems of Italy and Hungary. It is true that relations with Germany were adversely affected by the close Hungarian ties with Italy, since the Reich was at odds with Mussolini over Austria. But with the German-Italian *rapprochement* which began in 1936, Hungary found herself irrevocably linked with the Axis powers, in spite of the dangers which many of the conservatives, including Horthy, saw in this situation.

Internally, too, Gömbös was not as unsuccessful as he appeared on the surface. He was able to reorganize the Government Party and strengthen his own position in it, and he also created a 'Movement for National Unity' intended to stand behind this party and push it in the direction of establishing a one-party system. In the army, the civil service and the local bureaucracy his own supporters were steadily infiltrated into prominent positions, while government control over the press was increased and a number of new pro-government newspapers founded. The surveillance of the opposition, particularly through the mails and the telephone system, was also stepped up.

The high point of Gömbös's position came in early 1936 when he was able to persuade Horthy to dissolve parliament. He went to the country with a promise to break the stranglehold of the conservative forces and introduce radical changes, above all a new land reform. The new parliament, elected in March 1936, contained a majority of his Right-radical supporters, and Gömbös now declared in the Senate his intention of introducing a fascist regime. By his actions, however, he aroused the strong opposition of the conservatives, above all Bethlen, who resigned from the government, and even more important, Horthy himself. Horthy, annoyed by Gömbös's interference with the army and his schemes for a land reform, came to the conclusion that 'Gömbös was not a gentleman' and became determined to dismiss him. His power was effectively cut down and he was only allowed to remain in office because it emerged that he was mortally ill. When he died in October 1936, he was succeeded by a conservative aristocrat, Kálmán Darányi. However, though the regime remained a curious coalition of old-fashioned conservatives, it proved impossible to turn back from the path on which Gömbös had embarked, and the irony of Hungarian history was that from now on policies more or less in line with Gömbös's views were put through by people who disliked and distrusted what they were doing but who, under the pressure of events, could see no alternative.

Gömbös's period of office also saw the emergence of more extreme Right-radical groupings, partly as a result of disillusionment with the meagre results of his own half-measures, partly under the stimulus of the growing dynamism of Italy and Germany. There was a bewildering variety of these groups, which emerged, fused and split again with remarkable speed. But what they all shared was the feeling that what was needed was a radical attack on the old oligarchy and its allies, 'international Jewish financial power'. They called for radical land reforms, anti-Jewish legislation and an even closer linking of Hungarian foreign policy to that of the Axis powers. Of the different exponents of these views the most successful was a rather woolly-minded army officer, Ferenc Szálasi, who obtained a good deal of popular support for his 'Arrow Cross' movement, and who enjoyed a fair amount of patronage from a number of fascist-minded army officers, above all, General Jenö Rátz, the chief of the General Staff.

Hungary in the shadow of resurgent Germany

The main reason it proved impossible to abandon the policies initiated by Gömbös was the continuous series of foreign-policy successes enjoyed by the Axis powers, and above all by Germany. The remilitarization of the Rhineland in March 1936 meant that it was virtually impossible for France to fulfil her military commitments to her East European allies and this drastically altered the political situation. Hungarian politicians, even those who, like Horthy, believed that in a conflict between Germany and Great Britain the sea power was bound to win, saw themselves faced with a situation in which they had little choice. If they allied themselves with Italy and Germany they saw a real chance to regain some of the territory they had lost in 1918. Even if Germany eventually lost a war with Britain, the Reich was likely to remain for a long period the dominant power in Central Europe and they hoped that in a final settlement the justice of their claim to some at least of the territories they had lost at Trianon would be recognized. If, on the other hand, they made common cause with the states of the Little Entente and their allies in Western Europe, they saw few satisfactory prospects. They would have to abandon all hopes of revision, for even the Czechs, the most conciliatory of the Little Entente states, were only prepared to consider the most marginal frontier changes. They also exposed themselves to the hostility of Hitler, who had several strong cards to play against them. He could use the discontent of the 600,000 Germans in Hungary, and he could also count on the firm support of large sections of the Right-radicals.

In this situation it proved pitifully easy to embark on a path which involved Hungary for the second time in a generation in a disastrous war in alliance with Germany – this in spite of the fact that the three prime ministers who succeeded Gömbös were all originally aristocratic conservatives of relatively liberal stamp, Kálmán Darányi (October1936 to May 1938), Béla Imrédy (May 1938 to February 1939) and Pál Teleki (February 1939 to April 1941). Darányi found himself compelled to tighten more and more his ties with the Axis. In March 1938 he announced his intention of introducing anti-Semitic legislation. Imrédy took this position to its logical conclusion. He piloted through 'moderate' anti-Semitic legislation on the grounds that only in this way could more extreme measures be avoided, and supported, though in a somewhat half-hearted way, German policy towards Czechoslovakia.

As a reward for this, Hungary received parts of Southern Slovakia in November 1938, and later Sub-Carpathian Ruthenia, when Bohemia and Moravia were incorporated into the Reich. Imrédy now renounced his liberal views, and paved the way for Hungary's entering the anti-Comintern pact in January 1939.

Imrédy's growing Right-radical proclivities were responsible for his dismissal by the increasingly conservative Horthy in February 1939. But his successor, the relatively liberal and pro-western Count Pál Teleki, proved unable to change his policies. A second much more radical anti-Jewish law was passed in May 1939, and in August 1940 Hungary was granted two-fifths of Transylvania as a result of German pressure on Rumania. Teleki became increasingly unhappy about the consequences of his policy and committed suicide in April 1941, as a protest against the Regent's decision to allow the German army to cross Hungary in order to invade Yugoslavia, the decision which led the Western powers to break off relations with Hungary.

Under Teleki's successor, László Bárdossy (April 1941 to March 1942), Hungary not only became more closely linked with Germany, but also took the fateful step in June 1941 of declaring war on the Soviet Union. In the end the increasingly independent actions of the pro-German Hungarian army alarmed the Regent, who replaced Bárdossy in March 1942 by the pro-Western Miklós Kállay. Kállay's attempts to extricate Hungary from the war failed, and led in March 1944 to German occupation and the imposition of a pro-German puppet government under General Döme Sztójay. Horthy continued somewhat ineffectually to resist, and when he announced an armistice with the Soviet Union in October he was removed by the Germans, having been abandoned by the army which he trusted so blindly. The dual character of the regime was now finally ended, and a radical fascist government under the Arrow Cross leader, Szálasi, took office. It held power only for a brief two months, until the German and Hungarian troops were forced out of Hungary by the Red Army. An anti-German left-wing coalition was then established which soon fell under the complete control of the Communists.

The tragedy of Hungarian history in the interwar period lay in the strong commitment of all her politicians to the revision of the 1920 frontiers. It was this which led them to co-operate, though rather unwillingly, with Hitler and Mussolini and brought about the introduction of increasingly authoritarian internal policies. The commitment to revisionism at all costs, coupled with the experience of the Soviet republic, also blinded many people to the necessity of radical social reforms if Hungary was to emerge as a modern state. Nevertheless the ruthless suppression of all opposition and the hardships of rigid Soviet-style industrialization soon alienated most of the population from the Communist regime established after 1945, and led to the revolution of 1956. Since then, however, partly thanks to the restraint of the Hungarian people and partly because of the ability of the Communist leader János Kádár, a fair measure of liberalization has taken place. Today Hungary is almost certainly the freest of Russia's satellites and the mass of her people are better off than they have been at any time in this century.

Notes

1 According to the census of 1910: *1910 évi népszámlálása* (Budapest, 1912), pp. 18–19.
2 Based on C. A. Macartney, *October Fifteenth* (Edinburgh, 1956), vol. 1, p. 4.
3 N. Stone, 'Béla Kun', *History of the Twentieth Century*, No. 33, p. 923.
4 Macartney, *op. cit.*, vol. 1, p. 63.
5 Taking the years 1925–9 as 100 (see the Statistical appendix, Table 33, p. 177).
6 See the Statistical appendix, Table 36, p. 179.
7 Macartney, *op. cit.*, vol. 1, p. 43.
8 *Pester Lloyd*, 15 September 1932, quoted in Macartney, *op. cit.*, vol. 1, p. 48.
9 Macartney, *op. cit.*, vol. 1, p. 78.
10 *Ibid.*, p. 94.
11 *Ibid.*, p. 117.
12 *Ibid.*, p. 115.

Chapter 3

Austria

'A nation without a state'

The emergence of Austria, or, as it was first called, German-Austria, was an inevitable and unwanted consequence of the collapse of the Habsburg monarchy. The Germans had made up something like 35 per cent of the population of the non-Hungarian part of the monarchy and their importance in it had been even greater than their numbers would have justified, since they provided a large part of its administration and army officers, and since the dynasty, though in many respects standing above the national question, was never prepared completely to abandon them. It is true that there was considerable dissatisfaction among the Germans, whose dominant position in Bohemia and Moravia was progressively undermined by the Czech national revival and who feared that they would be swamped by the more rapid increase of the Slav peoples. Extreme nationalist views were thus far more popular among them than they were among the Germans in the Reich. They feared above all that the dynasty would make an alliance with the Slavs and abandon German interests, as had occurred during the premiership of Count Taaffe (1879–93), whose 'iron ring' had ended the predominance of the German liberals and who had governed through an alliance of Czech conservatives, Poles and German landowners. One of his ministers had even affirmed that 'it was possible to rule Austria without the Germans'.[1] However, with the success of the German street demonstrations which prevented the passing of the Badeni ordinances in 1897, which would have ensured complete equality for the Czech and German languages in Bohemia, these fears receded. From now until the outbreak of the war Austria was governed by non-parliamentary ministers, mainly officials, and no further attempt was made to undermine what the Germans regarded as their vital national interests. In 1914, apart from a small group who wanted the German areas of Austria (including Bohemia) to be incorporated in Germany, the overwhelming majority of the Germans were loyal supporters of the Habsburg monarchy.

The collapse of the monarchy in 1918 was a drastic blow to its German subjects. Over 3 million were incorporated into the new Czechoslovak state and the remainder were thus forced to proclaim their independence. As Clemenceau cruelly but accurately put it, 'Austria is what is left over.'[2]

The areas which made up the new state had no geographic unity. On the one hand there were the Alpine lands, with a largely rural and peasant population, clerical and conservative, with strong local and provincial loyalties and with little industry outside Styria. These areas had very little in common with the great imperial capital of Vienna, cosmopolitan and by now largely socialist, which, with its population of 2 million, made up one-third of the inhabitants of the new state. The industries of Vienna had depended to a very great extent on the importation of raw materials from areas which were now in the successor states, and its population included the many officials needed for the running of the 50 million strong Habsburg Empire, who were quite superfluous in the new state. Its adjustment to the new conditions in which it found itself was to prove a long and difficult process. Moreover the antagonism between 'Red' Vienna and the largely Catholic and conservative rural districts was never overcome and created many political difficulties.

It was widely believed that the new country was not viable. In the words of one of the socialist laeders, Karl Renner, 'Overnight, at one stroke, we became a nation without a state.'[3] It was this belief that led the National Assembly to resolve unanimously in November 1918 that 'German-Austria is a constituent part of the German republic.'[4] Union with Germany was, however, vetoed by the Allies, as was the name 'German-Austria' and the next twenty years were to see a series of attempts to create an Austrian national identity, which were ultimately to founder in the face of a combination of internal weakness and the dynamism of Nazi Germany.

Three political camps

The fundamental characteristic of the political life of the new state was one which it inherited from the Habsburg period, its division into three political groupings, distinct from each other not only in their general approach to politics but in their whole *Weltanschauung*. All these groupings, the Christian Social Party, the Social Democrats and the German Nationalists had emerged as a result of the collapse of organized liberalism in Austria in the 1870s and 1880s. The Christian Social Party had started as a radical Catholic organization, attacking both aristocratic and clerical conservatism, and capitalism, which it interpreted as a largely Jewish phenomenon. Its support came originally from the lower middle class and artisans in Vienna and the Austrian provinces, who felt threatened by proletarianization as a result of the development of capitalism, but who were unwilling to cast in their lot with the industrial working class. The party's social radicalism and anti-Semitism earned it the opposition both of the ecclesiastical hierarchy and of the emperor himself, who had three times refused to ratify the election of the Christian Social leader Karl Lueger to the office of Lord Mayor of Vienna. However in the period before the First World War the party gradually became more conservative, gaining a considerable peasant following and reconciling the Church hierarchy to its views. In the republic, it adopted a generally 'christian democratic' view, though its strong hostility to the Social Democrats led it to become rather more extreme than might have been expected. Its commitment to democracy did not extend to the belief that a purely socialist government should be allowed to emerge. Moreover it was not united. Though a large section of its adherents were hostile to the idea of union with a largely protestant (and now republican) Germany, it also included some supporters who favoured the Anschluss. On the question of a Habsburg restoration it was also divided.

The Austrian Social Democrat Party, the second of the great blocs, was nearly unique among European socialist parties in that it was able almost entirely to avoid the split into socialist and communist groupings which occurred everywhere after the Bolshevik revolution. This achievement was largely the work of its redoubtable leader, Otto Bauer, and it was not without cost. In order to retain the support of its left wing, the socialists had a ready recourse to radical phraseology which frightened the bourgeois majority in the state and masked the fact that the party was not really interested in social revolution. The use by Bauer of phrases like 'the present pause in revolutionary development', and the demand in the party programme adopted at Linz in 1926 for the establishment of a dictatorship of the proletariat, obscured the very real commitment of the socialists to the democratic constitution and was one of the main reasons for the political malaise of the republic. This was recognized by Bauer's right-wing trade-union opponents. One of these, Karl Renner, commented astutely, 'It is dangerous and a cause of confusion always to speak of revolution and simultaneously to uphold the view that the time is not ripe.'[5]

Indeed, although the Social Democrats were, until the Nazi conquest of power, strong supporters of an Anschluss with Germany, they were also the only true supporters in Austria of the democratic constitution established in September 1920. This commitment resulted from the very real gains which the socialists had made in the post-war period. A whole package of social legislation had been introduced, including the eight-hour day, workers' holidays, collective agreements, the limitation of work at night and for women and children, health insurance and provision for invalids. This had radically improved the position of the industrial working class. Moreover, the 1920 constitution had created a federal state, and the socialists were able to use the extensive rights granted to the provinces to introduce far-reaching reforms in Vienna, which was given provincial status. Their achievements here, in improving housing and in providing better education and recreation for the workers, were widely admired. But these achievements were the result of fiscal policies which taxed heavily the bourgeois elements in the city and were deeply resented. Political conflict was thus far more bitter in Vienna than anywhere else in Austria. 'Red' Vienna also became something of a symbol for the peasantry and bourgeoisie in the country as a whole. They saw in the situation there a foretaste of what lay in store for them if the socialists ever achieved power, and they did not like what they saw. Wild talk on the right of a 'march on Vienna' modelled on the 'march on Rome' alarmed the socialists and further worsened the political climate.

The third of the blocs, the German Nationalists, was neither as large nor as unified as that of the Christian Social Party or the Social Democrats. It is true that in the last pre-war elections (in May 1911) they had been the largest of the German groupings, with 108 seats against 76 for the Christian Socials and 49 for the Socialists. But a good deal of their support had come from the highly nationalist German areas in Bohemia and Moravia, and throughout the interwar period they were far weaker than the two rival groupings. In the elections of 1920, for instance, the Nationalist bloc won 24 seats, against 79 for the Christian Socials and 62 for the Social Democrats. The Nationalists were also internally divided. They were all agreed on the need for a union with Germany or, if this were impossible, on the need to align Austrian policy as closely as possible with that of Germany. But they were divided on how Austrian politics should be organized internally, both in the attitude to the democratic constitution and to the position of the Church. The largest nationalist group was the Pan-German People's Party, largely bourgeois in character, anti-clerical, and liberal in its economic policies. The Peasant League, though nationalist, was more concerned with the defence of rural interests, while the small National Socialist Party had the dubious distinction of being the precursor of the similarly named Right-radical movement in Germany.

The differences between the Socialists, many of whose leaders were Jewish, and the two other groups, were intensified by the role played by the 'Jewish question' in Austrian politics. Anti-Semitism had been an important aspect of the policies of both the Christian Social Party and the German Nationalists. It was intensified by the prominent position held by the Jews in Vienna, where they constituted nearly 10 per cent of the population and where their influence on the political, cultural and economic life of the capital was striking. A good deal of Austrian industry was owned by Jews, as were most of Vienna's great liberal newspapers, like the *Neue Freie Presse*.

'Autrichelieu'

For the first two years of its existence, the republic was governed by a coalition of Social Democrats and Christian Socials. Given the extreme hostility and suspicion with which the two parties regarded each other, this was always in danger of collapse, and it eventually broke down in June 1920. From now until the Anschluss, the Social Democrats were never again to hold office in the central government. At the same time, however, the Christian Socials were never able to win an over-all majority in parliament, and were forced to govern in coalition with the different German Nationalist groupings. For most of the twenties this bourgeois coalition was dominated by the enigmatic figure of Mgr Seipel, a political priest turned chancellor who firmly laid his impress on the Christian Social Party, and whose skill in intrigue earned him the nickname 'Autrichelieu'. He held the office of chancellor from May 1922 to November 1924 and again from October 1926 to April 1929.

Seipel's coalition achieved a good deal. In co-operation with the League of Nations, the finances of the new state were placed on a sound footing and by the end of 1922 the runaway inflation, which had reduced the Austrian crown to one fifteen-thousandth of its former value, was brought to an end. The measures necessary for this financial reorganization caused a great deal of hardship, and Austria's economy remained dangerously dependent on foreign loans, many of them short-term. By the mid-1920s however, the development of hydro-electric power had reduced the country's need to import coal, while the growth of new industries and the increase in tourism resulted in a modest but real economic revival.

Yet the government was not able to heal the country's deep political divisions. Seipel was intransigently hostile to the socialists, whom he regarded as quite incapable of sharing in the government of the country. His attitude was intensified by the opposition of the socialists to his economic measures: in particular, the subordination of the economic life of the country to League of Nations control. This confirmed his view that they were nothing more than irresponsible and demagogic agitators, willing for their own advantage to undermine the very structure of the state. Indeed, like many Christian Social politicians, he was not particularly convinced of the merits of democracy, and inclined towards corporate and authoritarian ideas, particularly when these were presented in a Catholic form, as in the works of the Viennese Professor Othmar Spann.

The result was a dangerous political stalemate in which the best organized political grouping in the country, which held the Vienna municipality and through its trade unions dominated the railways and key industries, was totally excluded from any share of political power. In addition, paramilitary organizations sprang up which further undermined political stability. Of these the largest and most significant was the right-wing Heimwehr (Home Guard). This had emerged as a series of local groups during the confusion following the collapse of the Habsburg monarchy and was intended to protect Germans from Slav, Hungarian and Italian incursions. It soon assumed a generally right-wing and anti-Marxist character, though it lacked any real ideological unity. Its ranks included representatives of all the principal non-Marxist groups, Christian Socials, German Nationalists, members of the Peasant League and monarchists. The only unifying factor was provided by its strong hostility to the socialists and its belief that liberal parliamentarianism had outlived its usefulness. The socialists feared that the Heimwehr would be used to undermine their remaining positions in the state and founded a rival organization, the Republikanischer Schutzbund (Republican Defence Organization).

From the mid-1920s clashes between these two rival armies became increasingly frequent. Following such a clash in the summer of 1927, a number of Heimwehr members were acquitted, because of lack of evidence, of causing the death of two socialists. On 15 July workers' demonstrations in Vienna against this verdict got out of control. The Vienna law courts were burnt down and in the consequent violence about eighty-five people, almost entirely workers, were killed. The socialists responded by calling a general strike. It was crushed by the government, which called in the army, and by Heimwehr strike-breakers. Civil war seemed imminent, and was only prevented by the socialists, conscious of their weakness, drawing back, and deciding to approach Seipel in the hope of achieving some compromise. Seipel, however, was in no mood to negotiate. He held the socialists reponsible for the violence which had occurred and believed, in addition, that the failure of the general strike had demonstrated their weakness. Moreover, he believed that he could make use of the Heimwehr to destroy the socialists, confident that he would be able to outmanoeuvre its not very clever leaders.

The Heimwehr grew enormously in power as a result of the riots. In October 1928 it was able, for the first time, successfully to challenge the socialist 'monopoly of the streets' by organizing a march through Wiener Neustadt, the reddest part of 'Red' Vienna. There appeared a considerable danger that the movement, whose fascist sympathies were becoming increasingly clear and which was getting a good deal of help from Mussolini, would be able to seize power on its own. Its hopes of power were increased when Seipel resigned in April 1929. Heimwehr demonstrations played a considerable role in the fall of his successor, Streeruwitz, and with the appointment in September 1929 of Johann Schober, the police commandant of Vienna who had ordered the police to fire on the workers, they believed their hope for power would soon be realized.

They were mistaken in Schober, however. Though glad of Heimwehr aid, he was not prepared to acquiesce in their demands. The movement was at this time becoming more and more openly fascist. In May it adopted a new programme rejecting 'democracy and Parliament', and was increasingly dependent on finance from Italy and Hungary. In September 1930 its new leader, Prince Starhemberg, was invited to join the new cabinet of Vaugouin as minister of the interior, which he did, as he disarmingly states, 'with the object of bringing about a *coup d'état*.'[6] The movement had, however, passed its peak and its lack of a clear ideology was proving an increasing weakness. Starhemberg was soon excluded from the cabinet and in the elections of November 1930 the Heimwehr won only 8 seats. The pathetic attempt of one of its leaders in Styria, Pfreimer, to organize a putsch in September 1931 further weakened its position. By the end of 1931 its political significance appeared to have diminished considerably.

Austria in the shadow of the great depression and Nazi Germany

The threat to the political stability of Austria now came from a new source. Austria's economic recovery had been heavily dependent on foreign loans, and it was thus extremely vulnerable to the economic downturn which began in 1929 and which reached its climax in central Europe in 1931. Schober, prime minister from September 1929, had many links with the pan-Germans, and wished to ensure their loyalty to his cabinet.

Therefore he argued that the only way out of the economic crisis lay in a customs union with Germany, which he concluded in March 1931. His proposal had to be abandoned because of the opposition of France and the Little Entente, who claimed that it conflicted with those clauses of the Treaty of Saint-Germain prohibiting an Anschluss. Before this happened, in order to increase the pressure on Austria, French deposits were withdrawn from the largest of the Austrian banks, the Creditanstalt Bankverein, which controlled a large proportion of Austrian industry. This precipitated a financial crisis in Austria. In order to prevent complete collapse the country was again forced to have recourse to the League of Nations. The loan granted at Lausanne carried with it the condition that the Anschluss should be renounced for twenty years. The new chancellor, Dollfuss, a representative of the young generation of Austrian politicians who had made his name in organizing the Christian Social Peasant Movement in Lower Austria (the area around Vienna), was willing to accept this. The German Nationalists were not. They had lost a good deal of popularity in the 1920s by associating themselves with Seipel's stabilization plan and its attendant hardships, and were not prepared to place themselves in this position again. Moreover the whole political position was being undermined by large-scale defections from the main nationalist groupings, the German People's Party and the Peasant League, to the National Socialists. This was clearly seen in the provincial election of April 1932, and by 1934 virtually the whole of the national camp had gone over to the Nazis. The Heimwehr also split, the pan-German elements within it becoming National Socialists.

In this situation the government's position was precarious. By making an agreement with the Peasant League and that section of the Heimwehr which was hostile to the Nazis, Dollfuss was able to create a bare parliamentary majority of one vote. His position was made still more difficult by the Nazi conquest of power in Germany in January 1933. Hitler, himself an Austrian, had always stressed that he regarded the union of Germany and Austria as one of the first priorities of his foreign policy. For the time being, however, because of Germany's weak international position and his own need to consolidate his power, he was thinking not so much of an Anschluss as of a general alignment of internal and foreign policy, a Gleichschaltung of the type which had occurred in Danzig. Germany's policy towards Austria was thus left from May 1933 to the Nazi party and its supporters in Austria, whose activities, liberally financed from the Reich, increased enormously.

Dollfuss was faced with a serious dilemma. His tiny parliamentary majority made government almost impossible, while fear of a Nazi triumph similar to that which had occurred in Germany in November 1930 led him to decide against risking an election, as was demanded by Hitler. This fear was almost certainly misplaced for, although the nationalist camp had gone over *en bloc* to the Nazis, both the Christian Socials and the Social Democrats were able to retain the bulk of their support. The refusal to allow elections was, in fact, a grave political blunder and it increased the willingness of the Nazis to resort to terrorist methods, buttressed by the belief that they had been denied victory through the ballot box. The Nazis' recourse to violence in the summer of 1933 made it impossible for Dollfuss, who was firmly committed to maintaining the independence of Austria, to consider a compromise with them. He had thus either to widen his support by bringing in the socialists or to resort to autocratic methods. Dollfuss was not hostile to democracy, towards which his past in the Lower Austrian peasant organizations predisposed him. He was, at the same time, a convinced disciple of Seipel and did not seriously consider an approach to the socialists, whom the rise of Nazism had made somewhat more conciliatory. His attitude hardened still more as a result of the socialists' opposition to the Lausanne loan, which he regarded as symptomatic of their unwillingness to compromise, and the tentative discussions he initiated with the Social Democrat leaders soon foundered. An approach to the socialists would anyway almost certainly have been vetoed by Mussolini.

Dollfuss was thus forced upon an autocratic path, and he was strongly encouraged in this course both by Mussolini and by the Hungarian prime minister, Gömbös, who feared the increase in French influence which would result from the socialists entering the government. Moreover, Mussolini and Gömbös were in a strong position, since they could use the Heimwehr, which received large Italian subsidies, to put pressure on Dollfuss not to come to terms with the socialists. Already in June 1932 plans had been laid, in co-operation with the Italians and Hungarians, to take violent action should he embark on such a course.

Dollfuss decided, as a result, to conciliate the Heimwehr, and in October 1932 one of its leaders, Starhemberg, again entered the cabinet, as secretary of state for security. In this capacity, he was able to transform the Heimwehr into a sort of auxiliary police force whose expressed aim was the destruction of the power of the Social Democrats.

From now on the transition to authoritarian rule and dependence on Italy was swift. On 4 March 1933 Dollfuss was able to make use of the fortuitous resignation of the Speaker and two deputy Speakers in parliament to declare the Assembly closed. Two weeks later he banned the National Socialists, whose agitation had reached a new peak of violence, and in September he proclaimed his intention of establishing a new constitution which would be directed not only against Marxism, but also against liberalism and democracy. In taking these moves, he was undoubtedly responding to the strong pressures of the Heimwehr, and the socialists did not exaggerate when they referred to Dollfuss as its 'prisoner'. The alliance was sealed by the creation of a 'Fatherland Front', intended to unite the Heimwehr and the Christian Socials and to create an effective right-wing response to the Nazi challenge. Its manifesto proclaimed:[7]

> All groups, all party organizations, that want to serve the
> fatherland, must join together and form a great and
> vigorous army united in one great and vigorous aim:
> Austria and her duty to survive, so that her mission in
> Central Europe may be accomplished for the good of every
> German.

These developments made a clash with the socialists inevitable. Dollfuss announced his intention of disarming the Schutzbund, and although he stated that he would not dissolve the Social Democrat Party, it was obvious that this was the Heimwehr's aim. Mussolini too was urging him to take action against the Left, arguing that this would increase his support and destroy the appeal of the Nazis. The crisis came in February 1934, when a local Schutzbund leader in Linz resisted a Heimwehr attempt to disarm his followers. Violence spread rapidly and led to a virtual civil war in Vienna, in the course of which over 300 people were killed. The Social Democrat Party and its trade unions were declared illegal, and most of its leaders went into exile. This was followed by the signing in March of the Rome Protocols, by which Austria became on paper an Italian satellite. In May, a new constitution was promulgated, authoritarian and corporative in character, which claimed to be based on the principles of the papal encyclical *Quadragesimo Anno* of 1931.

Although Dollfuss had destroyed his enemies on the left, the Nazis on the right remained and, after a renewed wave of violence in July, they attempted to take power in a *putsch* of which Hitler was given faulty information in advance. They hoped to capture the whole cabinet and force it to resign in favour of National Socialist sympathizers. The government got some wind of what was afoot, and only Dollfuss and two of his associates were in the Cabinet office when the trap was sprung. Thus, though Dollfuss himself was killed by one of the conspirators, the government was able to reorganize itself under Kurt Schuschnigg, the minister of education, and the rising, which did not reach any significant proportion outside Styria, where the insurgents were assisted by the Yugoslavs, was easily crushed.

Schuschnigg's '10 per cent chance'

Schuschnigg's position appeared strong on the surface. He had fought off the Nazi challenge and seemed to have the secure support of Italy. In fact, however, he was extremely weak and, as he later admitted, believed he had barely a '10 per cent chance' of maintaining Austrian independence.[8] He was never very happy about his dependence on Italy, refusing to accept other than financial aid from Mussolini, and his international position was thus rather isolated. Internally the regime remained, as it had been under Dollfuss, an uneasy coalition of the Heimwehr and the Christian Socials, and it failed to strike any deep roots. Its attempts to create corporations on the Italian model never got off the ground, and the Fatherland Front was never able to become a broad organization uniting the wide sectors of Austrian opinion that were hostile to a Nazi takeover. Its position was anyway somewhat weakened by Schuschnigg's desire to come to terms with the 'respectable' Nazis.

Schuschnigg was able, with considerable skill, to undermine the position of the Heimwehr, and in February 1936 he was able to force its leader, Prince Starhemberg, to leave the cabinet.

The organization itself was absorbed by the militia of the Fatherland Front and was thus effectively subordinated to government control. But this move was not followed by any significant widening of government support either on the Right or on the Left. The socialists, though they regarded the regime as a lesser evil than a Nazi takeover, were repelled by its clericalism and authoritarianism and remained bitterly hostile to the men they held responsible for the bloodshed of February. The Nazis too remained a significant force. It is true that they lost a fair amount of support as a result of the revulsion against their methods, which had been revealed in the Dollfuss murder. In addition, many of the more *enragé* party members were also confused and disillusioned by Hitler's reversion to correct diplomatic methods in his relations with Austria, as was symbolized by the appointment of Papen as ambassador in Vienna. But the hard core held firm, aided by subsidies from the Reich and the idealized picture of the reawakened German nation across the frontier. The government's repression of the Nazis and its creation of internment camps merely hardened the resolve of the more fanatical, while many crypto-Nazis established themselves in powerful positions in the army, the police and the civil service. Their neutrality in the civil war of February 1934 also won them a good deal of support, even among the socialists.

The foreign buttresses of the regime were also not as firm as they appeared. Gömbös's Hungary was certainly in no position to uphold the independence of Austria, and Mussolini's resolve was also weakening. The Italo-German conflict over Austria had frightened the Duce with the potential might of a resurgent Germany. He was determined to strengthen his position before Hitler could undertake an active foreign policy and it was this, above all, which led him to embark on the invasion of Ethiopia. He thus came into open conflict with the western powers when the League of Nations imposed sanctions, and the result was paradoxically to lead to closer ties with Germany. The inevitable result of an Italo-German *rapprochement* was, of course, the abandonment of the Italian protectorate over Austria.

Schuschnigg was aware of the weakness of his position. Like Dollfuss, he did not seriously consider a reconciliation with the socialists, which he regarded as suicidal, given both the internal and international position of Austria, and likely to alienate

Mussolini and further arouse the Nazis. His only alternative thus seemed an attempt to conciliate the Nazis internally while improving relations with the Reich. As early as April 1936 he suggested to his close associates the possibility of coming to terms with the 'national opposition', in this way isolating the extremists in their midst and saving a modicum of Austria's independence. His views were immediately reported to Papen, the German ambassador, and in July an Austro-German agreement was reached. According to its terms Germany recognized Austria's sovereignty, and both states promised not to intervene in the internal affairs of the other. Austria also undertook that her policies 'should always be based on principles corresponding to the fact that Austria has acknowledged herself to be a German state'. In the secret clauses, provision was made for the exchange of newspapers, an amnesty for Nazis, and for Schuschnigg to take two members of the 'national opposition' into his cabinet.[9]

Very little substance now remained to Austrian independence. The Nazi Party was able to increase its activity enormously, while the penetration of the administration continued rapidly. Moreover Schuschnigg's attempts to exploit what little freedom of manœuvre remained to him to secure Austria's independence enraged Hitler, who claimed that by toying with the idea of a Habsburg restoration he was disregarding both the letter and spirit of the July agreement. The crisis in Austro-German relations was brought to a head in January 1938 when the Austrian police discovered a plot by Nazi extremists against the Austrian government, the aim of which was to force Hitler's intervention. Hitler summoned Schuschnigg to Berchtesgaden on 12 February and in a fit of explosive hysterics and a studied display of intimidation induced Schuschnigg to make further concessions, including giving the Nazi Seyss-Inquart the ministry of the interior, which gave the Nazis control over state security.

Schuschnigg now came to the conclusion that only the most extreme measures could save Austrian independence. On 9 March he decided on a referendum in favour of a 'free and German, independent and social, Christian and united Austria'.[10] This was to be held three days later. He also approached the socialists for their support and they responded favourably. Hitler decided to act. He did not believe that the referendum would be fairly conducted, and feared that the result would go against him. He thus resolved to use his armed might to force its abandonment. The Austrian government did finally agree to give way, but too late to stop the invasion which took place on 12 March. No resistance occurred, and the country was incorporated into Germany as Ostmark, and was largely administered by Germans sent from the Reich, to the chagrin of many Austrian Nazis, who stood well to the left of the Nazis in the Reich and had expected far-reaching autonomy, with themselves in command. A plebiscite was held in which 99·75 per cent of the Austrians approved the Anschluss.

It has been claimed that the collapse of democratic Austria was the result of the fact that 'the democrats were not "Austrians" and the "Austrians" were not democrats'.[11] It is true that the Christian Socials' fear and suspicion of the Social Democrats was the overriding reason for the collapse of the state. Moreover, as Seipel often pointed out, Austria did not seem to many of her inhabitants a necessary and self-evident form of political organization. It is probable that a majority of Austrians after 1933 did not favour incorporation into Nazi Germany, although undeniably a substantial percentage welcomed it when it occurred. But although both Christian Socials and the Social Democrats were hostile to Nazi Germany, the divisions between them were too great for any real co-operation. The success of the Nazis in penetrating the army, the police and civil service further undermined the viability of the state. The only conceivable foreign guarantee of its independence lay in Italy, and when Mussolini moved close to Germany after Ethiopia, the end of Austria was only a matter of time.

Notes

1 Julian Dunajewski, the Minister of Finance, a Pole; quoted in C. A. Macartney, *The Habsburg Monarchy* (London, 1969), p. 659.
2 'L'Autriche, c'est ce qui reste', quoted in Introduction to H. Benedikt (ed.), *Geschichte der Republik Österreich* (Munich, 1954), p. 9.
3 Quoted in W. Goldinger, 'Die geschichtliche Ablauf der Ereignisse in Österreich von 1918 bis 1945' in Benedikt (ed.), *op. cit.*, p. 31.
4 K. R. Stadler, 'Austria', in S. T. Woolf, *European Fascism* (London, 1968), p. 106.
5 This was the comment of Karl Renner after the burning of the law courts in Vienna on 15 July 1927. Quoted in A. Wandruszka, 'Österreichs politische Struktur', in Benedikt (ed.), *op. cit.*, pp. 430–1.

6 E. R. Starhemberg, *Between Hitler and Mussolini* (London, 1942), p. 34.

7 L. Jedlicka, 'The Austrian Heimwehr', *Journal of Contemporary History*, vol. 1, no. 3, p. 142.

8 'Even a mere ten per cent chance was better than nothing', he wrote in his memoir, *Ein Requiem in Rot-Weiss-Rot* (Zürich, 1946), p. 304.

9 For the text of the agreement see *Documents on German Foreign Policy*, ser. D. vol. I, no. 152.

10 J. R. Gehl, *Austria, Germany and the Anschluss, 1931–1938* (London, 1963), p. 184.

11 A. J. P. Taylor, *The Habsburg Monarchy* (London, 1948), p. 258.

Chapter 4

Rumania

Before the First World War the dominant position in Rumanian politics had been held by the king, who possessed wide powers in terms of the constitution of 1866: he enjoyed the right to veto legislation, to summon and dissolve parliament and to appoint or dismiss the prime minister. His authority was further increased by the inchoate character of the Rumanian party system, which had rested on a fluid series of loose understandings rather than any hard-and-fast divisions of principle. In this respect it resembled far more the political sytem of early eighteenth-century Britain than the Western European models it claimed to follow. Of the two broad groupings the Conservatives were more clearly identified with the interests of the landowners, while the Liberals represented the urban elements who were profiting from Rumania's rapid economic development. But essentially both stood for the continued dominance of a small oligarchy of landowners, capitalists and officials, whose position was buttressed by a narrowly restrictive franchise, and who were hostile to any significant concessions to the peasantry which made up the overwhelming majority of the population.

The king, the shrewd and able Hohenzollern Carol I, was able to manœuvre between these two groupings, and by acting on the principle of 'To the most savage dog, the fattest morsel',[1] he was able to prevent any challenge to his dominant position. His power was further increased by the control he exercised over the electoral system. Elections were 'made' in the eighteenth-century English fashion – a new government was first appointed and then proceeded, with the support of the king and the bureaucracy, to organize a majority in the country. Carol was at one with the oligarchy in his hostility to any significant land reform, in spite of the extreme disparity between the small class of landowners and the large mass of ignorant and poverty-stricken peasants. The reforms introduced by Prince Alexandru Cuza in the 1860s had done little to alleviate the land question. In the fifty years before 1914, the growing commercialization of Rumanian agriculture, increasingly dependent on grain exports, had strengthened the position of the large landowners and had forced the peasantry into an economic subjection often described as neo-feudal. In 1905, for instance, 95 per cent of the agricultural plots in Rumania were smaller than ten hectares and comprised 40 per cent of the land. Against this, the 5,000-odd estates of more than one hundred hectares covered 49 per cent of arable land and 57 per cent if one included forests, orchards and vineyards.[2] It was these conditions which led in 1907 to a violent and bloody *jacquerie* in which at least 10,000 people lost their lives.

In foreign policy the state was linked by a secret alliance, whose existence was known only by the king and a small group of politicians, to Germany and Austria. The overriding motivation for this alliance was the fear of Russian aims and the resentment which had resulted from Russia's annexation of Southern Bessarabia in 1878. These feelings more than outweighed the bitterness many Rumanians felt at the treatment their compatriots were receiving at Hungarian hands in Transylvania. According to the Conservative, Dimitrie Sturdza, one of those most aroused by Magyar policy, no responsible Rumanian advocated the conquest of Transylvania because the maintenance of the Austro-Hungarian monarchy was 'a European necessity of the first order'.[3]

Even before 1914 this political system was beginning to change. The uprising of 1907 had shown the seriousness of the agrarian question, and the Liberals in particular began to advocate a far-reaching land reform. Already in 1914 the clause of the constitution preventing the expropriation of property had been abrogated. The restrictive nature of the political system came under fire, and there were a number of calls for the extension of the franchise. The pro-German orientation in foreign policy also grew increasingly unpopular, as fears of Russia faded and as bitterness grew at the forced Magyarization of Transylvania. Thus it was that Rumania remained neutral when war broke out, in spite of the desire of the king to uphold his commitment to Germany, and eventually entered the war on the Allied side in August 1916. The death of King Carol in October 1914 removed an important obstacle to change. His nephew, Ferdinand, was a much weaker personality and was quite incapable of the firm control exercised by his uncle.

The emergence of Great Rumania

The outcome of the First World War radically altered the whole nature of the Rumanian state, offering it great new opportunities, but also presenting it with new and complex problems. The Rumanian record during the war had not been particularly impressive. The country had been forced to sign an amnesty with Germany in December 1917 and had only re-entered the war in November 1918. In spite of this, Rumania profited enormously. She gained Bessarabia from Russia, Transylvania and some districts to the west of it from Hungary, and Bukovina from Austria. The population rose from 7·3 million in 1913 to 16 million, and the country more than doubled in area. These new areas enormously increased the wealth and potential power of Rumania. They also brought with them difficult problems. Pre-1914 Rumania had been a fairly homogeneous society. There was, it is true, a fairly large Jewish minority, particularly in Moldavia, whose hold over a good deal of the trade and commerce of the province had been largely responsible for the persistent anti-Semitism which had made the country notorious. But apart from this the country was marked by its national homogeneity. Now it included sizeable minorities. In 1910 in the areas annexed from Hungary (Transylvania and the districts west of it), there had been 2·1 million Hungarians and 732,000 Germans to the 2·9 million Rumanians.[4] Both in Bessarabia and in Bukovina there were substantial numbers of Ukrainians. According to the census of 1930, Rumanians constituted only 70·8 per cent of the population.[5]

The Rumanian constitution was highly centralized, on the general East European assumption that to give any significant rights to local areas would pave the way for the break-up of the state. This centralization, along with the introduction of rather inadequate and often corrupt bureaucrats from Bucharest, made even more difficult the thorny problem of inducing the minorities to accept life in the new state. It also considerably alienated the local Rumanians, who in both Transylvania and Bessarabia were highly dissatisfied with the quality of the administration with which they were provided. The international position of Greater Rumania was also not particularly secure. Its creation had only been possible because of the simultaneous collapse of Russia and the Central Powers, and the Soviet Union, Hungary and Bulgaria were all quite unreconciled to their territorial losses. The fear above all, of Soviet action to retain Bessarabia was perhaps the principal reason for the strength of the fear of 'Bolshevism', which did much to weaken the radical political forces in the country.

On the surface, the political structure of the new state differed markedly from that of pre-1914 Rumania. Fears that the peasants, encouraged by the Russian example, might take the situation into their own hands, as well as the need to destroy the power of the Magyar landlords in Transylvania and the Russians in Bessarabia, had led to the adoption of a fairly radical land reform. A ceiling of 100 hectares was put on land ownership, though many exceptions were made. Altogether 6 million hectares were expropriated, of which nearly 4 million were distributed to the peasantry. This did have the effect of containing agrarian discontent, but it failed in any sense to solve the peasant problem. Little effort was made to follow up the reform by providing the peasants with adequate capital or with the skills they needed if they were to farm their holdings effectively. Thus the rise in population soon brought pressure on the land back to its earlier level, while the severe impact of the great depression further undermined the position of the peasant proprietor.

The peasant not only received the land but was also en-franchised when universal male suffrage was introduced in June 1917. This seemed to make inevitable a break with the traditional pattern of Rumanian politics. In fact, much less changed than might have been expected. The king retained his large powers in the new constitution introduced in 1923, and he was still able, in conjunction with the army and the bureau-cracy, both of which remained firmly under his control, effectively to 'make' elections. Indeed, one of the main reasons for the persistent political malaise in Rumania was the contrast between the ostensibly western-style constitutional character of the regime, and its actual practices. This contrast soon became glaringly evident. The neat division of political life between the Liberals and the Conservatives did not survive the war. The Liberals, it is true, emerged strengthened under their inflexible but impressive leader, Ionel Brătianu, and were able to claim the credit for the great expansion of the country's territory. The Conservatives, however, were severely affected by the resentment which their pro-German stance during the war had provoked, by the introduction of universal suffrage, and because of their opposition to land reform. Throughout the interwar period, they remained an insignificant force. At the same time, however, a number of new parties emerged. Some of these, like Professor Nicolae Iorga's National Democrats, were little more than cliques around a dominating public figure. Two, however, stood outside the traditional political framework. Of these the Peasant Party represented the newly enfranchised rural population of the Old Kingdom (Regat), while the National Party was the spokesman of the Rumanian population of Transylvania. Both stood for the transformation of the political system from a pseudo-constitutional one to one in which the democratic institutions had real power, and both stressed the importance of upholding the interests of agriculture.

They received their first brief opportunity of wielding power in September 1919 when Brătianu, piqued at what he regarded as the unfair treatment he had received at the hands of the Allies, resigned. The king was not prepared to risk an open clash with the western powers, and he thus refused to support the Liberals in the elections of autumn 1919, which were thus subject to little official interference. The results were a great surprise. The Liberals lost heavily in the Regat and won scarcely any seats in Transylvania. Together, the National and Peasant Parties won a clear majority, and the king was thus forced, against his will, to appoint the National Party leader, Alexandru Vaida Voevod, as prime minister. Given the opposition of the crown and 'influential' circles, the position of this government was, from the start, precarious. It was assailed by the representatives of the old oligarchy for its 'Bolshevism' and was duly dismissed by the king in March 1920. In the new elections, the king's man, the 'peasant General' Averescu, by employing the well-tried methods of Rumanian campaigning, received a secure majority.

The weakness of the democratic forces was painfully evident in this crisis, which paved the way for the eventual return to power of the Liberals. In January 1922 Brătianu again became prime minister and his party held office (except for a brief period between March 1926 and June 1927) until 1928. They owed their hold on power not so much to their support in the country, which was minimal outside the Regat, as to the favour of the king, who had continued to regard Brătianu as his main political adviser even when he was in opposition, and to the ability of the bureaucracy to manufacture majorities in elections. They pursued a policy of rigid centralization in administration which soon alienated not only the national minorities, but also the Rumanians in the newly acquired territories. Their economic policies followed naturally from their belief that industrialization was vital if Rumania was not to remain poor and powerless. At the same time they were hostile to foreign capital, which they regarded as exercising excessive political influence and, by a series of laws, they severely restricted its scope within the economy. Given the relative scarcity of capital in Rumania, their schemes for industrial development thus came to depend on squeezing the peasantry by export premiums, inadequate provision of credit and high import duties. The results of this policy were disappointing. It is true that by 1929 the index of industrial production had risen to 117·3 (1913: 85·7)[6] but this increase had been achieved at the cost of a fall in the standard of living of the peasantry. Moreover, it had proved impossible to stabilize the currency, which fluctuated wildly.

The combination of administrative centralization and the fostering of urban against rural interests had the effect of driving the National and Peasant Parties together, so that the two groups united in October 1926, creating a formidable opposition to the Liberals, whose position was further undermined by the death in July 1927 of their strong supporter, King Ferdinand. Ferdinand's son Carol had reacted against his father's cold inflexibility by becoming a thoroughgoing rake and man-about-town. The court had succeeded in having an early 'unfortunate' marriage of his dissolved, and had arranged a wedding between Carol and Helene, the daughter of the Greek king. This union did not prove happy, and Carol soon became involved with the very attractive and intelligent Magda Lupescu, the half-Jewish daughter of a chemist in Moldavia. Carol's rift with the court was widened by his resentment of his father's subservience to the Liberals, above all to the overweening Brătianu. Brătianu, feeling his position would be threatened if Carol came to the throne, was able to play on the court's anxiety at the heir's behaviour, and induced Ferdinand late in 1925 to issue an ultimatum: Carol must either abandon his mistress or renounce the throne. Carol chose Lupescu, and went into exile with her; thus on Ferdinand's death in 1927 a regency was established on behalf of Carol's six-year-old son, Michael, over which it proved more difficult for the Liberals to establish control. The death in November 1927 of Brătianu further undermined the Liberals' hold on power.

The National Peasant government, December 1928 to October 1930

The plight of the Liberals made possible the return to office of the National Peasant Party, which won a great victory in the relatively free elections of December 1928. The stage seemed set for the transformation of Rumania's political system and the introduction of a real measure of democracy. As the new prime minister, Iuliu Maniu declared, 'Our first aim will be to give the principles of the Constitution their real meaning and impart a character of strict legality to the working of the administration.'[7]

Maniu announced a decisive break with Liberal politics; more credit was to be provided for agriculture, local institutions were to be granted increased powers, and censorship and martial law were ended. Maniu also abandoned the Liberals' policy of industrial protectionism and announced his intention of welcoming foreign capital. Yet although a number of successes were achieved, particularly in the floating of a large foreign loan in February 1929 which made possible the stabilization of the currency, the government soon ran into difficulties. Its attempt to allow a fair degree of autonomy for the new provinces was bitterly criticized by the Liberals, and in June 1929 a somewhat ridiculous plot against the regime by a group of fascist army officers was discovered. Moreover, the economic situation was not propitious. Though the 1929 harvest was excellent, the value of exports was severely affected by the catastrophic fall in world grain prices. At the same time, the influx of foreign capital provided many new opportunities to get rich within the government. These were liberally taken advantage of by many of the National Peasant leaders who, unlike the scrupulously honest Maniu, shared the low standards of public morality which had made Rumania notorious. The claim of the National Peasants to have driven the corrupt Liberals from the Temple came to seem less and less credible.

What finally destroyed the government was the return of King Carol in June 1930. Maniu, a sincere believer in the virtues of a constitutional monarchy, had long hoped to engineer a compromise with the king and end the unsatisfactory regency. He was also not above hoping to use the case of Carol to embarrass the Liberals, and indeed the king's return caused a deep split in that party. Maniu demanded, however, as a condition of Carol's return that he abandon Madame Lupescu. After some hesitation, the king refused to comply and Maniu thus resigned in October 1930, hoping in this way to force him to give way.

However he had chosen the wrong issue on which to challenge the king. As Hugh Seton-Watson has pointed out, 'Bourgeois sexual morality is probably less esteemed in Roumania than anywhere else on the continent.'[8] The king was able to ride out the storm and appoint a government sympathetic to his own position. Indeed, the failure of the National Peasant government was a significant stage in the process by which even the purely formal character of Rumanian democratic institutions was undermined. The disappointing inability of the National Peasants to modify the conditions of Rumanian political life had many causes – political inexperience, economic difficulties, the hostility of the army and the bureaucracy. Above all, however, its weakness was the result of the political failings of its dominant figure, Iuliu Maniu. He had spent his life first as an attorney at the Uniate Metropolitanate in Blaj and as professor at the Blaj Theological Academy, and then as defender of the rights of the Transylvanian Rumanians in the unsympathetic atmosphere of the Hungarian parliament at Budapest. From his clerical contacts, he absorbed a strong belief in moral rectitude, an attitude not easily understood in the permissive atmosphere of Regatine Rumania. From his years in the Hungarian parliament he had derived a preference for the rigid adherence to principle which was possible if one was in continuous opposition, but which made the exercise of power extremely difficult. Above all he suffered from a paralysing inability to take decisions which was a source of perpetual exasperation to his political associates. The fact that he remained the party's leader up to and during the Second World War goes far to explain its inability to exercise the influence which its position in the country would seem to have assured it.

The king dominant within the constitution, October 1930 to February 1938

From the fall of the National Peasant government in October 1930 until his abdication in September 1940, King Carol controlled Rumanian political life. Nevertheless it was only in February 1938 that he actually introduced a dictatorial system. Until then he aimed merely at exercising the vast powers which he enjoyed in terms of the constitution. He had few clear political ideas apart from admiration for Mussolini, and a rather naive and vague belief that he was 'the first peasant, the first labourer and the first public servant of the realm'.[9] He had no real desire to rule as dictator – the difficulties which King Alexander had encountered in Yugoslavia were a strong warning against embarking on such a course – but at the same time he deeply distrusted the 'old' parties, in which he included the National Peasants. As he told Wickham Steed in 1937, the political parties were 'sterile, their leaders fit only to criticize'. His functions as king would be to 'discipline them and harness them to constructive work'.[10]

His principal political tactic was to appoint governments headed by leading political figures, but ultimately responsible to him rather than to their party. He was able with some ease to exploit the divisions within the two major parties, and by January 1934, after a series of changes of government, he seemed at last to have found a suitable prime minister in the person of the Liberal Gheorghe Tătărescu. Although this administration was nominally Liberal, there was no doubt that it was ultimately responsible to the king. Carol had apparently achieved the difficult task of creating a stable government without recourse to unconstitutional methods.

However this stability was illusory. It is true that the political power of the king increased markedly between 1930 and 1938. He gained the allegiance of prominent members of both the Liberals and the National Peasants and already from 1931 he asserted his right to preside over the cabinet once a week. Within the administration and the army, he placed his own supporters in key posts. Moreover neither of the two main parties was in any position to challenge his dominance. Yet his continued relationship with Madame Lupescu, who had become the head of a highly influential palace clique, and his amassing of a vast personal fortune, stimulated considerable popular resentment of his activities.

At the same time, extremist political movements were becoming increasingly significant in the country. These derived their inspiration to some extent from the growth of Right-radical movements elsewhere, but owed much more to Rumanian conditions. The widespread fear of Russian intentions in Bessarabia, coupled with the high percentage of non-Rumanians, above all Jews, in the party leadership condemned the Communists to ineffectual weakness. As a result, the persistence of the great depression and the resulting misery of the peasantry strengthened the various fascist groups. The blatant contrast between the high-flown pretensions of the Rumanian constitution and the nationalist rhetoric taught in the schools on the one hand, and the sordid reality of Rumanian political life on the other, lent force to calls for a fundamental revolution. The group which profited most from this situation was known at different times as the League of the Archangel Michael and the Iron Guard. Led by Corneliu Zelea Codreanu, an extreme nationalist of partly Ukrainian and partly German origins, it was a radical populist movement which differed from most European fascist groups in its strong belief in the primacy of peasant interests. The league had no clear programme. As Codreanu put it, 'The country is dying for lack of *men*, not programmes.'[11] It did, however, display many fascist characteristics; it encouraged the cult of the leader Codreanu, who was invested with almost Christ-like attributes, it was strongly nationalistic and anti-Semitic, it believed that parliamentary government was merely a screen behind which the Judeo-capitalist oligarchy perpetuated its rule, and it favoured close links with Nazi Germany. Its calls for a radical land reform won it a good deal of support in the countryside, where many resented the increasing conservatism of the National Peasants. As the Iron Guard grew in strength, a number of politicians became interested in reaching some sort of arrangement with Codreanu, a development which was most obvious in the Liberal Party. Carol himself was to some extent subsidizing the Guard in the belief that this would further weaken the older parties.

Tătărescu's government lasted until November 1937. It pursued the traditional Liberal policy of fostering industry at the expense of agriculture and had some success in stimulating the economic revival. But it struck no significant roots in the country, and its power rested almost entirely on the use of police and administrative methods of repression. At the same time the growing divisions within the National Peasant party, between those who favoured co-operation with the king and those who wanted an all-out struggle for the establishment of democratic institutions, appeared to strengthen the government. Tătărescu thus decided to go to the country in November 1937, confident that the weaknesses of his opponents and the support of the king would ensure him an easy majority. His calculations proved radically mistaken. To the general surprise, Maniu, still the dominant figure within the National Peasants, announced a 'non-aggression pact' with the Iron Guard, aimed at ensuring that the elections would be relatively freely conducted. From the long-term political viewpoint this was a serious error of judgment because it associated the one group clearly committed to democratic reforms with the anti-democratic and unparliamentary Iron Guard. Nevertheless, it achieved its main objective in that it was able severely to limit the amount of pressure the government could employ in the elections. Tătărescue failed to win the necessary 40 per cent of the votes needed to obtain a parliamentary majority, his share of the polls amounting to 36 per cent against 21 per cent for the National Peasants, 16 per cent for the Iron Guard and 9 per cent for a smaller nationalist and anti-Semitic group, the National Christian Party.

The royal dictatorship, November 1937 to September 1940

Carol's response to this situation was to appoint a government headed by Octavian Goga, the leader of the National Christians.

The appointment of this blatantly minority government was a further stage in the establishment of a royal dictatorship. The king's reasons for his action are fairly obvious. He had no desire again to entrust power to the Liberals after the débâcle of the recent elections, and his inability to reach an agreement with Maniu precluded the appointment of a National Peasant government. He hoped moreover, through the establishment of an extreme nationalist and anti-Semitic regime to steal some of the thunder of the Iron Guard.

The Goga cabinet, which included a number of prominent politicians, including General Antonescu, prime minister from 1940 to 1944, and several defectors from the National Peasants, proved a disaster. The main characteristic of its brief period in office was its virulent anti-Semitism and its open incitement of pogroms. Foreign protests led Carol to dismiss Goga in February 1938 and openly to assume power himself in a government of national union headed by the Orthodox patriarch. A new constitution was introduced which enormously increased the power of the crown, diminished the power of parliament, and abolished the party system. Direct universal suffrage was abandoned and individuals voted according to their profession or social class, an open concession to corporative ideas. However, the new cabinet lacked a clear political character, and was for the most part made up of politicians from the older parties who had become adherents of the king. Though Carol had not been unwilling to use the Iron Guard to undermine the power of the older parties, once he had established his dictatorship, he came increasingly into conflict with it. He resented, above all, its social demagogy, its attempts to limit his power and its openly pro-Axis stance in foreign policy. As a result, after an outbreak of anti-government violence, the Guard was declared illegal and in November 1938 Codreanu and thirteen of his associates were 'shot while trying to escape'. The Guard's assassination of the prime minister, Armand Calinescu, in September 1939 unleashed a further wave of persecution against its members.

Carol's position appeared unassailable. What destroyed him was the development of the international situation. Since the dismissal, under German and Polish pressure, of the pro-Western foreign minister Nicolae Titulescu in August 1936, the determining of foreign policy had lain with the king. Though he regarded the eventual victory of Britain and France in a war with Germany as highly probable, he was resolved to safeguard Rumania's position and, above all, her hold on Transylvania by a policy of neutrality. His intention of pursuing such a policy was considerably strengthened by the western surrender over Czechoslovakia, and in November 1938 the king visited Berlin, where he had a very successful series of talks with the Nazi government. Relations between Rumania and the Reich deteriorated as a result of the attack on the Iron Guard, but again improved in March 1939, when a far-reaching economic agreement between the two states was concluded. Nevertheless Rumania was still able to use the German bogy to get a British guarantee for her independence, though this was intended merely as a useful bargaining counter against the Reich. However, Rumania's position was clearly threatened by the conclusion of the Nazi-Soviet pact in August 1939, which in a secret protocol had in fact recognized the Russian 'interest' in Bessarabia.

Stressing her neutrality, Rumania was able to keep out of the war in September 1939. For some time the policy of balancing between Germany and the Allies seemed to be successful. It was described by its leading exponent, the foreign minister Gafencu as 'guaranteed by London, armed by Berlin'.[12] But with the fall of France in June 1940 the chickens finally came home to roost. Carol was now faced with a difficult choice. The prospect of standing alone seemed impossible, bearing in mind Rumania's military weakness and the encouragement Germany would then have given to Hungarian ambitions in Transylvania. An alliance with the Soviet Union, which was insistently pressing for the return of Bessarabia, was unacceptable both on social grounds and because of the obvious provocation it constituted to Germany. It is thus not surprising that in the summer of 1940 Carol took the decision to throw in his lot with the Germans. A new and more totalitarian constitution was introduced, a single 'Party of the Nation' was set up to which members of the Iron Guard were admitted, and the pro-German Ion Gigurtu entered the cabinet.

This switch did not save Carol. He was forced in June 1940 to cede Bessarabia and southern Bukovina to the Soviet Union, and in August, under Axis pressure, had to abandon southern Dobrudja to Bulgaria and northern Transylvania to Hungary. All in all, the country had lost one-third of its territory, and its humiliation was increased by the fact that no resistance had been offered to these cessions. Thus in September General Antonescu, who had been called in by the king to strengthen his position, turned against him, partly on German prompting, and forced him to give up his dictatorial powers. A few days later Antonescu, acting in co-operation with Maniu and the Liberal leader Constantin Brătianu (brother of Ionel), compelled Carol to abdicate. Antonescu, however, resisted Iron Guard pressure to abolish the monarchy and merely forced the new King Michael to grant 'absolute powers' to the prime minister. The monarchy, as in Italy, thus remained as a rival focus of loyalty, a factor which was to prove important as the disastrous consequences of the alliance with Germany became increasingly clear.

The Antonescu regime

Antonescu's coup had been supported by Maniu and Constantin Brătianu in the belief that he would re-establish a constitutional regime. In this they were disappointed. It is true that the ambitious and able Antonescu had been a Francophile in the 1930s, but the weakness and pusillanimity of the Western Powers had turned him into an ardent protagonist of the German orientation. He had come, too, increasingly to hold the view that democracy could not work in Rumania, and that what was needed was a strong autocratic and nationalist regime. His clash with Carol, as a result of which he had lost the post of minister of war in March 1938, had led him to cultivate his links with the Iron Guard, with whom in fact he had little in common. In many respects he resembled Pétain, a soldier who saw as his primary responsibility the ending of the corrupt political system which had preceded him; he may also have seen himself as an intermediary between the Germans and Rumania.

The new regime, like that in Hungary, was really a com- promise between old-fashioned conservatives like General Antonescu and the fascists of the Iron Guard. These groups did not coexist easily, and a clash between them was not slow in coming. On the face of it, the position of the Guard seemed strong. Their leader, Horia Sima, was made deputy prime minister, five other Guardists entered the cabinet and the Guard became the sole official political organization and was entrusted with the 'moral and material uplift of the Rumanian people'.[13]

Its members were quick to use their position of strength to initiate the social revolution for which they had waited so long. In November 1940 Sima's followers unleashed a ferocious anti-Jewish pogrom and attempted to murder a large number of their political enemies. Though their plans misfired they did kill several prominent politicians and sixty-four former secret policemen who, in the Carolist period, had been responsible for the repression of the Guard. However the crude louts of the Iron Guard were no match for Antonescu. The general, who had no prior knowledge of what was about to take place, was furious, and in his decision to crush the Guard, he was able to win the support of the Germans, who had had troops in Rumania since October 1940, and who were above all interested in the maintenance of peaceful conditions in Rumania so that the flow of oil for their war effort would not be disrupted. As a result, in January, after considerable bloodshed, Antonescu was able to destroy the power of the League. Many of its members fled to Germany, where they remained to be exploited as a potential government-in-exile should Antonescu try to move out of the German orbit. A straight military dictatorship was now established. It was this regime which in June 1941 took the decision to join the Nazi attack on the Soviet Union, and it was inevitably involved in the German defeat. In August 1944 King Michael, together with the Liberals, the National Peasants, the Socialists and the Communists, overthrew Antonescu and withdrew from the war. The new regime was at first a genuine coalition, but Rumania had been assigned to the Soviet sphere of influence and the government thus soon came under strong Soviet pressure. By early 1945 all political power was in the hands of the Communists, until now quite insignificant, who proceeded to organize a people's democracy firmly under Soviet control.

Notes

1 The German ambassador wrote to Chancellor Caprivi in February 1891 that this was the maxim on which the king operated. Quoted in R. W. Seton-Watson, *A History of the Roumanians* (Cambridge, 1934), p. 372.

2 H. L. Roberts, *Rumania: Political Problems of an Agrarian State* (New Haven, 1951), p. 6.

3 Quoted in Seton-Watson, *op. cit.*, p. 378.

4 *Ibid.*, pp. 566–7.
5 See the Statistical appendix, Table 9, p. 163.
6 Taking 1955–9 as 100 (Statistical Appendix, Table 33, p. 177).
7 Roberts, *op. cit.*, p. 131.
8 H. Seton-Watson, *Independent Eastern Europe 1918–1941* (Cambridge, 1945), p. 204.
9 Roberts, *op. cit.*
10 *Ibid.*, p. 189.
11 E. Weber, 'Romania' in E. Weber and H. Rogger (eds), *The European Right* (London, 1965), p. 527.
12 G. Ionescu, *Communism in Rumania, 1944–1962* (London, 1964), p. 58.
13 Roberts, *op. cit.*, p. 235.

Chapter 5

Yugoslavia

The emergence of Yugoslavia

The Kingdom of Yugoslavia, or as it was called until 1929, the Kingdom of the Serbs, Croats and Slovenes, was a product of the First World War. The three nations which made up the majority of the population had relatively little in common in their political or cultural traditions. It is true that the Serbs and Croats spoke virtually the same language, though, they wrote it with different alphabets. In every other respect, however, they differed widely. The Serbs were Orthodox in religion and, because of the support they had received from Russia, were strongly Russophile. Their political goal before 1914 had been the unification of all the Serbs still under Turkish and Austrian rule in a Greater Serbia. They had achieved this objective in relation to Turkey as a result of the first Balkan war (1912), but by 1914 there were still large numbers of Serbs in the Habsburg monarchy, in Bosnia, the Vojvodina and Southern Croatia. Their situation was particularly onerous in Bosnia, which had only finally been annexed by Austria in 1908 and where a small group of Moslem beys still ruled over a population of largely Orthodox serfs. It was among the Orthodox population of Bosnia that pan-Serbian ideas had their strongest support in the monarchy, and it was from this group that came the youths who planned and executed the assassination of the Archduke Franz Ferdinand. Serbian political life had been considerably democratized as a result of the revolution of 1903, which had

deposed the Obrenović dynasty and brought Peter Karadjordjević back to the throne. But the country retained many
Balkan features, inherited from the 400 years of Turkish rule:
corruption, police brutality and a rather inefficient civil service
remote from the mass of the population.

The Croats, on the other hand, were Catholic and looked
towards western Europe for their political models. From the
eleventh century Croatia had been ruled by Hungary, and it
had escaped the worst effects of the Turkish conquest of the
Balkans. In 1868 the Hungarians, after reaching the Ausgleich
(compromise) with the Habsburg state, had granted a fair
degree of autonomy to Croatia, which obtained its own parliament and local administration, but this autonomy was continually threatened by the policies of the governor appointed by
the Hungarians. The conflicts which resulted caused a considerable decline in the strength of the pro-Hungarian elements in
Croatia. By 1914 there were two dominant political orientations.
The nationalists, divided among themselves, denied the existence
of any common interests between Serbs and Croats. They
wanted to unite all the areas in which Croats were in a majority
in Austria-Hungary in a Croatian province which would have
equal status with Hungary and the Austrian lands. The supporters
of the Yugoslav (Yugo = 'South') idea stressed the unity of all
the south Slavs in the monarchy – they did not think, however,
in terms of a union with Serbia but of a recasting of the structure
of Austria-Hungary to ensure their national rights within it.
By 1914 the Serbo-Croat coalition, dominated by 'Yugoslavs',
had emerged as the strongest political force in the Croat
parliament.

The Slovenes spoke a language quite different from Serbo-
Croat. They were staunchly Catholic and did not find Austrian
rule particularly onerous, though they did come into conflict
with the German minority in the areas in which they lived,
a clash which resembled, on a smaller scale, the Czech-German
conflict in Bohemia. They were deeply distrustful of the
Orthodox Serbs and hoped for a change in the internal policies
of the monarchy to obtain their national objectives.

The First World War greatly stimulated the Yugoslav
movement and gave it a strongly anti-Habsburg character. In
1914, a number of leading Habsburg 'Yugoslav' politicians
had left the country to establish a Yugoslav National

Committee whose aim, declared in its manifesto of May 1915, was 'the liberation of our people from the foreign yoke and their union in a single free nation'.[1] The Serbian prime minister, Nikola Pašić, who thought exclusively in the older pan-Serb terms, looked with considerable suspicion on this movement. But the occupation of Serbia and the fall of the Tsarist monarchy, the strongest foreign supporter of the pan-Serb idea, induced him to come to terms with Ante Trumbić, the leader of the Yugoslav National Committee, in July 1917. They agreed that the war was to be fought for the union of the Serbs, Croats and Slovenes and that the new state was to be a 'constitutional, democratic and parliamentary monarchy'[2] under the Serbian Karadjordjević dynasty. Universal suffrage would be introduced and there would be equality for the two alphabets, three national flags and three religions of the new state.

The agreement was couched in the vaguest terms, and it allowed the highly adroit and experienced Pašić to impose his own conception of unity on the new state. The constitution which he was able, though with some difficulty, to force through parliament in July 1921 was highly centralized, and provided no adequate recognition for the national diversity of the country. It gave great power to the king, who was to choose the prime minister and whose control over the army was already effectively established as a result of the crushing in mid-1917 of the 'Black Hand', a group of army officers suspected of plotting against him. A pro-royalist group, the 'White Hand', was set up within the army and throughout the interwar period the king could rely on the senior officers to do his bidding, thus to a considerable extent belying the democratic appearance of the constitution.

Problems of the new state

From the start it was the national question, and, above all, the relationship of the Croats to the state, which was the key issue of Yugoslav politics. The elections of November 1920 had brought a great surprise in Croatia. The restrictive Hungarian franchise, by which only about 25 per cent of the population had the vote, had masked the support enjoyed by the Croat Peasant Party of Stjepan and Antun Radić. Before 1914 the overwhelming majority of the Croat deputies in Parliament had belonged either to the Serb-Croat coalition or to the nationalist Pure Right Party. Now, however, with the establishment of universal suffrage, the Croat Peasant Party swept the board.

The party was not basically anti-Yugoslav. Its leaders were strong believers in south Slav unity and looked with particular favour on the activities of Stamboliiski, a peasant leader in Bulgaria. But they were, at the same time, extremely suspicious of rule from Belgrade. As republicans, they distrusted the Karadjordjević dynasty and as agrarians, demanding primacy for peasant interests, a radical land reform and the reduction of taxation, they looked with dislike on the bureaucratic clique which they believed, with some justification, to be in control in Belgrade. They demanded the creation of a federal structure in the new state and refused to recognize the 1921 constitution, which they held to be pan-Serb, as a legitimate political framework. The party had been built up by the two Radić brothers, Stjepan and Antun. Stjepan was the fiery demagogue and Antun the political theorist and tactician, a combination which had proved extremely effective. Unfortunately for the political stability of Yugoslavia, Antun died in 1919, and the entire responsibility for leading the party thus fell upon Stjepan Radić. It was not a responsibility for which he was well fitted. A man of great emotion, he shifted his political position with bewildering rapidity. Even those Serbian politicians who would have liked to come to terms with him were often hard pressed to know exactly what he wanted. Moreover, as Croat dissatisfaction with the new state failed to diminish, the Croat Peasant Party changed in character, becoming less of a peasant organization and more of a spokesman for the claims of the Croat people. Thus it came more and more to take the form of 'an uneasy marriage of peasant democrats and bourgeois reactionaries'.[3]

The Croat problem was not, however, the only difficulty to face the new state. Serbia had been devastated by the war, and the rebuilding of its war-shattered territory was to prove a long and difficult task. The loss of 1 million of its population was painfully felt. At the same time, the marked divergence in the level of economic development between the different parts of the kingdom, from relatively highly developed Slovenia to backward Macedonia, made the creation of a single economic unit difficult. The failure to deal effectively with the peasant problem also underlay a good deal of the instability in the country. Yugoslavia was one of the most highly agricultural countries in eastern Europe with nearly four-fifths of the population dependent on agriculture for their livelihood. A fairly radical land reform was introduced in February 1919, in terms of which ultimately about 2 million hectares of land were redistributed. This was not enough to solve the problem, however, for outside central Serbia the peasantry was too poor to profit by it. In 1931, for instance, over two-thirds of the peasantry had less than ten hectares of land,[4] and the pressure on resources was further increased by the rapid rise in population. The slow growth of industry and the limited opportunities for emigration proved quite inadequate to absorb the surplus agricultural population.

The complexity of politics was increased by the divisions in Serbia, as expressed in the rift between Pašić's Radicals, now increasingly conservative, and the more left-wing Democrats led by Ljuba Davidović. Davidović held power briefly in late 1924 but his attempts to investigate corruption and to diminish the power of the new vested interests which had grown up in Belgrade led him to clash with the king, who dismissed him early in 1925. Radić and the Croat Peasant Party oscillated in the period with chameleon-like rapidity between fundamental opposition to the Yugoslav state, co-operation with the Serbian opposition of Davidović, and collaboration with the government. Radić even joined the cabinet for a brief period early in 1926.

Such little stability as the system enjoyed was provided by Pašić, who was able to carry on a parliamentary government by a coalition of the Radicals, the Slovenes, who were given virtual autonomy, and the Bosnian Moslems, who were promised that the land reform would be only mildly implemented. Pašić's death in December 1926 removed one of the few men who had the strength, ability and unscrupulousness to make the system work.

With the elections of early 1927, which gave the Radicals and their allies a working majority, the polarization of political life had reached a dangerous point. The country was now clearly divided into two blocs. The 'Belgrade' bloc was made up of those groups which favoured the centralized political system: the Serbian Radicals, the Bosnian Serbs, some of the Serbs in

Croatia and Vojvodina, the Slovenes and the Moslems. The 'Zagreb' camp included all the supporters of decentralization: the Croats, the Macedonian and Albanian minorities, some Montenegrins and some Serbs from Croatia and Vojvodina. Politics grew progressively more heated until in June 1928 a Radical deputy from Montenegro, in a fit of fury in Parliament, drew a pistol and killed two Croat deputies, also wounding Radić who died several weeks later. For another six months the Belgrade coalition was able to carry on, but by December it was forced to throw in its hand.

The initiative now lay with the king. 'The machine no longer works', he informed the correspondent of *Le Matin* in January.[5] He attempted first to come to terms with Vladko Maček, who had succeeded Radić as leader of the Croat Peasant Party. Maček demanded the division of Yugoslavia into five federal units: Slovenia, Serbia, including Macedonia and parts of Bosnia, Croatia, Vojvodina and Montenegro. Each was to have its own parliament and to control its own trade and finance, education and postal services. Each was also to have its own army, which was not to be used outside the province without the consent of the local parliament. This would have left virtually no substance to the unity of the country and was as unacceptable to the king as it was to the main Serbian parties. Alexander thus saw no alternative to the introduction of a royal dictatorship.

The royal dictatorship

There is no doubt that Alexander's intentions in introducing his dictatorship were honourable. He had been disgusted by the way in which parliamentary democracy had functioned in the ten years since the war, and, brought up in St Petersburg, had little sympathy for, or understanding of, constitutional niceties.[6]

> Is not that dictatorship [he asked] when a party leader, who has not even got a programme, decides of his sovereign power that this or that one of his friends shall be elected in a constituency of whose first needs he is utterly ignorant? Or when a party leader gets a crowd of his followers nominated as officials, although they have no aptitude to recommend them except their support of that politician

who, in return, enables them to live at the expense of the country?

His aim was to re-create a common Yugoslav patriotism which would overcome the inherited allegiances of the past. The country was now to be called Yugoslavia, and no longer the Kingdom of the Serbs, Croats and Slovenes. Political parties organized on a regional, particularist or religious basis were forbidden. Little was to be left of the country's democratic institutions. It is true that the new constitution introduced in September 1931 did allow a residual role to parliament, but ultimate power now clearly lay with the king, to whom ministers were responsible. The new electoral law, by which the party that won a majority of the votes obtained two-thirds of the seats, further increased the power of the government, which was able quite effectively to influence election results by administrative pressure.

In spite of its autocratic character, the king's regime was at first well received. The democratic constitution had clearly failed, and the former Habsburg subjects, in particular, hoped Alexander would end the Serbian monopoly of high office. Maček, for instance, expressed his relief that 'the waistcoat [the 1921 constitution] has been unbuttoned. . . . By the wisdom of the King, the Croats will become free in their free Croatia'.[7] The dictatorship was also strengthened by the economic situation. Yugoslavia was not at first severely hit by the world economic crisis. The harvests of 1929 and 1930 were abundant, while Yugoslav industry, protected by high tariffs and still aided by German reparations, developed rapidly. At the same time, the regime had a number of achievements to its credit. Various measures were introduced to aid agriculture, including the establishment of an agrarian bank to provide cheap credit for the peasants. The division of the country into thirty-three departments was done away with, and nine provinces which corresponded more closely to national divisions were established, with a marked increase in administrative efficiency. Ordinary crime diminished and brigandage, that persistent scourge of the Balkans, was done away with.

Nevertheless, the royal dictatorship was not a success. Alexander's heavy-handed attempt to create a common Yugoslav patriotism aroused considerable resentment. The forcible amalgamation of the Serb and Croat *sokols* (political-gymnastic unions), the measure compelling Serbian regiments to give up their treasured Serbian battle flags in exchange for Yugoslav ones, and the transfer of the national holiday from 28 June, the anniversary of the Battle of Kossovo, to 6 September all created widespread irritation. The regime also tended to become increasingly pan-Serb in character. It was difficult to find backing for the government in Croatia, whereas the party divisions in Serbia did create opportunities to win over a fair number of politicians. The political party created by the king to support him drew its adherents from dissident members of all the three main Serbian parties, but this 'Yugoslav Peasant Radical Democratic Party' had little following in the rest of the country. Even in Serbia its position was not strong, and the king came more and more to depend on the senior army officers and older politicians of the Radical Party whose experience in pre-war Serbia gave them virtually no basis for understanding the nature of Croat demands. In this situation nationalism grew in strength in Croatia. The Croat Peasant Party became much more a national than a peasant movement. On its right, generously financed by Italy and Hungary, there developed the fascist *Ustaša* which sought to obtain the independence of Croatia through an armed uprising.

The regime was also undermined by the delayed, though severe, impact of the great depression from late 1931. Agricultural exports fell drastically, and in September 1931 a bank moratorium was declared. There was little the government could do on its own to deal with the crisis, although a moratorium on peasant debts was introduced in 1932. Peasant discontent grew rapidly and culminated in a desperate rebellion by the starving country people of southern Croatia and the Dalmatian hills in September 1932. Opposition in the towns also grew. In the winter of 1932 the leading Croat politicians were joined by the Serbs of Bosnia and Vojvodina in issuing a 'Zagreb manifesto' which demanded the application of the principle of popular sovereignty, the ending of Serb hegemony, and the protection of the peasantry. It enjoyed a wide measure of support, even from such traditionally pro-government elements as the Slovenes and the Bosnian Moslems. The small, underground Communist Party, banned by the government in 1921, also grew in strength among a wider circle of sympathizers. One of its most important centres of support was among the students of Belgrade University. Its experience in conspiratorial techniques was to prove invaluable in the difficult conditions of guerrilla warfare in which it was involved after 1941.

The reply of the government was repression. Maček and Ante Korošeć, the Slovene leader, were arrested and Mehmed Spaho, the principal Moslem spokesman, was interned. In April 1933, Maček was sentenced to three years' imprisonment. His trial heightened the already widespread hostility to the government in Croatia. In Serbia too, opposition was growing in force.

This was the situation when Alexander was assassinated in Marseilles in October 1934 by a Macedonian terrorist acting with Italian and Hungarian connivance. It has been argued that he was aware of the failure of his dictatorship and was contemplating a return to a constitutional system. This, however, remains an open question.

The regency

Alexander was succeeded by his eleven-year-old son, Peter, and a regency was proclaimed under his cousin, Prince Paul. Western-educated, and lacking any real understanding of the issues of Yugoslav politics, Paul was not particularly well equipped to deal with the pressing problems which the state faced. At the same time, alienated by what he regarded as the 'barbarity' of much of Serb life, he was well placed to achieve some compromise with the more westernized Croats. It was to the search for such a compromise that the entire period of his rule was devoted. He was also far more interested in foreign affairs than in the rather sordid internal politics of Yugoslavia. He favoured the policy, to some extent already embarked on by Alexander, of loosening Yugoslavia's ties with France and looking to Germany, at first without results, as the country's 'natural protector' against Italian hostility.

In internal politics Paul started by relaxing the dictatorship, and released Maček from prison. Nevertheless he did not favour a return to constitutional government, and his prime minister, Bogoljub Jevtić, who had been Alexander's foreign minister, announced that the 1931 constitution with its autocratic features would remain in force. However, he did allow the opposition to participate in the elections of February 1935 and abandoned the sponsorship of the Government Party, putting up instead a list of his personal adherents.

The elections did not go particularly well for Jevtić. In spite of strong pressure, his list won 1·7 million votes (301 seats) against 1 million for the opposition (67 seats) and the disparity of seats and votes precipitated a political crisis. The Croats declared that they would boycott the parliament, while the Serbian opposition also increased their demands for a restoration of constitutional rule. Paul decided to approach Maček, who responded fairly sympathetically, accepting the dynasty and a common army and foreign policy, but demanding the democratization and federalization of the state. It soon became clear that the major obstacle to an agreement was Jevtić, with his strongly pan-Serb views. As a result, he was dismissed in August 1935 and replaced by Dr Milan Stojadinović, a Serbian radical who was believed to hold moderate political views and to favour a *rapprochement* with the Croats.

Stojadinović proved a disappointment to those who believed he would foster the re-establishment of a constitutional system. His real political sympathies were authoritarian, and he aimed, above all, to make the royal dictatorship more palatable, while leaving the power of the Regent undiminished. As Ciano, the Italian foreign minister, wrote in his diary in March 1937, 'Stojadinović is a Fascist. If he is not one by virtue of an open declaration of party loyalty, he is certainly one by his conception of authority, of the state, of life.'[8] He abandoned Alexander's attempt to establish by force a common Yugoslav patriotism and returned rather to Pašić's principle of ruling by means of a coalition of what was left of the old Serbian Radicals, the Slovenes and the Moslems, who were organized in a new pro-government party, the Yugoslav Radical Union (JRZ).

Stojadinović did somewhat relax police pressure, he released something like 10,000 political prisoners and he allowed the Croat Peasant Party to function. But he was in no hurry to come to terms with Maček. Indeed he even attempted to undercut his support by enacting a very liberal *concordat* with the Catholic church, but was forced to let this lapse because of Serbian opposition. At the same time, he further loosened Yugoslavia's ties with France, courting Germany and now also Italy, which had for the moment abandoned its support of Croat separatism.

Stojadinović enjoyed at first a certain measure of support, particularly as the economy revived and foreign trade, primarily with Germany, increased significantly. Like everyone before him, however, he was defeated by the Croat problem. His policy of winning the Croats by kindness failed, above all because the Croats were interested in deeds, not words. Maček himself came increasingly to argue that the resolution of the Croat problem could only come about as a result of the re-establishment of a democratic system. Thus in autumn 1937 he sponsored an agreement between the Croat Peasant Party, the Independent Peasant Party (composed of former Habsburg Serbs) and the Serbian Radical, Democratic and Agrarian Parties. This agreement was greeted with great enthusiasm in Serbia. The main argument for the establishment of the dictatorship had been the failure of the democratic parties to solve the Croat problem. Yet now they had shown their ability to reach a compromise with Maček.

Stojadinović did not change his course as a result of this agreement. He continued to flirt with both the fascist powers, hoping to play off each against the other, and toyed with the idea of introducing fascist-style institutions in Yugoslavia. He also showed some diplomatic ability in bringing to an end in January 1937 the long-standing dispute between Yugoslavia and Bulgaria. The surrender of the Western Powers at Munich seemed to bear out the wisdom of his policy of courting Germany and Italy and, on the strength of this, he went to the people in December 1938. The election results showed both the strength and weakness of his position. He won 1·6 million votes against 1·4 million for the opposition (306 seats to 67). But while he received 70 per cent of the votes in Serbia, the Croat Peasant Party obtained 80 per cent in Dalmatia and Croatia.

The regent was by now increasingly unhappy with Stojadinović. The fate of Czechoslovakia had shown the fragility of multi-national states and had demonstrated the urgency of coming to terms with the Croats. Paul therefore dismissed Stojadinović in February 1939 and appointed as Prime Minister Dragiša Cvetković, a former Radical politician who had been prominent in the Yugoslav National Union, where he had organized the fascist-style government trade unions.

In April Paul ordered Cvetković to open negotiations with Maček. The pressing character of the Croat problem had already been shown in the previous month, when a group of Croat extremists appealed to Hitler for help in obtaining autonomy. Loyal to his agreement with Mussolini that the Mediterranean was to be an Italian sphere of influence, Hitler refused. There were two ways the situation could be dealt with. The solution of the Croat problem could be made part of a general demo-cratization and the abandonment of the dictatorship or an agreement could be reached directly with Maček, thus cutting the ground from under the Serbian opposition. It was inevitable that Paul, deeply fearful of Bolshevism and unwilling in the unsettled international situation to attempt risky internal experiments, should have opted for the latter. Maček hesitated at first to throw over his former allies, but seeing the impossi-bility of inducing the Regent to modify his views, decided to negotiate on Paul's terms.

Agreement was reached in August 1939, in terms of which a new province of Croatia was to be created. Just under three-quarters of its population (29 per cent of the country) would be Croats. The historic office of governor was re-established, with fairly extensive powers, while an assembly, with authority over all matters except foreign affairs, defence, commerce and public security, was set up in Zagreb. The existing central parliament was dissolved, and the government undertook to prepare a new electoral law, and laws dealing with the freedom of the press, and of assembly and association. The cabinet, still headed by Cvetković, became a coalition. Six Croats entered, and Maček was given the position of deputy prime minister. Ivan Šubašić, a well-respected Croat of pro-Yugoslav views, became Governor of Croatia.

On the face of it, this seemed an admirable and statesmanlike agreement. Yet it had serious weaknesses. No further measures to democratize the state were introduced, and the Serbian opposition was bitterly antagonized by Maček's *volte-face*. In Croatia, too, there was a fairly large body of unreconciled opinion, which now saw the chance to establish an independent state. Nevertheless, it was not internal weakness which destroyed the compromise, but the development of the international situation. Yugoslavia continued to follow a policy of neutrality between the Axis and Western powers after the outbreak of war in September 1939. This policy became impossible to follow once Germany became directly involved in the Balkans in late

1940. The need to secure the German southern front in the case of the planned invasion of Russia meant that Hitler had to come to Mussolini's aid after the debacle of the Duce's invasion of Greece in October 1940. Germany now needed Yugoslav neutrality during her proposed invasion of Greece, and after what was virtually an ultimatum, Yugoslavia signed the Anti-Comintern Pact in March 1941. This surrender to German pressure was unacceptable to Yugoslav and, above all, Serbian public opinion and on 26 March the Regent was overthrown by a group of army and air-force officers, who created a government largely Serbian in character and representing the older democratic politicians.

Hitler was now determined to crush Yugoslavia along with Greece. After a brief campaign, the country was overwhelmed in April 1941. Large areas were annexed by Germany, Italy, Bulgaria and Hungary, while Croatia was made independent under Italian and subsequently German control. A rump Serbia dominated by Germany was also set up. During the war the country was the scene not only for brutal foreign occupation but of a bitter three-way civil war among the Croats, the Communist partisans and the royalists. As a result of this civil war the partisans, led by Tito, who were most fully committed to the Yugoslav idea and who gained support from the peasants whose land had been confiscated, emerged as the rulers of the country, only to be faced with the perennial problem of reconciling the conflicting aspirations of Yugoslavia's different nations.

Notes

1 'Manifeste du comité Yugoslave à la nation et au parlement britannique' in Adriaticus, *La Question Adriatique* (Paris, 1920).
2 H. C. Darby and R. W. Seton-Watson, 'The Formation of the Yugoslav State' in S. Clissold (ed.), *A Short History of Yugoslavia* (Cambridge, 1966), p. 162.
3 H. Seton-Watson, *Independent Eastern Europe 1918–1941*, (Cambridge, 1945), p. 227.
4 See the Statistical appendix, Table 17, p. 167.
5 *Le Matin*, 15 January 1929. Quoted in R. W. Seton-Watson and R. G. D. Laffan, 'Yugoslavia between the Wars', in Clissold (ed.), *op. cit.*, p. 175.
6 Quoted in Seton-Watson and Laffan, *op. cit.*, p. 176.
7 *Ibid.*, p. 177.
8 M. Muggeridge (ed.), *Ciano's Diplomatic Papers* (London, 1948), p. 104.

Chapter 6

The Czechoslovak exception

The countries so far discussed were not the only ones in Eastern Europe where Western-style constitutions failed. In *Bulgaria*, for instance, democracy collapsed as early as 1923. Here defeat in the First World War, in which Bulgaria had been allied with the Central Powers, had led, as in Hungary, to a loss of faith in the established authorities. As a result, power fell in August 1919 to the veteran peasant leader Alexander Stamboliiski, who had been imprisoned for opposing the war with Russia. His radical agrarian regime introduced a land reform which did away with the few remaining large estates in the country, and he also attempted a number of other innovations. The urban politicians distrusted Stamboliiski's somewhat boorish brand of demagogy and his regime was also compromised by a certain amount of corruption. What brought him down were his indiscreet threats after his victory in the elections of April 1923 to cut down radically the powers of the king, and the hostility of *émigrés* from Macedonia to his plans for establishing friendly relations with Yugoslavia. Stamboliiski was overthrown and murdered in June 1923 as a result of a military coup in which the king may have been implicated.

From now until 1934 the dominant influence over the government was exercised by IMRO (Internal Macedonian Revolutionary Organization), the terrorist organization which aimed at winning back Macedonia for Bulgaria. In May 1934, however, a group of younger army officers, led by Colonel

Damian Velchev took power and were able, with the support of of the king, to destroy the power of IMRO, which had done so much to disrupt Bulgarian political life. Velchev soon fell out with King Boris, who took personal power in April 1935. The king did allow a certain amount of liberalization, particularly after 1938, and he did end the running sore of Macedonian irredentism by establishing friendly relations with Yugoslavia in 1937. Yet right up until its collapse as a result of the Nazi defeat, the regime remained autocratic and repressive, unresponsive to popular demands.

The history of *Greece* in the interwar period was perhaps more troubled than that of any other country in Eastern Europe. The clash during the war in which the pro-German King Constantine had attempted to keep the country neutral, against the efforts of the Cretan Eleutherios Venizelos to intervene on the Allied side, had left deep scars. So too had the unsuccessful attempt in the immediate post-war period to carve out a Great Greek Empire on both sides of the Aegean. This had led to ignominious defeat by Turkey, to the overthrow of the monarchy and to the judicial murder of six prominent royalist politicians in 1922. It had also caused the influx of huge numbers of Greek refugees from Turkey. These made up nearly one-fifth of the population of the country and their absorption contributed in a large way to the country's already difficult economic situation.

Given this background, it is not surprising that Greece should have experienced a series of political convulsions. The first of these came in the aftermath of the defeat by Turkey, when a group of republican army officers led by colonel Nicholas Plastiras took power in a coup and dethroned the king. This republic proved incapable of achieving political stability and, as a result, in January 1926 a shortlived dictatorship was established under General Theodore Pangalos. Pangalos too lasted little more than six months and was succeeded by the veteran radical Venizelos, who was able to establish the republic on a firmer footing. His position in turn was undermined by his inability to deal with the great depression, and his political collapse resulted in the return of King George in November 1935, following several abortive coups by republican army officers. Though the King had originally intended to embark on a conciliatory political course, he soon became convinced of the need for strong measures and acquiesced in the establishment of an authoritarian regime headed by General Metaxas, modelled on those of Italy and Germany. This 'Fourth of August Regime' lasted until Greece's defeat by Germany in April 1941, when its adherents split between those who favoured collaboration with the Germans and those who wished to continue resistance.

Albania, the smallest of the Balkan states, was never able to establish its independence on a firm basis. The country had been set up in 1912 as a result of pressure from Austria-Hungary and Italy, and in order to deprive Serbia of the outlet to the sea on the Adriatic that she had sought in the first Balkan War. Albania lacked the resources to maintain any sort of independent existence and from the start it was the scene of bitter international rivalries, as the Austrians and Italians struggled against each other to establish a sphere of influence there. The country also faced almost insuperable political problems. The deep divisions between Moslems, Catholics and Orthodox, and between the still largely tribal mountaineers of the north and the more developed plainsmen of the south created a serious bar to the establishment of a stable constitutional system. So too did the general economic and cultural backwardness, and the strong distrust of all governments caused by five centuries of Turkish rule. Land reform, particularly in the south, where the landowners were largely Moslems and the peasants Orthodox, posed difficult problems.

Thus after the First World War the country was riven by serious political conflicts, while Italy and Yugoslavia struggled to obtain a dominant position. In December 1924 an able and unscrupulous tribal leader, Ahmed Zog, seized power, aided by a good deal of Yugoslav military aid. In spite of these links with Belgrade, Zog decided to look to Italy for military and economic aid, believing that the Italian connection would be less dangerous to the country's independence than close ties with Yugoslavia which had always coveted northern Albania. Italy rapidly acquired a dominant position in Albania, and Italian backing enabled Zog to consolidate his position and make himself king in September 1928. His regime tried to introduce a number of reforms, including a redistribution of land, but it made little impact on the highly conservative structure of Albanian society. At the same time his attempt to keep Italian influence under control increasingly broke down, and the *de facto* Italian protectorate was finally converted into direct control when the country was occupied by Mussolini in April 1939.

In the Baltic, too, democratic institutions did not prove firmly based. *Lithuania*, *Latvia* and *Estonia* were all small countries, very frightened of losing the independence they had achieved in 1918 as a result of the simultaneous collapse of Russia and Germany. In all of them the pervasive atmosphere of insecurity gave strength to calls for the establishment of 'strong' dictatorial regimes. This was particularly the case in Lithuania, whose relations with Poland were poisoned by the dispute over Vilna, while in both Estonia and Latvia there was strong suspicion of Russian and German intentions. The Baltic states also faced serious political problems. All had introduced highly democratic constitutions with advanced systems of proportional representation, which were not calculated to work well, given the general lack of political experience. All had introduced radical land reforms which had considerably alleviated peasant discontent, but they were still confronted with serious economic difficulties, since such industry as had grown up in them was closely linked with the now inaccessible Russian market.

Constitutional government broke down first in *Lithuania*. Here a moderately left-wing cabinet had taken power in June 1926, but had rapidly alienated the Right by what was regarded as its excessive concessions to the national minorities and its 'softness' towards the communists and the Soviet Union. It was thus overthrown by a military coup in December 1926, and a strongly right-wing regime, headed by Augustinas Voldemaras took power. Many leading politicians were arrested and strong measures were taken against the opposition, particularly after an unsuccessful revolt in September 1927 and an attempt on Voldemaras's life in May 1928. The regime became somewhat milder in character in September 1929 when the President Antanas Smetona was able to oust Voldemaras and to replace him by Juozas Tūbelis. Democratic institutions were not, however, re-established and the regime remained a nationalist dictatorship, ultimately dependent on the army. It was gravely weakened by its acceptance of a Polish ultimatum in March 1938 compelling Lithuania to open diplomatic relations with Poland, and even more by the German annexation of Memel (Klaipéda) in March 1939. As a result, Smetona forced Tūbelis to resign and a new cabinet under General Jonas Cernius was created, in which two of the main opposition parties were represented. This semi-constitutional government remained in power until Lithuania was incorporated in the Soviet Union.

In *Latvia*, the extreme political fragmentation of the country, with its multiplicity of parties, led to frequent changes of government, but the constitutional system managed to survive until the great depression. Attempts were made in 1933 by the right-wing parties to increase the power of the president. When these were rejected by parliament, the prime minister, Karlis Ulmanis, with the help of the supreme commander of the Latvian army, J. Balodis, and a right-wing paramilitary organization, the Latvian Home Guard, declared the Assembly dissolved in May 1934 and banned political parties. His dictatorship, which lasted until the incorporation of Latvia into the Soviet Union, was relatively mild, although a number of leaders of the Social Democrats and a small fascist group, the Perkonkrusts, were arrested. The regime proclaimed the intention of promulgating a corporate-style constitution, but this was not done before its collapse, although attempts were made to create a single front of national unity.

Estonia, too, was not able to work its highly advanced constitution successfully. Between 1920 and 1934 there were twenty different governments and, in December 1924, an unsuccessful communist rising took place in Tallinn. The great depression hit the largely agricultural economy of the country hard and led to considerable discontent, with demands for a reform of the constitution to create a powerful presidency. A right-wing extra-parliamentary organization of war veterans, the League of Soldiers of the War of Liberation rapidly grew in strength and was able to secure the passing by referendum in October 1933 of a new constitution with a more powerful executive. Civil war seemed close as the League of Soldiers nominated its own candidate, General Larka, for the now all-powerful office of president. Fears of this type provoked the prime minister, a veteran nationalist politician, Konstantin Päts, to seize power in March 1934 with the help of General Laidoner. The presidential election was called off, political parties were banned and 500 of the League of Soldiers activists arrested. Päts's regime lasted until 1940, and although the new constitution it introduced in January 1938 did allow a good deal of scope for opposition, it remained in its essence autocratic and ultimately dependent on the army. It did, however, enjoy a good deal of popular support, particularly among the peasantry, who had profited from the economic revival since 1934.

Ultimately the fate of the Baltic states came to depend on the development of the international situation. The Russo-German non-aggression treaty of August 1939 had assigned them to the Russian sphere of influence, and in September and October 1939 the Soviet Union forced all three states to sign pacts of mutual assistance with her. The Soviets were given the right to station troops in them and their independence, was, to all intents and purposes, abrogated. The ultimate Soviet annexation followed logically ten months later in August 1940, and was confirmed by the defeat of Nazi Germany.

In *Finland* democratic institutions did survive, though they were close to collapse on a number of occasions. This was primarily the result of the divisions left in the country by the civil war which had followed the achievement of independence, and which culminated in a White victory in May 1918. In the nineteenth century the Grand Duchy of Finland, though ruled by the Russian Tsar, had enjoyed a wide measure of autonomy. As a result Finnish nationalism had, in its initial stages, been directed against the native Swedish landowning and bourgeois classes. From the 1890s, however, the Tsarist government began to undermine the autonomy of Finland, and this gave to Finnish nationalism a strongly anti-Russian character which was exacerbated by Finnish claims to the areas east of the Grand Duchy, such as Karelia, Ingria and the Kola peninsula which were, for the most part, inhabited by Finnish-speaking peoples. At the same time, the development of industry in Finland and the unhappy situation of many small tenant-farmers caused the emergence of a strong Social Democrat Party with very radical views. This group cultivated links with the Russian Social Democrats, principally the Bolsheviks, and strongly opposed the nationalism of the bourgeois parties. The revolution in Russia precipitated a clash between the socialist and nationalist forces in Finland, in which the former enjoyed the backing of the Bolsheviks and the latter were given substantial support first by the Germans and subsequently by the Allies.

The adherents of the right won the civil war but in the new state they regarded themselves as cheated of their victory. They felt, first, that the Treaty of Dorpat (Tallinn) concluded in mid-1919 had unnecessarily renounced Finland's claim to East Karelia in favour of the Soviets. In addition, in August 1918 the radical wing of the Social Democrats had seceded and established the Finnish Communist Party. Its leaders were able to entrench themselves under Soviet patronage in the Soviet autonomous region of Karelia. This prototype for the communization of Finland constituted a continuous irritant to the right and strengthened still further its desire to create a 'Greater Finland' incorporating the Finnish-speaking areas of the Soviet Union. The Social Democrat Party continued to operate legally in Finland, but was regarded with great hostility and suspicion by the right, which was able to prevent its inclusion in the govern-mental coalition. This meant that throughout the 1920s demo-cratic cabinets could only function with great difficulty and could barely summon a majority in parliament.

The great depression led to a growth of communist strength and this stimulated the emergence of a powerful anti-communist organization, the Lapua movement, which gained the patronage of the White leaders in the civil war, such as Gustaf Mannerheim, P. E. Svinhufvud and S. K. Paasikivi. But once the right had secured the enactment of new and more stringent anti-com-munist laws, the conservative Whites broke with their Right-radical supporters and were able to reduce them to political insignificance. A Right-radical uprising in February 1932 failed dismally, and popular support for the right waned. In 1936 a democratic alliance of the Agrarians and Social Democrats was victorious in the national elections and created a government. By this time the recovery of the Finnish economy had further undermined the support of the fascists, now organized mainly in the People's Patriotic Movement. They were even more compromised by the Winter War, when the Soviet Union tried to reduce Finland to satellite status, since in this war Finland was supported by the democratic west and abandoned by Nazi Germany, to whom the Right-radicals had looked for backing. When Finland entered the war against the Soviet Union on the German side, the People's Patriotic Movement joined the coalition, but played only a small role in the government. This coalition, from which the radical Right was now excluded, was able to reach an armistice with the Soviet Union in September 1944, and established a fairly satisfactory *modus vivendi* with the Soviet Union which has lasted to the present day.

There was however one country in the area which was relatively successful in working its democratic institutions. This was *Czechoslovakia*. At the outset the prospects for stable political development here did not seem particularly bright. The state was set up on the assumption that there was a single Czechoslovak nation. In fact, however, great differences in social and economic development and in political culture separated the Czechs and Slovaks, whose languages, though similar, were by no means identical. The Czechs had lived under the relatively mild rule of semi-constitutional Austria, and since 1867 they had not been subjected to any strong pressures to abandon their nationality and become German. The areas in which they lived were the most highly developed in the Dual Monarchy and had included 80 per cent of the cotton mills, 85 per cent of the wool mills and 90 per cent of the linen mills in its non-Hungarian parts.[1] Substantial heavy industry had also grown up, particularly around Plzeň, where the Škoda armament works provided most of the weapons of the Austro-Hungarian army. This economic development had brought about a considerable alteration in the social structure of the Czech lands. Until the early nineteenth century they remained territories in which a German or Germanized aristocracy ruled over Czech-speaking serfs, a result of the Habsburg reconquest of Bohemia in the Thirty Years War. But by 1914 a fairly substantial middle class, both Czech and German, had grown up together with a similarly mixed industrial proletariat. The Germans were still by far the wealthier and more powerful community, but the Czechs were increasing both in numbers and in influence. In all the large towns, outside the overwhelmingly German frontier areas, the Czechs constituted a substantial majority of the population. Politically, too, they had gained a good deal of valuable experience, particularly since they had abandoned in 1879 the futile policy of boycotting the central parliament. They had also built up a highly developed intellectual and cultural life, centred around Prague, with its Czech university and national theatre.

The position of the Slovaks was quite different. They had never been able successfully to establish an independent national existence, and from the tenth century they had been ruled by Hungary. The largely mountainous regions in which they lived had witnessed little industrial development in the nineteenth century, and in 1914 these parts were still overwhelmingly agricultural. The Slovaks were almost exclusively peasants and the dominant group in the area was the Hungarian landowners, many of whom possessed vast estates. The urban population was almost entirely German or Jewish.

After the granting of home rule in Hungary in 1867, the Slovaks had been subjected to strong pressure from the Hungarians. Slovak secondary schools were closed down and the number of primary schools in which Slovak was the language of instruction was drastically reduced. Considerable inducements were also offered to enable Slovaks to become Magyar. Though this policy was ruthlessly implemented, and though it did enjoy some success, it was not able to destroy the existence of Slovak national sentiment which, aggravated by the all-pervasive land hunger, became increasingly anti-Hungarian. In 1905 a Slovak National Party, strongly Catholic in character and led by a Catholic priest, Father Andrej Hlinka, was established and soon became a significant political force. Unlike the situation in the Czech lands where the Catholic Church, because of Hussite memories and its close links with the Habsburgs had never been a powerful force, Slovak nationalism from the first had a strongly Catholic and clerical character.

There was little in common between the highly developed and sophisticated Czech lands and the backward mountains and forests of Slovakia. There had been a number of attempts before 1914 to foster links between Czechs and Slovaks, but these had never got much beyond the pious expression of common 'Slav' sentiment, except among the Slovak Lutheran minority. Indeed, neither the Czechs nor the Slovaks had thought before 1914 in terms of political independence. What the Czechs sought was to establish themselves securely in control in Bohemia and Moravia, and to acquire for the Czech lands at best a status similar to that the Hungarians had achieved since 1867, and at worst one comparable to what the Poles had obtained in Galicia. The great nineteenth-century Czech historian and politician, Palacky, had recognized the Czechs' need of the Habsburgs when he asserted: 'If Austria did not exist, it would be necessary to create her in the interests of humanity itself.'[2] The Slovaks did not even have such clear-cut aims. Their overwhelming pre-occupation was to survive the denationalizing pressures of the Magyars and most still hoped for a transformation of the

Habsburg monarchy, perhaps under the Archduke Franz Ferdinand, which would end Magyar hegemony in Slovakia.

What made possible the creation of Czechoslovakia was, of course, the collapse of Austria-Hungary in 1918. A significant proportion of the leading Czech politicians decided quite early in the war that a victory for the Central Powers would be a disaster for the Czechs and would even seriously endanger their national existence. From late 1914 onwards they began to work for the break-up of the Habsburg Monarchy. The leader of this group was Thomas Masaryk, a Slovak from Moravia and the most outstanding product of the Czech national movement. Before 1914 he had been the leading figure in a small but influential group of politicians called the 'Realists', who had opposed what they regarded as excessive Czech chauvinism and had attempted to foster closer links between Czechs and Slovaks. Masaryk himself, the son of a coachman, had become professor of philosophy at the Czech University of Prague and was a man of real personal integrity. He had aroused the ire of Czech chauvinists by exposing as forgeries some early Czech chronicles which had been used to prove that the Czechs were the earliest people in Northern Europe to have writings of this type. He had spoken out against a Hungarian ritual murder trial and had exposed the falsity of documents upon which the Austrian government had based its case against a group of Serbs and Croats accused of links with Serbia in the Zagreb treason trial of 1909. At the University of Prague, he had a magnetic influence not only on the new Czech generation, but also on the south Slav, Slovak and Rumanian students who came to study under him. A Slovak himself, Masaryk was a strong believer in Czecho-Slovak unity both on cultural grounds and because it was only by the establishment of a 'Czech-Slovakia' that a state strong enough to maintain an independent existence could be established.

In June 1918 Masaryk was able to reach an agreement in Pittsburgh with the leaders of the large Slovak community which had established itself in the USA. He promised them that the new state would establish a Slovak Diet, would create an autonomous administrative and legal system in Slovakia and would employ the Slovak language in administration and in the schools in Slovakia. It was on these terms that the most important Slovak leaders decided in late October 1918 to accede

to Czechoslovakia, acknowledging at the same time the existence of a 'Czechoslovak' nation. Masaryk's promises proved
easy to make, but difficult to implement. Given Hungarian
policy, there were few qualified Slovaks, and the administration
of Slovakia was entrusted mainly to Czechs, who antagonized the
Catholic Slovaks by their anti-clericalism and their inability to
understand local susceptibilities. As in all the new states, it was
felt that federalism would inevitably lead to political weakness
and the Slovak diet and administration promised in the Pittsburgh agreement were never set up. It is true that by the local
government reform of July 1927 a provincial assembly was set
up in Slovakia, but it had relatively narrow powers and its scope
for action was further reduced by the existence of a partially
nominated executive committee. Economically too Slovakia
suffered from the union with Bohemia and Moravia, since its
economic ties had been with the Magyar plain to which it had
exported timber and wood products, and where its peasantry
had been able to find work.

In this situation it was not surprising that there should
have been a fair amount of discontent in Slovakia. This was
mostly expressed through the Slovak People's Party, led by
Father Hlinka, the successor of the Slovak National Party. The
People's Party was clerical in character and derived its support
above all from the clergy and peasantry, although it did have a
fair number of adherents in the towns. It was suspicious of the
secular character of the Czechoslovak state, and demanded
autonomy for Slovakia in fulfilment of the promises of the
Pittsburgh agreement. It did, however, include a more radical
element which wanted complete independence. As resentment
grew against the policies of Czech centralization, its support
increased, so that its share of the vote rose from 21 per cent in
the elections of April 1920 to 32 per cent in November 1925.
In October 1929 its following fell slightly to about 28 per cent.
The Communists too provided another focus for discontent in
Slovakia, winning nearly 20 per cent of the votes there in 1925.

The new state was confronted not only with the problem of
coming to terms with the Slovaks, but also with that of integrat-
ing its substantial national minorities. In 1930, for instance,
Czechs and Slovaks made up only 66·2 per cent of the population
of the state.[3] The Czechs alone constituted barely 46 per cent.
Of the minorities, the greatest difficulties were caused by the

5-million-strong German community concentrated in the border areas of Bohemia and Moravia. Here, particularly in north-western Bohemia, Germans constituted a solid bloc of between 90 per cent and 100 per cent of the population. Partition of Bohemia and Moravia on national grounds, as had been advocated by Masaryk before 1914, was ruled out both by the Czechs and by the French in 1918. It was argued that large-scale partition was unfeasible since the German population of Bohemia was not economically self-sufficient and would be compelled, even if it became part of Germany, to retain its close economic links with the Czech areas. This would inevitably compel Germany to take an interest in the Czech lands, either by achieving economic domination of them or by taking them over directly. Some minor border rectifications were considered, but these were rejected by the French on strategic grounds, and by the Germans who took the view that if they were to be compelled to live in Czechoslovakia, it was to their advantage that their numbers be as large as possible.

The Czechs were thus faced with the problem of reconciling their own national aims with those of the Germans, a task which had ultimately proved beyond the ability of the Habsburg monarchy. They declared themselves willing to go very far to satisfy justifiable German demands. In his note to the Powers of May 1919, Eduard Beneš, the country's foreign minister and Masaryk's closest collaborator, declared it his intention to 'make of the Czecho-Slovak Republic a sort of Switzerland, taking into consideration, of course, the special conditions in Bohemia'.[4] The Czechs took on far-reaching obligations in relation to the Germans, as indeed to all the minorities. Minority schools were to be established where necessary, all public office was to be open to the minorities, law courts were to be mixed and 'Germans will have the right to plead before the highest courts in their own language'; local administration was to be carried on in the language of the local minority, and though the official language of the state was to be Czech, 'in practice the German language will be the second language in the country'.[5]

Given the long history of national conflict in Bohemia, it was not surprising that the relations between Czechs and Germans in the first years of the republic were marred by considerable tension and bitterness, and that the promises made by the Czechs proved difficult to keep. As a moderate Sudeten German,

Dr Gustav Peters, has observed, the Sudeten German regards the Czech as[6]

a half-educated . . . creature, to some extent saved by
German influence, who is politically intolerable and
unreliable, socially never satisfied and always pushing for
his nation, while the Czech sees in the German the invader,
the remorseless conqueror, the apostle of German world
hegemony, who only lives in the land in order to subjugate
the Czech people socially, politically and in every other way.

The Czechs, who had suffered considerably during the war because of Habsburg doubts of their loyalty, were determined to show the Germans that they were now masters in Bohemia. At the same time, their nervousness lest the Sudeten areas should secede led to a considerable amount of violence. In March 1919 demonstrations in the German areas against the government's decision to forbid them to participate in the Austrian elections led Czech troops to fire on crowds, with over fifty deaths. The Czechs were anxious to undo all the Germanization attempted in these areas since the Battle of the White Mountain in 1620. They passed a land reform, more radical on paper than it turned out in practice, which was intended to end the dominant position of the German landowners in the Czech lands (and incidentally of the Magyars in Slovakia and Ruthenia). They founded many new Czech primary schools in largely German areas and subjected the German population to a large number of irritating pinpricks, as when German shop signs were prohibited in Prague, and French replaced German as the foreign language at the Czech-Austrian frontier station of Břeclav. Economically, too, the industries of the German areas suffered from the erection of tariff barriers following the break-up of the Habsburg monarchy, and from the economic difficulties of Germany, their other main customer.

Of the other minorities, the 705,000 Hungarians in southern Slovakia wanted only to return to Hungary, while the 75,000 Poles in former Austrian Silesia were a constant focus for Polish government agitation. The 460,000 Ruthenians in Sub-Carpathian Ruthenia had, like the Slovaks, been promised autonomy in October 1918, a promise which was never fulfilled. Discontent grew, and this, increased by the widespread land hunger, made Ruthenia an area in which the Czech Communist Party, which called for the incorporation of Ruthenia into the Soviet Union, had considerable success.

Stabilization

In spite of the difficult problems which it faced, the Czechoslovak state functioned well in the 1920s. The land reform of April 1920 did a good deal to alleviate the land hunger of the peasantry, both in the Czech lands and in Slovakia. It provided for the expropriation of all land in large estates of over 150 hectares (250 hectares where forest land was concerned) and granted rather low compensation to the landowners. Though never as far-reaching in practice as it appeared on paper, it further contributed to the powerful position which the capable and well-organized peasantry in the Czech lands had built up since the abolition of serfdom in 1848. The financial reform of Alois Rašin, in accordance with which the old depreciated Austria crowns were called in early in 1919 and replaced by a new Czechoslovak crown, also helped to prevent the occurrence of a runaway inflation of the type which did so much to undermine political stability in Germany, Austria, Poland and Hungary.

The state was also able to achieve a fair amount of political stability. In February 1920 a new constitution was adopted wihch, unlike that of Poland or the Baltic states, provided for a strong executive. The election of the widely respected 'President-Liberator' Thomas Masaryk as head of state contributed still further to the power this office enjoyed. The new state was thus able quite easily to defeat the challenge to its authority posed by the Communist Party, formed in 1920 by the secession of the majority of the pre-war Czech Social Democrat Party. A Communist-led general strike in December 1919, which the Communists hoped would lead to their seizing power, failed dismally.

Indeed political life here was remarkably free of the upheavals which were so evident elsewhere in Eastern Europe. After a brief period of radical reform under the aegis of the two Socialist-dominated cabinets of Vlastimil Tusar (July 1919 to September 1920), power passed to the more broadly based Pětka, the five-party coalition which dominated Czech politics throughout the interwar period. The unity of the major Czech parties had been fostered by the difficulties they had experienced before 1914 in making their point of view heard in the Austrian parliament. It was further buttressed by the precarious character of Czech independence, and by the obvious hostility to the new state of a significant number of the parliamentary representatives of the national minorities, above all the Germans and the Hungarians. The pre-eminent party in this coalition was the Agrarians, the representatives of the prosperous and conservative Czech peasantry with its long established and highly organized system of co-operatives, whose position had been strengthened by the land reform. Agrarian dominance was clearly established with the creation in October 1922 of a cabinet headed by the peasant leader Antonìn Svehla.

A rival focus of power was constituted by the 'castle group', the network of advisers which surrounded President Masaryk. They tended to be rather more radical than the Agrarians and came, to a large extent, from the moderately left-wing National Socialist Party. The group was strongly committed to the principles of western constitutional democracy and wielded more power than its numbers might otherwise have warranted because of the exceptional esteem enjoyed by Masaryk. It thus provided a useful counterbalance to the more down-to-earth, interest-group politics of the Agrarians.

In power, the Agrarians tended to foster rural interests through high agricultural tariffs, the stabilization of farm prices and the holding down of industrial prices. They succeeded well in subordinating the army to political control, thus avoiding the problems of Poland, and attempted to alleviate the conflict with the Vatican which had arisen as a result of the secularizing policies embarked on between 1918 and 1920. In this sphere, they enjoyed a good deal of success, particularly after the Socialists left the government coalition in October 1926. Prosperity returned, and in this favourable economic climate the grievances of the minorities and of the Slovaks tended to diminish. In 1925 the Slovak Agrarian Party united with the Czech Agrarians and thereby became, in a sense, the governing party of the state. Within the German community, the 'Activist' point of view, the belief that one should accept the existence of the Czechoslovak state and work within legal bounds won increasing support. In November 1926 the German Agrarian Party joined the coalition, followed in October 1926 by the German Clericals and in December 1929 by the German Social Democrats. In January 1927 the Slovak People's Party also joined the cabinet, though it soon withdrew.

The crisis of Czechoslovak democracy

The depression hit Czechoslovakia hard, closely linked economically as it was with Germany and Austria, the two centres of the crisis in Europe. Its effects were made worse by the rigid adherence of the conservative Agrarians to a policy of deflation. It was only in February 1934 that the government took the long overdue step of devaluing the Czech crown, and then only by an inadequate 16 per cent. A certain economic revival did result, but this still lagged considerably behind the more rapid recovery of the German economy.

These economic difficulties greatly exacerbated the national conflicts in the state. Slovakia was especially badly affected, particularly after the denunciation in December 1930 of the Hungarian-Czechoslovak trade treaty. Normal trade between the two countries was only resumed in June 1935, and the Slovaks suffered heavily from the disruption of the links with their natural market. Moreover, the policy of agricultural protection and of artificially supporting grain prices, while it helped the more prosperous Czech peasants, bore hard on the large population of agricultural and forestry workers in Slovakia, who had to buy grain in the market. The weak and vulnerable Slovak metal industry also suffered severely.

These economic difficulties considerably increased the support for Slovak nationalism, and within the Slovak People's Party the younger elements, who favoured complete independence, grew in strength at the expense of those who demanded only autonomy within Czechoslovakia. Already in 1928 Voytěch Tuka, one of the leaders of the party, claimed that the proclamation of Turčansky Sväty Martin in 1918, as a result of which Slovakia had acceded to the republic, had contained a secret clause in terms of which the union was only to be valid for ten years, and that since the Czechs had failed to introduce autonomy, they now possessed no legal rights in Slovakia. The Czech government reacted strongly to this challenge to its authority: putting Tuka on trial for treason, they were able successfully to prove that he had received a good deal of financial support from Hungary, and were thus able for a time to discredit the more extreme elements. But little was done to alleviate the basic problems and discontent grew. In 1933 Hlinka, the leader of the Slovak People's Party, again affirmed that he had no desire to see the return of Hungarian rule. But, at the same time, he bitterly attacked the Czech government for failing to introduce autonomy as it had promised, and affirmed ominously, 'there are no Czechoslovaks: we wish only to be Slovaks'.[7] From 1935 the party began to make common cause with the other minorities, above all with the Germans.

For the depression had again tilted the balance against the Activists in the German areas. The industries of these parts, to a considerable extent producing consumer goods, suffered very severely, while the tourist trade declined catastrophically, particularly after the imposition of stringent exchange control regulations by Nazi Germany. The rise to power of Hitler in Germany and the Nazi revolution was watched with uncritical adulation by large sections of the Sudeten German population, among whom the national conflict had long fostered an extreme chauvinism. Already in 1931 the Czech authorities had felt it necessary to ban Nazi and Nazi youth uniforms, and in the summer of 1932 had brought to trial a number of the leaders of the Nazi youth movement Volksport on a charge of plotting an armed rebellion. The following year the Sudeten Nazis, fearing that the government would ban them, dissolved their organization and went underground. They re-emerged in a new form in 1934 as the Sudeten German National Front. This organization, ably led by the skilful and totally unscrupulous Konrad Henlein, aimed at uniting all the German nationalist forces in Czechoslovakia in a broad alliance. It succeeded in bringing together Catholic, Austrian-style fascists, old-fashioned nationalists, and adherents of German-style Nazism. It displayed considerable skill in its political tactics, calling itself 'neo-activist' and disclaiming any intention of destroying the Czechoslovak state. Its aim was merely 'a considerable decentralization of the administration in favour of districts with a German population'.[8]

Its broad nationalist appeal, coupled with the widespread discontent in the German areas and the persistence of the depression, gave it wide support. In the elections of May 1935 it won a decisive victory, obtaining about 62 per cent of the German votes, seriously undermining the position of the

Activist parties. After a certain amount of inner conflict, the Sudeten German Party, as it was now called following Czechoslovak pressure, was remodelled in the summer of 1936. The dominance of the National Socialist elements was now assured and the organization also became almost entirely subject to orders from Berlin.

The reaction of the Czechs to this new situation was twofold. On the one hand they attempted to tighten the links with their allies, France and, after 1935, the Soviet Union. They therefore rejected an accommodation with Germany of the type which had been achieved by Poland since January 1934 and by Austria in the agreement in July 1936. An understanding of this sort was indeed offered by the Germans, though how seriously they intended it has been questioned. There were a number of politicians, particularly in the Agrarian Party, who favoured the adoption of such a course. However it was rejected both by Beneš, who succeeded Masaryk as president in November 1935, and by the new prime minister, the Slovak Agrarian Milan Hodža, on the grounds that such a move would mean abandoning the democratic character of the state. Indeed, the immediate result of the adhesion of Czechoslovakia to the Franco-Russian alliance in 1935 was Operation Schulung, Hitler's first plan for invading the country. In his mind power politics, and not an interest in Henlein, had always been paramount.

Internally the Czechs attempted to cut the ground from under the Slovak and German nationalists by encouraging pro-Czech politicians in these areas and by attempting to alleviate the more obvious grievances. No real attempt was made however to introduce autonomy in Slovakia, and the Slovak People's Party remained unreconciled. In relation to the Germans, a major effort to meet their demands was made and culminated in the agreement reached with the Activist parties in February 1937. This promised a number of important economic and political concessions: greater equity in the allocation of public works, easier access for Germans to the civil service and subsidies for German educational and cultural organizations. Nevertheless it was unable to halt the rapid Nazification of the German minority, which was accelerated in February 1938 when Hitler declared himself to be responsible for 'the protection of those German people who are not in a position to secure, along our frontiers, their political and spiritual freedom by their own efforts',[9] and still more after the German annexation of Austria in March 1938.

The outcome of the crisis faced by Czechoslovakia is well known. Under strong pressure from Britain and France, the Czechs agreed in September 1938 to cede to Germany their predominantly German areas. They were also subsequently forced to acquiesce in the loss of the Hungarian and Polish minorities and to grant autonomy to Slovakia and Ruthenia. The state which emerged from these changes was totally dependent economically and politically on Nazi Germany and it did not prove lasting. In March 1939, when the Czech government finally tried to reassert its waning authority, which Hitler was undermining, in Slovakia, Hitler allowed the state to be destroyed. Bohemia and Moravia were incorporated into the Reich as a protectorate, Slovakia was made nominally independent under German tutelage, and Ruthenia, after one day's 'independence', was given to Hungary as a sop for the loss of Slovakia, and also to conciliate Russia.

In spite of its ultimate collapse, the achievements of the Czech republic in the interwar period were considerable, and its political life contrasts very favourably with that of the other states of Eastern Europe. The breakdown of its political system was overwhelmingly due not so much to its inner weaknesses as to the tensions caused by the victory of the Nazis in Germany. There were a number of reasons for the greater success of the Czechs in running a constitutional system. In the first place, the country had a far more balanced economic situation than the other states of the area. A good deal of industrialization had taken place in the Czech lands, and only 33 per cent of the population in the republic as a whole were dependent on agriculture for their livelihood. Moreover, at least in the Czech lands, the peasantry was prosperous and well-organized. The Pětka, the group of five leading parties which in coalition governed the country for almost the entire interwar period also contributed to Czech stability, as did the dominant position of the Agrarian Party, representing the level-headed and down-to-earth peasantry. Finally the personality of Thomas Masaryk, the beloved 'President Liberator', did much to mitigate the bitterness of political conflict. It was the decision of the Western Powers to force the Czechs to capitulate to Nazi demands that brought about the collapse of the state. This, together with six harsh years of German occupation, left a residue of bitterness which partly explains the Communist Party's emergence as the most powerful political group after 1945, and its successful seizure of power in 1948.

Notes

1 E. Wiskemann, *Czechs and Germans* (London, 1938), p. 161.
2 R. W. Seton-Watson, *A History of the Czechs and Slovaks* (London, 1943), pp. 186–7.
3 See the Statistical appendix, Table 5, p. 160.
4 'Note on the Regime of Nationalities in the Czecho-Slovak Republic', Paris, 20 May 1919. Quoted in Wiskemann, *op. cit.*, p. 92.
5 *Ibid.*, pp. 92–3.
6 Quoted in Wiskemann, *op. cit.*, p. 118.
7 Quoted in H. Seton-Watson, *Independent Eastern Europe 1918–1941* (Cambridge, 1945), p. 178.
8 M. W. Graham, 'Parties and Politics', in R. J. Kerner (ed.), *Czechoslovakia: Twenty Years of Independence* (Berkeley and Los Angeles, 1940), p. 163.
9 In his Reichstag speech of 20 February. Quoted in W. Shirer, *The Rise and Fall of the Third Reich* (London, 1960), p. 333.

Chapter 7

Epilogue

The failure of the democratic constitutions established in Eastern Europe after 1918 is not difficult to explain. Democracy is not only a constitutional framework, but also a habit of mind, a willingness to accept that one's point of view may not necessarily prevail, and an ability on the part of politicians to accept long periods out of office. It has only proved successful, with a few exceptions, in the wealthy countries of Western Europe and North America where class divisions have not been too deep-rooted and where there has been a long tradition of relatively stable political evolution. The conditions which existed in Eastern Europe after 1918 were hardly conducive to the emergence of effective democratic institutions. The countries of the area were for the most part poor, and in many cases their poverty had been intensified by the devastation caused by the war. They were racked by deep class divisions, both in the towns themselves and between the towns and the countryside. For most part they lacked any real political tradition, and even in countries like Serbia and Bulgaria, where independence had long been achieved, the habit of regarding the state as a means for satisfying the personal needs of oneself and one's kin died hard. In the words of one pre-war Bulgarian politician: 'What God gives is for all, but the blessings which the state may confer are first for our kin. That is how we understand democracy. So it was yesterday, is today and will be tomorrow.'[1]

In all of Eastern Europe there was a need for radical social reforms to narrow class divisions. Yet the adoption of such

127

reforms was seriously impeded by the widespread fear of communism in the governing élites. This fear, derived above all from memories of the Hungarian and Estonian Soviet regimes and from the Polish–Soviet war, led to the labelling of any left-wing movement as communist. Fears that the 1918–21 territorial settlement would not prove lasting, and that it would be undone by German, Hungarian, Bulgarian or Soviet revisionism, increased the pervasive atmosphere of insecurity and further undermined democratic institutions. In the light of the serious foreign situation, calls for national cohesion fell on fertile ground. Fears that the national minorities' demands for the redress of their many grievances were merely a pretext for the revision of the Versailles frontiers in Eastern Europe were a major factor in preventing a fair assessment of their claims. Their deep dissatisfaction and willingness to resort to violence, as in the case of the Macedonians or the East Galician Ukrainians, obviously contributed to the fragility of democratic institutions.

In a number of countries of Eastern Europe, above all Hungary, Rumania, Slovakia and Poland, the development of the Jewish problem contributed to the weakness of democracy. Anti-Semitism, the 'socialism of the idiot', found eager support in these countries where intermediary occupations such as trading and small scale money-lending were largely in Jewish hands. This went along with the widespread belief that there was a Jewish conspiracy to take over the world, and with accusations that all left-wing organizations were the tools of this conspiracy. These views seem to us almost lunatic today, but they commanded the support of significant sections of the Eastern European middle classes and intelligentsia, above all the university students, and they were given a tremendous fillip by the ease with which the Nazis were able to dispossess the wealthiest and, in many ways, most assimilated Jewish community in Europe. The accusations of the young Right-radicals that the Polish, Hungarian and Rumanian governments had sold out to the Jews were a continuously disrupting factor in politics, as was their extreme willingness to have recourse to anti-Jewish violence.

Perhaps the major factor in exposing the weaknesses and contradictions of the new states was the great depression. The catastrophic fall in grain prices which resulted from the worst agricultural depression for eighty years had a devastating effect in the largely agricultural countries in Eastern Europe. It had much to do with the increasing repressiveness of the Piłsudski regime in Poland, the fall of Bethlen in Hungary and the failure of King Alexander in Yugoslavia, to mention only a few examples. It contributed everywhere to the growth of extremist movements, mostly on the Right, though also on the Left, and strengthened the widespread belief that liberal capitalism as a system was bound to collapse.

The breakdown of democracy in Eastern Europe was closely connected with the failure of the French system of alliances. It is true that the French system had no specifically ideological overtones, but those most critical of its operation in Eastern Europe were also, in many cases, those who favoured close links with the newly resurgent Germany of Hitler. In Hungary and Rumania, above all, the young Right-radicals strongly pressed for close links with Nazi Germany, not only to advance the interest of their nations, but also because of their hatred for liberal democracy, as embodied in France. The progressive triumph of Germany contributed greatly to the belief in Eastern Europe in the 1930s that democracy as a political system was weak and played out.

On the surface, there is no clear pattern in the regimes which emerged from the collapse of democracy. The Piłsudski regime in Poland was the product mainly of the persistence of the pre-war conflict of orientations and, at least until the clash with parliament in 1929–30, remained largely constitutional in nature. The Yugoslav regime under Alexander also had a rather archaic character and had little in common with the one-party states which developed in Italy and Germany. Even under the regency attempts to develop a one-party system were rather half-hearted, and were abandoned with the fall of Stojadinović. In Bulgaria, too, although brutal repressive measures were taken against the Agrarians and the Communists, some elements of the constitutional system remained, and the regime was far more like a pre-1914 Balkan royal dictatorship than a truly fascist one. Fascist ideas had more success in Austria and Hungary. Developments here were closely linked with the evolution of the situation in Italy. In Hungary, the regime had from its inception a dual character. It was partly an attempt to re-create the political system which had obtained in pre-1914 Hungary. At the same time, the counter-revolutionaries who had overthrown the Soviet regime of Béla Kun adopted a good deal of the ideology of the radical Right, with their belief in the rottenness of liberal democracy and the Jewish conspiracy. These two elements fought for power and though for the most part it was the older conservatives who triumphed, they tended also to take over the ideas of the young fascists, particularly their pro-Italian and pro-German orientation in foreign policy and their anti-Semitism. In Austria, the increasingly authoritarian character of the Dollfuss regime had much to do with pressure from both Italy and Hungary, though the situation was complicated by the fact that the young Right-radicals tended to be pan-German. In Rumania after 1938 fascist ideas also became popular in governmental circles and gained in strength after the abdication of King Carol. However here too, even more than in Hungary, it was the old-fashioned conservatives like General Antonescu, rather than the younger Right-radicals of the Iron Guard, who emerged victorious. The short-lived Slovak and Croat regimes were both more openly fascist, though in both there were elements which resented the subordination of their national interests to those of Italy and Germany.

In spite of the extremely varied characters of the different regimes, certain common features emerge. Though efforts were made to foster government parties in most countries these were by and large unsuccessful, and the regimes thus lacked the demonic dynamism so apparent in Nazi Germany. At the same time, Right-radical views became increasingly popular among sections of the intelligentsia, particularly those whose career prospects had appeared blighted by the great depression and by the large number of Jews in certain professions. However, these Right-radical views never gained significant popular support outside Rumania, where the Iron Guard had some characteristics of a mass movement, and some areas of Hungary. In spite of this, one of the main characteristics of the 1930s in Eastern Europe was the growing belief in the power of Nazi Germany and the conviction on the part of ever-increasing numbers of politicians that some *modus vivendi* with Hitler would have to be found. Along with this belief went a contempt for western values and the complementary view that closer links with Germany meant the adoption of some aspects of the German political system, especially its anti-Semitism and its authoritarian character. The belief became increasingly common that fascism, loosely defined as a nationalist one-party regime, was the wave of the future, and this affected even those to whom the Nazi *Weltanschauung* was anathema. But though there were many politicians who hesitated to commit themselves to Hitler, the alternative of an alliance with the Soviet Union, then undergoing the worst of the purges, was attractive to few leaders outside Czechoslovakia, and even there was looked on with considerable reservations by many. Schemes for combined action by all of Eastern Europe against both Russia and Germany never had any chance of success given the depth of national antagonisms, while plans such as those of the Polish foreign minister, Beck, for a Third Europe, which rested on the destruction of Czechoslovakia, only made the path easier for Hitler.

The Second World War saw the establishment of German domination in Eastern Europe, a process which reached its height with the initial successes of the war against the Soviet Union in 1941. The nations in this Nazi 'New Order' fell into two groups. On the one hand, there were the Nazi-allied or satellite states. Of these, Hungary, Bulgaria and Finland all owed to the Nazis the achievement of long-held territorial ambitions. Rumania was compensated for the loss to the Hungarians of Northern Transylvania with the reacquisition of Bessarabia and Northern Bukovina and new territory east of the Dniester River. Slovakia and Croatia both achieved their independence as a result of Nazi assistance. All of them retained, until very late in the war, a fair measure of internal independence and the pre-war élites were, for the most part, not displaced.

The situation was much worse in the countries directly administered by Germany. In March 1939, with the collapse of the rump Czecho-Slovakia established by the Munich agreement, what was left of Bohemia and Moravia was incorporated into the Reich. Parallel Czech and German administrations were created, but ultimate power clearly lay in the hands of the German Reichsprotektor. The Czech authorities who collaborated, mostly in the hope of alleviating the harshness of German rule, were quickly reduced to the status of implementers of German orders. The occupation bore differently on the different sectors of population. The industrial workers and peasantry benefited economically from incorporation into the Reich. Unemployment fell, wages rose, and the price of agri-

Map 6 Territorial changes, 1938–41

cultural produce remained satisfactory. It was the intelligentsia and middle class who bore the brunt of Nazi denationalizing policies, and it was among them that resistance first got under way. During the period of occupation something like 38,000 Czechs were killed, and by 1945 hatred of the Germans was widespread in all classes, particularly as it had become evident that the ultimate aim of Nazi policy was the destruction for ever of the Czechs as a nation.

In Poland, German policy was even harsher. The territory assigned to Germany by the Soviet-German Friendship Treaty of September 1939 was divided into two areas. The western part, which went considerably beyond the German frontier of 1914 and included the great textile town of Łódź, was directly annexed to the Reich. Its population was subjected to a ruthless campaign of Germanization, and Jews and refractory Poles were deported. The Poles who remained were treated as second-class citizens. They had to wear a yellow badge marked 'P' to indicate their nationality, while the Polish language was prohibited in the administration and schools. Many were deported to the interior of the Reich as labourers. Plans to settle large numbers of Germans had, however, to be postponed until the end of the war. In the rest of German-occupied Poland, a 'General Government' was established, directly administered by the SS and the Gestapo. The aim of German policy was to reduce the area to an agricultural appendage of the Reich, and attempts to enlist the collaboration of the Poles were only half-heartedly pursued, even after the war turned against the Germans on the Eastern front. In the words of the German governor, Hans Frank, 'Poland shall be treated as a colony; the Poles shall be the slaves of the Greater German World Empire.'[2] All attempts at resistance were brutally crushed, and raw materials and industrial plants were ruthlessly plundered. The General Government was also the centre for the German 'final solution' of the Jewish problem by mass murder. By the end of the war, Poland had lost over 6 million people, half of them Jews, and 38 per cent of her material resources had been destroyed.

The German treatment of Yugoslavia was almost as brutal. After the Yugoslav defeat in April 1941 Croatia, including Bosnia and Herzegovina, but without the Dalmatian coast, which went to Italy, was made independent. Slovenia was partitioned. The northern two-thirds went to Germany, where a policy of Germanization, with deportations and the proscription of the Slovene language, was pursued. In the southern one-third, the Italians adopted a policy of fascist indoctrination, rather than directly attacking the Slovene national identity. Montenegro was made nominally independent under Italian military control, while Macedonia was divided between Bulgaria and Italian-ruled Albania. The western part of the Vojvodina was annexed by Hungary, while the eastern part was directly ruled by its large German minority. Serbia, now reduced to an area smaller than that it had possessed in 1878, was given nominal independence under German control. In Greece, which in 1941 lost its part of Thrace to Bulgaria, a nominally in-dependent government, controlled first by Italians and, from September 1943, by the Germans, was established.

Resistance to Nazi rule developed most rapidly in those countries directly administered by Germany. This was partly the inevitable consequence of the harshness of German control, but also owed a certain amount to the existence of Polish, Czechoslovak, Yugoslav and Greek governments-in-exile esta-blished under Allied auspices, principally in Great Britain. Though more slowly, resistance to German rule also developed in Slovakia, Bulgaria and Croatia, and finally even in Rumania and Hungary. The resistance movements were nowhere united and several countries experienced what were in effect civil wars in the closing stages of the war. The main division was between those who favoured a return to a more democratic and pro-western version of the pre-war regimes, and those who advocated the introduction of radical social changes, particularly on a communist model. These two groups differed not only in their views of how their countries should be ruled in the post-war period, but also in the tactics to be employed in fighting the Germans. The leftist movements favoured suicidal direct attacks on the Germans, in the belief that the inevitable Nazi over-reaction to their activities would radicalize the population as a whole. The moderate groups favoured a more cautious strategy, both because of their unwillingness to expose their people to vicious German reprisals and because they wished to preserve their forces for the post-war struggle for power. This was, broadly speaking, the pattern in Poland, Yugoslavia, Greece and Albania. In Poland, the non-communist forces emerged as the most powerful group, in the other three countries this position was held by the Communist groups. Czechoslovakia falls somewhere between. The Communists were powerful here, both in Bohemia-Moravia and also in Slovakia, but so too were the non-communist forces. The government-in-exile was, moreover, able to create a coalition composed of both these groups. In Bulgaria, pro-Russian sentiments and disillusionment with participation for a second time in a generation in a German-dominated coalition strengthened the Communists, while in Rumania and Hungary, traditionally anti-Russian, non-communist elements were unquestionably stronger.

Thus the immediate post-war period would, even without Great Power intervention, have seen a struggle for power between Communist and non-communist forces in Eastern Europe. In fact, however, the fate of the region was settled by the wartime agreements between the Soviet Union, Great Britain and the USA, and the subsequent deterioration of relations between the wartime allies. By mid-1948 the whole of the area, including East Germany, but with the exception of Greece and Finland, had gone communist. All these states, except for Yugoslavia and Albania, were also under firm Soviet control. This had come about, outside Yugoslavia and Albania, where real revolutions had occurred and partisan guerrillas had seized power, through the creation of popular front regimes from which the non-communist elements were progressively squeezed out, with the help of the Red Army, by what the Hungarian communist leader, Mátyás Rákosi, referred to as 'salami tactics'.

The reasons for this development have aroused a great deal of controversy in recent years. At the height of the Cold War it was widely assumed in the west that the Soviet takeover in Eastern Europe was the result of a master plan for expansion on the part of Stalin. It was only western realization of the more or less unlimited character of Stalin's aims which led western statesmen to adopt a policy of containing the Soviet empire within the limits it had reached. An earlier realization of the character of Soviet policy could, it was argued, have set tighter limits on the extent of Soviet control. This view has been challenged in recent years by a revisionist school of historians, particularly strong in the USA. They have argued that Stalin, rather conservative in his objectives, aimed only at creating a zone of friendly states on his western border in order to achieve security for the Soviet Union against a revived Germany. The

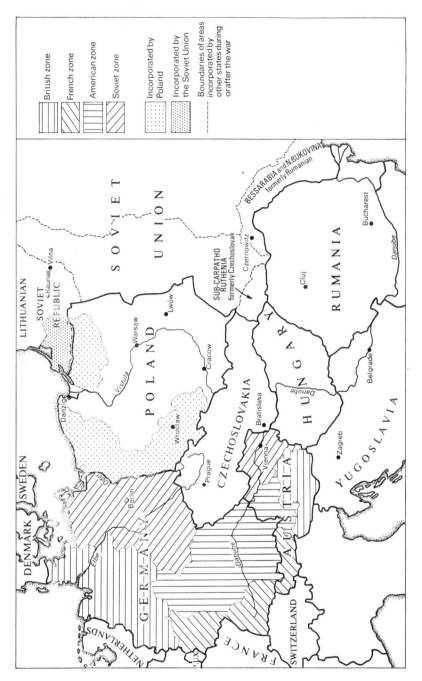

Map 7 Territorial changes resulting from the Second World War

western powers were at first willing to concede this to him, but, particularly after Yalta, with the change in the presidency and the acquisition of the atomic bomb, the USA began to draw back from its undertakings, and it was this which led Stalin to tighten his hold over the area in which he was dominant.

Certain points can be made about this controversy. Though Stalin's objectives were certainly not limitless and were clearly tempered by his realization, as he told Djilas and Tito, that Russia could not fight a major war for fifteen years,[3] he did have a number of aims. In the first place, he wished to preserve the territorial acquisitions made by the Soviet Union in the period of co-operation with Nazi Germany between August 1939 and June 1941. He wanted to retain the Baltic states, primarily on strategic grounds, and Eastern Poland, Bessarabia and Southern Bukovina so that all Ukrainian and Byelorussian people would be contained within the Soviet Union, and no rival nationalist focus for them could emerge. This objective was accepted by the western powers as the inevitable consequence of Stalin's participation in the war. Second, he aimed at the establishment of a set of friendly states on the western border of the Soviet Union. This objective was also more or less conceded by the Western powers in relation to south-eastern Europe, for it followed fairly inevitably from the decision taken at the Teheran Conference in November 1943 that Eastern Europe would be liberated from the east. If the percentage agreement, made between Churchill and Stalin in Moscow in October 1944, meant anything, it also implied the concession to the Soviets of a dominant position in Rumania and Bulgaria and a strong position in Hungary and Yugoslavia, in return for a recognition that Greece, vital for imperial communications in the Eastern Mediterranean, lay in the British sphere of influence, a division of interests to which Stalin by and large adhered.

Poland, for which the British had after all gone to war, was a more difficult problem. From mid-1943 the British had decided that they would have to accept the Soviet position on the eastern Polish border. They hoped to induce the Polish government-in-exile in London to agree to this by ensuring that Poland was compensated for the loss of territory east of the Curzon line by accretions in the west at the expense of Germany. In this way it was hoped to resolve the problem of the future government of liberated Poland in a manner favourable to the government-in-exile. These positions formed the basis of the decisions taken over Poland at Teheran, and, along with the agreement that Poland was to be liberated by the Red Army and not the Western Allies, in fact settled the Polish issue. The compromise foundered on the refusal of the Poles to accept the loss of the territories east of the Curzon line, and on their perhaps well-founded distrust of Russian intentions. By November 1944 the British had effectively abandoned the London Poles, and at Yalta in February 1945 a face-saving compromise was patched up, whereby the communist-dominated Lublin government, with some additions from the London Poles, was to be recognized as the ruler of Poland. Free elections were also promised.

It seems fairly clear that although there had been some bitter disputes, conflicts over Eastern Europe were not central in the breakdown of the wartime alliance. However, a problem was created by the lack of a common political language between the west and the Soviets. Western politicians conceived of a sphere of influence in nineteenth-century terms: the countries affected would have to subordinate their foreign policies to that of the predominant power, but would preserve a fair degree of internal autonomy. To Stalin, almost paranoid in his suspicion, anyone not completely for him was against him. Soviet acts of repression in Eastern Europe thus considerably strengthened western suspicion of Stalin's objectives. Moreover, the heavy Soviet hand in Eastern Europe, and the way the Soviets compelled their newly liberated 'allies' to sell raw materials and finished products to the Soviet Union at sub-economic prices to facilitate her recovery, stimulated opposition in Eastern Europe. Stalin came increasingly to the view that the only political element he could trust in Eastern Europe were Moscow-trained communists, securely under his control. The Hungarian elections of autumn 1945 were crucial in this respect, since in them the Hungarian Communist Party won only 17 per cent of the vote, as against 57 per cent for the Smallholders' (Peasant) Party.[4] This seems to have convinced Stalin that he could not trust the electoral process to produce the sort of regimes he wanted.

It was over the German question that the breakdown came. Stalin's objectives here were twofold: to make use of large-scale reparations from Germany to rebuild the war-shattered Soviet economy and to establish a Soviet say in the administration of Germany so as to ensure the creation of a 'friendly' state there.

By 1945 it had become apparent that the various plans worked out during the war for the division of Germany into a number of smaller countries, and for the 'pastoralization' of the German economy were impracticable. This was not so much because the Western Allies wished to be lenient to Germany – the sheer cost of administering Germany soon made it obvious that, unless the German economy was revived, European economic rehabilitation would be severely hampered. Thus when they met in Potsdam in June 1945, the Allies reached agreement, in theory at least, on the maintenance of Germany as an economic unit, with Berlin as its capital. It was because of this view that Germany should be administered as a whole that the position of Berlin as the centre for the four-power administration of Germany was left very vague. The vital question of access rights was hardly dealt with at all.

Conflict soon arose over the level of reparations. The Russians were determined to extort all they could, even though their actions would have led to the reduction of Germany to economic chaos. This soon led to Allied protests and to General Clay's refusing to allow the transfer of goods from the American zone of occupation to Russia. From then on mutual suspicions grew rapidly, particularly since the Russians took the view that the principle that German reconstruction should take precedence over their own economic needs was hostile to the spirit of the alliance. The further deterioration of relations was also linked with economic questions. In the post-war period the USA, which was very much influenced by the belief in the negative effect before the war of restrictions on international trade, was thinking of an economic policy for the whole of Europe, designed to remove such restrictions. The European Economic Commission in Geneva was intended to promote these policies. By 1947 it had become obvious that a massive injection of American aid was needed if a European recovery was to be achieved. To meet this need the Americans formulated the Marshall Plan. Participation in this plan was open to Russia and to her allies and satellites in Eastern Europe, but the Russians forbade Poland and Czechoslovakia to participate, believing that the Marshall Plan was an attempt to create a West European bloc which would undermine Soviet control in Eastern Europe. The rejection of Marshall Aid in July 1947 precipitated a political crisis in Czechoslovakia, which was still ruled by a real popular-front coalition. This culminated in a communist takeover in February 1948, in which the Czech communists, rather than the Soviets, played the principal role. However, this development caused widespread disillusion with Soviet intentions in Western European circles. The expulsion of Yugoslavia from the Cominform, which showed that no country, no matter how communist, would be allowed any significant autonomy in relation to the Soviet Union, further increased the awareness in Western Europe that an 'Iron Curtain' now divided the continent. The immediate result was a crisis in Berlin, which because of the vagueness of the Potsdam agreement was on the wrong side of the curtain, and the Berlin blockade followed. As a result, 1948 saw a serious deterioration of East–West relations and the beginnings of Stalinism in Soviet-controlled Eastern Europe. Already in September 1947, Stalin had established the Cominform, a body including the Communist parties of Eastern Europe as well as those of France and Italy and which was intended to subordinate their policies firmly to Soviet control. In January 1949 the Comecon was set up, to co-ordinate economic policy. In April 1949 the North Atlantic Treaty Organization came into being, affirming the American commitment to defend the *status quo* in Western Europe, and in June 1950, the Korean War broke out.

The Stalinist attempt at the totalitarian reshaping of the societies of Eastern Europe thus took place in an atmosphere of mounting international tension and in a situation in which the outbreak of a general war between the Soviet Union and the USA was widely feared. The Stalinist period was marked by considerable uniformity in the political and social development of Eastern Europe. Major decisions were taken in Moscow and Soviet 'advisers' were prominent in all ministries and especially in the security forces and the army, whose members had usually to swear an oath of allegiance to the Soviets. The dominant role of the Soviet Union in the bloc was constantly stressed, as was the fact that the Soviet model was the only possible one for the countries of Eastern Europe. The cult of Stalin was zealously propagated, with towns named after him and statues of him erected in all the countries of the area. In his wake, a number of lesser Stalins, such as Bierut in Poland, Gottwald in Czechoslovakia and Chervenkov in Bulgaria promoted minor cults of their own.

Political life was dominated by the unchallenged rule of the party, and the central committee with its *apparat* and the security forces were the only domestic sources of power. The Stalinist concept that the transition to socialism was characterized by a sharpening class struggle was used to justify the large-scale arrest of pre-war political figures who were often condemned in show trials to cow the population. Organized religion, in particular the Catholic Church, was especially suspect, and its leaders in Hungary, Poland and Czechoslovakia were subjected to harassment and imprisonment. A 'class viewpoint' was officially introduced in several countries in the distribution of food and consumer goods, and children of worker and peasant origin were similarly favoured in access to higher education. In cultural life, the norms of Soviet-style 'socialist realism' were rigorously adhered to.

Non-communists were not the only people who suffered from the political atmosphere of the time. Stalin's clash with Tito, which resulted in essence from his pathological suspicion of the Yugoslav leader, as indeed of any independent communist, led to the expulsion of Yugoslavia from the Cominform in June 1948 and the unsuccessful attempt to provoke an internal coup to displace him. It was followed by a search for national deviationists throughout Eastern Europe, which culminated in the show trials of László Rajk in Hungary, Traicho Kostov in Bulgaria and Vladimir Clementis in Czechoslovakia, and to the imprisonment of Władysław Gomułka in Poland. The people involved in these purges, who in some cases lost their lives, were largely communists who had remained in their native countries during the war, rather than move to the Soviet Union. Their 'crime' in Stalin's eyes was, he believed, that they were not entirely under his control and might at some stage resist his demands. The 'anti-cosmopolitan' and 'anti-Zionist' campaign in the Soviet Union of 1951–2 unleashed a second series of purges in Eastern Europe, mostly of Jewish communists of a predominantly leftist orientation. The most prominent victims were Rudolf Slánský in Czechoslovakia and Ana Pauker and Vasile Luca in Rumania.

In the economic field, the period was marked by the adoption of centralized planning on the Soviet model and by a pronounced emphasis on mining, metallurgy and the production of machine tools. Impressive increases in production were registered and much wartime devastation was soon made good, but at the cost of the standard of living of the population as a whole, and of the creation of severe imbalances in the structure of the economy. In agriculture, the land reforms which followed liberation were succeeded by widespread collectivization, which inevitably led to a decline in agricultural efficiency and imposed a further strain on the standard of living of the towns. Another feature of the economic situation in these years was the deliberate down-grading of traditional economic links with the west and the reorientation of the trade of Eastern Europe towards the Soviet Union. Given the dominant Soviet position, this involved a fair degree of economic exploitation. Most countries of the area were compelled to export raw materials and finished products to the Soviet Union at sub-economic prices. By an agreement of August 1945, Poland was compelled to deliver annually 13 million tons of coal (later halved) to the Soviet Union at a price of $1·25 per ton, at a time when Denmark and Sweden were prepared to offer $12 and later $16 per ton. Other Polish coal was bought by the Soviet Union at $14 per ton when Western European prices were over $18 per ton. Polish yarn was bought by the Soviet Union at $1 per kilo when Sweden was offering $2·87 per kilo.[5]

One final characteristic of this period was the extensive militarization of society. Fear of a major war was widespread, and with the Soviet acquisition of the atomic bomb in 1949, her satellites were to provide a large section of the conventional armed forces of the bloc. In Poland, for instance, the army increased rapidly from 100,000 in 1946 to 500,000 in 1950, while defence expenditure grew from 1,000 million złoty in 1948 to 6,600 million in 1952. Between 1951 and 1955, defence pro-duction comprised 11·0 per cent of all Polish industrial invest-ment.[6]

The rigidities of the Stalinist system could not long outlast the death of Stalin himself in March 1953. Its undermining in Eastern Europe was the result both of the impact of events in the Soviet Union and of pressures for change in the area itself. Stalin's system of personal terror did not survive him, and his death was followed by the establishment of the principle of collective leadership and the rejection of the cult of the per-sonality. It did not lead to any immediate liberalization in Eastern Europe, however, and ill-judged schemes of economic reform in Czechoslovakia and East Germany, which further undermined the standard of living of the workers, led to serious rioting in Plzeň in May and, more seriously, in East Berlin in June. The unrest in Berlin very nearly led to the collapse of the East German government, which was only able to maintain itself with the help of Soviet military intervention. The near disaster gravely undermined the position of Beria, head of Soviet security, and contributed to his fall in June, which led to the drastic weakening of the security apparatus and to demands for similar changes in the Soviet Union's satellites. Malenkov's 'New Course', with its stress on consumer goods rather than heavy industry, led to reforms everywhere in Eastern Europe. In Hungary the dogmatic Stalinist, Mátyás Rákosi, was forced to bring the liberal Imre Nagy into the leader-ship as premier, while retaining the first-secretaryship; in both Czechoslovakia and, to a lesser extent, Poland significant economic reforms and some political liberalization were intro-duced.

Malenkov's fall in February 1955 did not lead to a new hard line in Eastern Europe, and although Rákosi now regained power at Nagy's expense, he was unable to rule as ruthlessly as before. Indeed, Khrushchev's attempt from May 1955 to achieve a *rapprochement* with Yugoslavia appeared to legitimize the concept of 'separate roads to socialism' and increased demands for change in Eastern Europe. One of Tito's conditions for the re-establishment of satisfactory relations seems to have been the removal of a number of Stalinist leaders in Eastern Europe, of whom the most important was Rákosi. The climate of unrest was greatly heightened by Khrushchev's secret speech at the twentieth congress of the Communist Party of the Soviet Union in February 1956, in which he bitterly and graphically denounced the crimes of Stalin. He again stressed the concept of 'separate roads to socialism' and though he probably intended this to refer only to Yugoslavia, in Eastern Europe it was taken in a wider sense.

The pressures for change in Eastern Europe were of various types. From economists there came criticism of the rigid character of the centrally directed economic system and demands for more flexible methods of economic planning. Workers resented the low standard of living, peasants wanted the end of collectiviza-tion. Writers and intellectuals wished to diminish the crudities of Stalinism in the cultural field, while many party members were disillusioned with the way their countries were being governed and, in particular, at the continual subordination of their interests to those of the Soviet Union. These pressures were felt everywhere in Eastern Europe but were rather weak in Czechoslovakia, Rumania and Bulgaria and the party leaderships were able to keep them under control. It was in Poland and Hungary, where in the figures of Gomułka and Nagy there existed the leadership of alternative communist governments and where the existing Party apparatus was demoralized, that the pressure for change became uncontrollable.

The course of events in these two countries was, however, drastically different. In Poland the death in March 1956 of Bolesław Bierut, the first secretary of the party and the man most closely identified with Stalinism, made possible the election of Eduard Ochab, a moderate liberal, as first secretary. The extent of popular discontent with the regime was made obvious in June, when riots broke out among industrial workers in Poznań in which at least fifty-three people were killed. Although these began as a protest against economic conditions, they soon came to involve political demands. By early October pressure for change from below had built up considerable force and enjoyed a wide measure of support in the party. Władysław Gomułka, who had been restored to his membership of the party in July 1956, came to appear increasingly as the only man who could achieve a peaceful reform of the communist system. He was therefore elected first secretary of the party at the end of October in spite of strong Soviet pressure against him, and he set up a new and liberal Politburo. He was able to convince the Soviets that he would not let the situation get out of hand and was thus able to prevent Russian intervention, but at the cost of gradually abandoning the more liberal aspects of his programme.

In Hungary, Ernö Gerö, who had replaced Rákosi as first secretary in June 1956, refused to give way to popular demands. When demonstrations against him assumed large proportions in October, he ordered the police to open fire. This failed to subdue the population and drastically undermined his own position as the demonstrators were joined by armed workers and units of the Hungarian army. The Soviet troops in Hungary, supported by a few thousand security policemen, were unable to restore order. They made an armistice and this allowed

Nagy to emerge as leader of a popular democratic government, representing not only the Communists, but the pre-war Socialist and Smallholders' parties. This government left the Warsaw Pact and established a multi-party system, but was crushed by Soviet military intervention early in November. A new pro-Soviet regime was established under János Kádár, who deserted Nagy at the last minute.

The events of 1956 seemed to teach two contradictory lessons in Eastern Europe. In the first place, it was now obvious that any attempt to leave the Soviet bloc or dismantle the apparatus of Communist power would be followed by Soviet intervention and could expect no more than verbal support from the west. At the same time, reforms which did not involve a challenge to the 'leading role of the Communist Party' and which stressed the willingness to remain within the Warsaw Pact established in May 1955, which gave the Soviets the right to maintain troops in the countries of their East European allies, were apparently tolerated. The growing Soviet preoccupation with the rift with China also tended to diminish the tightness of Russian control in Eastern Europe. As a result, the years after 1956 were followed by increasing divergences in the development of the states of Eastern Europe.

In Poland, the high hopes raised by Gomułka's return to power were largely unfulfilled. It is true that collectivization was ended, and a rather uneasy *modus vivendi* was established with the Catholic Church, which, under the redoubtable leadership of Cardinal Wyszyński, remained a power in the land. Gomułka also ended close Soviet control of Polish political life. However, always a conservative and not especially intelligent communist, he came to see 'revisionism' as the main danger in Poland, and thus the intellectual freedoms achieved in 1956 were gradually whittled away. It was above all his fear of 'revisionism' which made him one of the strongest proponents of armed intervention in Czechoslovakia in the summer of 1968. His hostility to economic experimentation together with Poland's unsatisfactory economic growth led to a feeling that the country was stagnating. As a result, he came under attack from a younger and more nationalistic group within the party. This group, known as the Partisans, because of their wartime record in the Communist resistance in Poland, were led by General Moczar. They saw their rise to power obstructed by the many

Jews who still held important positions in the party. Gomułka's speech in July 1967 attacking pro-Israeli Jews was thus exploited by them to unleash an anti-Zionist (a new euphemism for anti-Jewish) purge in 1968. In consequence, most of Poland's remaining 30,000 Jews left the country. Student demands for Czech-style reforms in spring 1968 gave Moczar, with his calls for firmer action to deal with the revisionist 'danger', the chance to challenge Gomułka's position, but with Russian support Gomułka was able at first to fight off this attack. In December 1970, however, he was faced with widespread rioting and loss of life in northern Poland in response to a crassly implemented economic reform which involved substantial increases in the price of food. This unrest was exploited by Edward Gierek, first secretary of the party provincial committee in Silesia, who allied himself with Moczar and was able to replace Gomułka as first secretary. Gierek, an intelligent pragmatist who had won considerable respect for the efficiency with which he had run the highly industrial province of Silesia, has proved a fairly successful ruler. In 1971 he was able to rid himself of General Moczar, and has since introduced a number of significant economic reforms, above all improving the position of the peasantry. Though not a 'liberal' in the cultural field, he has allowed the emergence of a freer atmosphere than prevailed in Gomułka's last years.

In Hungary, the collapse of the revolution was followed by several years of severe repression. The writer's circles, foci of opposition to the regime, were closed down, and a new pro-government Writers' Association created. Several writers such as Tibor Déry and Gyula Háy were imprisoned for their participation in the revolt. The workers' councils were suppressed, and in June 1958 repression reached a climax when Nagy and a number of his associates were sentenced to death. At the same time, János Kádár was not the man to reintroduce the Stalinist system in Hungary. He had been imprisoned and tortured by Rákosi and realized that the old methods would not work. Thus, in spite of the strength of the Stalinist elements within the newly established Hungarian Socialist Workers' Party, he embarked on a 'new course' in 1961. Its watchword, expressed in a speech by Kádár in December of that year, was 'He who is not against us is with us'.[7] Kádár showed considerable skill in easing the dogmatists, such as Imre Dögei and György Marosan, out of prominent positions in the party, and, unlike Gomułka, was always open to advice and persuasion. Though he re-established collectivization in 1959, in other respects he showed considerable flexibility and a willingness to experiment in economic matters. The introduction of fairly large-scale economic reforms brought a significant increase in the standard of living of the population. This, together with the abolition of class and party criteria in selection for most jobs and admission to university, brought a much more relaxed atmosphere. Intellectual life, too, was allowed a certain amount of freedom. The large aims of 1956 had been brutally crushed and the Hungarians were now reconciled to making their country, 'the merriest barracks in the socialist camp'. Kádár increasingly evoked a grudging respect and, indeed, admiration from the population.

In Rumania, Gheorghe Gheorghiu-Dej, a 'native' communist who had remained in the country during the war, established a dominant position in the party as early as 1952 with the purging of the 'cosmopolitan' group of Ana Pauker and Vasile Luca. From 1962 he attempted, with considerable success, to establish a position of independence in relation to the Soviet Union. This seems to have been motivated primarily by resentment at Comecon schemes for the distribution of industry in Eastern Europe which would have left Rumania primarily an agricultural state. Gheorghiu-Dej was able with some skill to neutralize the pro-Soviet elements in the leadership. He made adroit use of the Sino-Soviet dispute, establishing very friendly relations with China, and also with the USA. His bid for independence was probably only possible because of the tight control he exercised over the party, and was not followed by any major domestic liberalization. On his death in March 1965 he was succeeded by Nicolae Ceauşescu, who has continued and developed his policies. Though Rumania's independence came under considerable pressure from the Russians following the invasion of Czechoslovakia, its substance has, for the most part, been preserved. A good deal of economic growth has been achieved, but in the political and cultural fields, possibly in emulation of the Chinese cultural revolution, Ceauşescu has taken a fairly hard line.

In Bulgaria liberalization has probably gone less far than anywhere else in Eastern Europe. The relaxation which followed Todor Zhivkov's final ousting of the Stalinist, Vulko

Chervenkov, in November 1961 was soon reversed. Zhivkov, essentially an unimaginative and conservative bureaucrat, has maintained a domestically repressive policy, while closely following the Soviet lead in foreign affairs. An attempted coup aimed at establishing a more 'national' communism was foiled in April 1965, largely as a result of information provided by Soviet military intelligence in Bulgaria.

The German Democratic Republic occupies a special place in Soviet Eastern Europe. In the first place, while unification was still a possibility the Soviets were not prepared to allow too far-reaching changes to be implemented. The majority of the population were strongly committed to reunification, and in the existence of the western enclave in West Berlin had before them the easy possibility of leaving East Germany, of which large numbers of them availed themselves. It was these conditions which made the German Democratic Republic, in the words of an astute commentator 'an international problem rather than a nation state'.[8] In the late 1950s these conditions ceased to operate. Probably by 1957 the Soviets had decided that unification on their terms, with the whole of Germany neutralized, was impossible. From this the decision in August 1961 to build the Berlin Wall and close the escape route to the west followed logically. It had important consequences. As in the case of Hungary in 1956, the western powers failed to react, and were probably secretly relieved. The population of East Germany realized that the prospect of reunification and the early end of Communist rule was clearly chimerical, and there was a widespread feeling in favour of making the best of the situation. The economic reforms introduced by Ulbricht in 1965, coupled with the access which the DDR enjoyed to the EEC in terms of the Treaty of Rome, were followed by a rapid economic upsurge. By 1972, the country was the fifth economic power in Europe and the ninth in the world. This made it a vital trading partner, not only for the Soviet Union, but also for Czechoslovakia and Poland. It also created a real feeling of pride among its population in their achievement, accomplished in spite of extremely heavy Soviet reparations. 'Normalization' of relations with the Federal Republic of Germany, which led to a treaty recognizing the existence of two German states while conceding the special position of Berlin, thus finally legitimized the division of Europe established between 1945 and 1948. Today, under the rather more flexible leadership of Erich Honecker, the DDR is a power in its own right. Though still repressive internally, it can be expected to play a larger role in the politics of the Soviet bloc in the next few years.

It was in Czechoslovakia that the most dramatic events in recent years have occurred. For a very long time the Czechoslovak Communist Party, under the uninspired but able bureaucratic control of Antonín Novotný, was able to resist demands for de-stalinization and liberalization. But from 1961 the forces for change gradually became stronger and more difficult to control. As in Poland and Hungary before 1956, a number of factors contributed to this development. In the first place, the delayed recognition of the injustices which had been committed in the name of 'socialist legality' during the Stalinist period created a loss of confidence and provoked considerable discontent within the party. Resistance to the slavish following of the Soviet model and calls for a 'specific' Czech road to socialism grew in strength. Among intellectuals and, in particular, writers and journalists, there emerged renewed demands for a relaxation of censorship and greater freedom of expression. This discontent coincided with a severe economic crisis, resulting from the difficulties of applying orthodox central planning in a highly developed economy. In 1962–3, the GNP actually fell, and the current economic plan had to be abandoned. A radical economic reform was adopted in January 1965, but its implementation seemed to be hindered by the conservatism of some leading party functionaries. Finally, discontent grew in Slovakia because of increased centralization and the abolition in 1960 of a number of Slovak institutions, including the Slovak Board of Commissioners. This feeling was exacerbated by Novotný's obvious hostility to Slovak aspirations.

Between 1961 and 1968 the tide of reform ebbed and flowed. It became a flood in January 1968, when Alexander Dubček replaced Novotný as first secretary of the party. The changes which were now introduced, had they been allowed to take effect, would have fundamentally altered the character of the communist system in Czechoslovakia. Provision was made for a great deal of inner party democratization, the legitimacy of forming factions within the party was explicitly recognized and the 'leading role' of the party in society was redefined in a looser sense. A large number of conservatives, particularly at higher levels, were replaced by reformers, censorship was abolished and non-party political organizations were permitted to function. The powers of the secret police were curbed and the role of the national assembly was greatly increased. Slovakia was given federal status.

The working out of these innovations was cut short with the invasion by the Soviet Union and her four Warsaw Pact allies in August 1968. The Soviets seem to have been particularly uneasy about the weakening of the 'leading role' of the party, and feared the impact of the Czechoslovak reforms on the rest of Eastern Europe and indeed on the Soviet Union itself. Apprehensions that West Germany might exploit the Czechoslovak situation may also have played a role. In spite of initially successful passive resistance by the Czechs and Slovaks, the Soviets have been able, by constant pressure, to impose their concept of 'normalization' on Czechoslovakia. The reformist leadership has been entirely purged, though Gustáv Husák, a Slovak who was imprisoned in the 1950s, has retained the post of first secretary in spite of persistent criticism from the hardliners. Recently some attempts to win over the population have been made, but real progress in this field has still to be achieved.

The invasion of Czechoslovakia and the formulation of the 'Brezhnev doctrine' recognizing the right of the Soviet Union to intervene in Eastern Europe if it believes 'socialism' to be threatened, seemed to many to presage a new era of tighter Soviet control. In fact, however, their worst fears have not been realized. Pressed both by their own economic difficulties and by their fear of China, the Soviets have pursued a policy of *rapprochement* with West Germany which should increase, if only slightly, the freedom of manœuvre of the states of Eastern Europe. Nevertheless, the Soviets seem less sensitive to changes in Hungary, Rumania and Bulgaria, which are not directly linked to the German question. The Soviets also seem to have realized the disadvantages of using purely military means to achieve their objectives. Another invasion like that of Czechoslovakia would prove extremely costly in terms of prestige, and in December 1970 the Soviets were quite prepared to see Gomułka fall. It has even been implied that the responsibility for the invasion lies with Pyotr Shelest, the recently deposed Ukrainian party secretary. Soviet policy seems now to be to use economic integration under Comecon to establish her control over Eastern Europe. The Soviets are also unhappy about the fact that they largely supply Eastern Europe with raw materials, taking in return manufactured goods. The ambitious plan for huge steel and other plants in Byelorussia serving the Soviet Union and also Eastern Europe is thus aimed at reversing this pattern of trade and at creating a real and irrevocable degree of economic integration. Whether this new method of control will work, given the persistence of nationalist sentiments in Eastern Europe, remains open to question.

Five countries in Eastern Europe have managed to remain outside the Soviet orbit. In Austria, the experience of German rule created a deep distaste for pan-German sentiments and forged a bond between the Christian Socials and Social Democrats who suffered together in the concentration camps. Austria's democratic system seems today to be firmly based. In Greece, however, the bitterness and division created by the civil war at the end of the Second World War proved, in the end, too much for democracy. Although a western-type democratic system was established, political hatreds remained deep and unreconcilable. Fears that a victory by Papandreou in the 1967 elections would pave the way for communism played a major role in the decision of the faction of colonels to take power and overthrow the constitution. Their regime was, however, singularly barren and has been replaced by a more liberal government. As yet it seems impossible to predict what direction the new regime will take. In Yugoslavia, national communist forces took power under Tito and successfully weathered the breach with Stalin in 1948. Tito's regime has many achievements to its credit, but has been plagued by the persistence of national antagonisms, exacerbated by the economic divergences between the advanced north-western republics and the more backward areas of the south-east. In 1966, with the fall of the security chief, Ranković, the regime embarked on an ambitious programme of economic and political liberalization. This ran into serious economic problems, and also saw the growth of local nationalism, particularly in Croatia. The crushing of Croatian nationalism has led to a general political retrenchment, and with Tito in his early eighties, many question marks hang over the future of Yugoslavia. Albania owed its ability to move out of the Soviet orbit to its geographic position beyond Yugoslavia. After a long flirtation with China, its leaders have begun to cultivate its neighbours, and Albano-Yugoslav and Albano-Greek relations have improved markedly in the last few years.

Finland was relatively leniently treated by the Soviets at the end of the last war, being forced to cede only small areas in Karelia and the extreme north. Communism remained a strong force here, however, with the Communists prominent in the government coalition. In May 1948 a crisis occurred similar to that in Czechoslovakia in February. The final outcome differed, however, with the resignation of the Communist minister of the interior and a loss of Communist support in the subsequent election. But Finland was not vital to the Soviets (Molotov once referred to the country as a 'peanut') and Soviet–Finnish relations did not deteriorate significantly. Finland has recognized the limitations imposed on her foreign policy by her neutrality, and her democratic institutions seem today to be firmly established. Indeed the Soviets seem at times to trust the Finnish President, Kekkonnen, more than people like Gierek or Husák.

How far do the specific features of Eastern Europe which were mentioned in the Introduction still persist today, nearly thirty years after the Second World War? Since 1945, industrialization has made great progress throughout the area. Though agriculture is still everywhere of much significance, the predominance it enjoyed in the interwar years no longer exists. In Poland, for instance, the percentage of the population gaining its living from agriculture in 1970 was only 29·5 per cent, in Hungary it was 25·7 per cent and in Rumania 50·1 per cent. In Yugoslavia in 1971 it was 36·4 per cent. Only 10·5 per cent of the population in 1970 in Czechoslovakia was made up of co-operative farmers and small farmers.[9] In Poland in 1971 the percentage of the population in urban areas was 52·7 per cent, in Hungary (1970) 45·1 per cent, in Rumania (1971) 41·1 per cent. Along with the move from the countryside to the towns has come a marked fall in the birth rate, which has eased the pressures which rapid population growth created before 1939. This has gone furthest in Czechoslovakia, with a natural increase in population in 1969 of 4·3 per thousand and Hungary with 3·0 per thousand. In both these countries, indeed, the slow growth of the population has begun to cause social problems. In Poland in 1971 the natural increase was 8·7 per thousand, having fallen sharply from the high level of the immediate post-war period. In Rumania, the figure in 1971 was 10·0, a significant decline after the rapid growth of the late 1960s. Yugoslavia still has a very high rate of population growth (18·7 per thousand in 1969) and this has much to do with the persistent economic malaise of the country.

The shift to the towns has been accompanied by an industrial revolution, particularly in north-eastern Europe. According to official figures, industrial production has increased over six times in Poland and Hungary between 1950 and 1970 and over eleven times in Rumania. In Yugoslavia in 1969 the level of production was over nine times that of 1939, while in Czechoslovakia between 1937 and 1970 a sevenfold increase occurred. All this has meant that the area is now increasingly facing the problems all industrial countries have to deal with, though in a specifically communist context. At the same time, everywhere in the area, with the exception of Albania, it has been recognized that the Stalinist model of central planning is no longer applicable, and various schemes for economic reform, involving the introduction of some sort of market determination of prices, economic decentralization and a greater stress on consumer goods have been widely introduced. These have often involved a diminution of job security previously enjoyed by the workers. It was a scheme of this type which provoked the riots in northern Poland in December 1970, and in future years the politics of economic reform may well force the governments of the area into greater consultation with the workers.

Though agricultural questions are no longer predominant, they remain among the most difficult of the issues which the states of Eastern Europe have to resolve. The rapid increase in industrial production has nowhere been paralleled by a similar growth in agricultural efficiency. In Yugoslavia, the level of agricultural production in 1970 was actually significantly below that of 1930–9, in Czechoslovakia the level of 1970 was only 22·3 per cent above that of 1936, and in Hungary, if we take the index of agricultural production in 1950 as 100, it had risen by 1970 to 146, compared to 111 between 1934 and 1938. Similar figures could be cited for Poland and Rumania. There are a number of reasons for this development. In Poland and Yugoslavia, where peasant proprietorship has survived, the governments have been reluctant to encourage the emergence of large and efficient holdings, though this attitude is now changing. The peasants, too, have remained rather suspicious, believing that government attempts to help them by fostering co-operative ventures are only the first stage of collectivization. In the other countries of the area, though collectivization had made possible fairly intensive investment in agriculture, it has brought with it the familiar problems of creating incentives among the peasantry to work for a system which at worst they regard as a new form of serfdom and at best as depriving them of their land and reducing them to the status of industrial workers. The next few years may well see more schemes, like that already introduced in Hungary, for improving the productivity of the collectives.

On the surface, the problems of national minorities seem to have played a smaller part in the politics of Eastern Europe since 1945 than they did in the interwar period. Yet they have by no means disappeared. It is true that the territorial changes whereby the Soviet Union extended its border westwards have left virtually no Ukrainians or Byelorussians in Eastern Europe. Ukrainian nationalism is thus today a problem for the Soviets rather than for the Poles, Rumanians and Czechs. In Poland, the events of the war left almost no non-Poles in the country. Yet, there still remain perhaps a quarter of a million Germans in the areas annexed from Germany, whose desire to emigrate to West Germany has created some problems in the 'normalization' of relations between the two countries. In Czechoslovakia the Slovak question remains a key issue, and, in spite of some expulsions immediately after liberation, there is still a large Hungarian minority in Southern Slovakia. In Rumania too, the Hungarians remain a large group in Transylvania, and their treatment has caused some friction between the Hungarian and Rumanian governments. A significant German minority also remains here, though the Germans were for the most part expelled from Hungary and Yugoslavia. Bulgaria has retained the southern Dobrudja, formerly a Bulgarian pocket in Rumania, and has allowed a small proportion of her Turkish minority to leave for Turkey. It is in Yugoslavia that national problems have proved most difficult to deal with. We have already noted the problems created by the Croat resurgence. The large number of Albanians in the Kossovo region and Macedonia have recently begun to assert their rights, Macedonian nationalism is a significant force and the Moslems of Bosnia have also begun to develop a distinctive national identity. All these problems are likely to play an important role in the inevitable crisis which will follow the death of Tito, now over eighty.

The Jewish problem has also persisted in a rather curious way. The Nazi 'final solution' left relatively few Jews in Eastern Europe, and most of them emigrated between 1945 and 1956 to Israel, Western Europe and the USA. Yet Jews played a prominent part in the Communist parties of Poland, Czechoslovakia, Hungary and Rumania, and some were purged as a result of the East European reverberations of the 'anti-Zionist' campaign in the Soviet Union in 1951–2. The Arab-Israeli war of 1967 provoked further 'anti-Zionist' purges in Poland, and there has been a tendency in Czechoslovakia since the Soviet invasion to blame the reform movement on 'Zionist machinations'. Jews have been prominent among the reformers who have lost their positions since 1968. In Hungary and Rumania, however, there are still a number of Jews in significant positions.

Eastern Europe between the wars had many of the problems the Third World has today. The lack of political experience, the overwhelmingly rural character of most of its countries in 1918, the pre-eminence of the national question in its politics, all these suggest parallels with the politics of Latin America and of the new countries which have emerged in Asia and Africa since the Second World War. But there is one respect in which Eastern Europe in the interwar period was unique. This is the fact that because of its geographic position it was of vital importance to a number of great powers, France, Italy, Germany, the Soviet Union and even, at times, Great Britain. It is the fact that individual countries were racked not only by social and economic conflict, but also by differences of orientation in foreign policy, which makes the history of the interwar period so complex. This situation no longer obtains, as most of Eastern Europe today is effectively under the control of the Soviet Union. Any further developments will come about not so much as a result of internal transformations, since any attempt to move out of the Soviet sphere would be ruthlessly crushed, as from changes in the Soviet Union itself. The people of Eastern Europe are materially better off than in 1914, and as nations most enjoy rather more autonomy. But they are still not truly masters of their own destiny.

Notes

1 Quoted in G. C. Logio, *Bulgaria, Past and Present* (Manchester, 1936), p. 42.
2 Quoted in H. Seton-Watson, *The East European Revolution* (London, 1950), p. 75.
3 M. Djilas, *Conversations with Stalin* (London, 1962), p. 91.
4 H. Seton-Watson, *op. cit.*, p. 193.
5 In 1946, only 8 million tons were to be delivered (R. Hiscocks, *Poland: Bridge for the Abyss*, London, 1963, pp. 127–8).
6 *Ibid.*, pp. 150–2.
7 J. F. Brown, *The New Eastern Europe* (New York, 1966), p. 44.
8 *Ibid.*, p. 33.
9 For these and subsequent figures, see *Rocznik statystyczny* (Warsaw, 1969, 1970, 1971); *Statistická ročenka ČSSR* (Prague, 1969, 1970, 1971); *Statistical Yearbook* (Budapest, 1969, 1970, 1971); *Anuariul statistic al Republic Socialiste România* (Bucharest, 1969, 1970, 1971); *Statistcki Godišnjak Yugoslavije* (Belgrade, 1971, 1972).

Statistical appendix

National composition of some East European states

The following census returns give a fair indication of the national composition of some of the states of Eastern Europe. The criterion for determining national identity (nationality or mother tongue) is indicated. Pressure to obtain satisfactory census results was universal in Eastern Europe and it can be assumed that these tables exaggerate the numbers of the dominant nationality and underestimate those of the minorities. Percentage figures of the religious composition of the various states have also been provided.

Table 1   *Composition of the population of Poland according to the 1921 census (nationality)*[1]

Nationality	Number (000s)	%
Poles	18,814	69·2
Ruthenians	3,898	14·3
Locals[2]	49	0·2
Byelorussians	1,060	3·9
Jews	2,110	7·8
Germans	1,059	3·9
Lithuanians	69	0·3
Russians	56	0·2
Czechs	31	0·1
Others	16	0·0
No details	13	0·0
	27,177[3]	99·9[3]

[1] Based on *Rocznik statystyki Rzeczypospolitej Polski* IV (1925–6), p. 26, table 5.

[2] Many people in Byelorussian areas, when asked their nationality, replied 'Local'.

[3] Figures rounded up.

Table 2   *Religious denominations in Poland*[1] *in 1921*

Religion	%
Roman Catholic	63·8
Greek Catholic	11·2
Orthodox	10·5
Protestant	3·7
Other Christian	0·3
Mosaic	10·5
	100·0

[1] Based on *Rocznik statystyki Rzeczypospolitej Polski* IV (1925–6), p. 26, table 5.

Table 3   *Mother tongue of population of Hungary in 1920*[1]

Mother tongue	Number (000s)	%
Hungarian	7,147	89·6
German	551	6·9
Slovak	141	1·8
Rumanian	24	0·3
Ruthene	1·5	0·0
Croat	37	0·5
Serb	17	0·2
Others	61	0·7
	7,979·5	100·0

[1] *Az 1920 evî népszdmldlds* (Budapest, 1923), vol. 1, p. 12.

Table 4   *Religious denominations in Hungary in 1920*[1]

Religion	%
Roman Catholic	63·9
Greek Catholic	2·2
Calvinist	21·0
Lutheran	6·2
Greek Orthodox	0·6
Unitarian	0·1
Jews	5·9
Others	0·1
	100·0

[1] *Az 1920 evî népszdmldlds* (Budapest, 1923), vol. 1, p. 17.

Table 5   *Ethnic divisions in Czechoslovakia[1] (Nationality) in 1930*

Ethnic division	Number (000s)	%
Czechoslovaks[2]	9,757	66·24
Russians and Little Russians	569	3·86
Germans	3,318	22·53
Magyars	720	4·89
Jews	205	1·39
Poles	100	0·68
Gypsies	33	0·22
Rumanians	14	0·10
Yugoslavs	6	0·04
Others and unknown	8	0·05
	14,730	100·00

[1] *Annuaire statistique de la République tchécoslovaque* (Prague, 1938), p. 8.

[2] The census takers did not distinguish between Czechs and Slovaks. The census of 15 December in 'independent' Slovakia showed a population of 2,635,564 (H. Seton-Watson, *Independent Eastern Europe 1918–1941*, Cambridge, 1945, p. 414).

Table 6   *Religious divisions in Czechoslovakia in 1930*[1]

Religion		%
Roman Catholic		73·54
Greek Catholic		3·97
Protestant		7·67
Czech Brothers	2·02	
German Protestants	0·90	
Lutherans in Silesia	0·32	
Lutherans ⎱ in Slovakia and Sub-Carpatho	2·77	
Calvinists ⎰ Ruthenia	1·49	
Moravian Brothers	0·04	
Czech Baptists	0·03	
Congregationalists	0·04	
Methodists	0·05	
Others	0·01	
Orthodox		0·99
Czechoslovak Church		5·39
Old Catholic		0·16
Other Christians		0·05
Jews		2·42
Without confession		5·80
Unknown		0·01
		100·00

[1] *Annuaire statistique de la République tchécoslovaque* (Prague, 1938), p. 9.

Table 7   *Nationality of population in Yugoslavia according to the census of 1931*[1]

Nationality	Number (000s)	%
Serbo-Croats[2]	10,731	77·01
Slovenes	1,135	8·15
Germans	500	3·59
Magyars	468	3·36
Rumanians and Vlachs	138	0·98
Albanians	505	3·63
Turks	133	0·95
Other Slavs (Czechs, Slovaks, Poles, Russians, Ukrainians)	193	1·39
Jews	18	0·12
Gypsies	70	0·51
Italians	9	0·07
Others	32	0·23
	13,934[3]	99·99[3]

[1] Based on W. Markert (ed.), *Osteuropa-Handbuch Jugoslawien* (Cologne, Graz, 1954), p. 16.
[2] Under Serbo-Croats were included Montenegrins, Bosnian Moslems, Macedonians, Bulgarians.
[3] Figures rounded out.

Table 8   *Religion of population of Yugoslavia according to the census of 1931*[1]

Religion	%
Orthodox	48·7
Roman Catholic	37·4
Uniate	0·3
Protestant	1·7
Other Christian	0·2
Moslems	11·2
Jews	0·5
	100·0

[1] Based on W. Markert (ed.), *Osteuropa-Handbuch Jugoslawien* (Cologne, Graz, 1954), p. 175.

Table 9 *Population of Rumania according to the census of 1930*[1] *(nationality)*

Nationality	Number (000s)	%
Rumanians	12,981	70·8
Hungarians	1,426	8·6
Germans	745	4·2
Russians	409	2·3
Ukrainians, Ruthenians	382	3·3
Bulgars	366	2·1
Gypsies	263	1·5
Turks and Tatars	177	0·9
Jews	728	4·1
Others	418	2·4
	17,895	100·0

[1] *Breviariul statistic al României* (Bucharest, 1939), pp. 53–60.

Table 10 *Religion of population in Rumania in 1930*[1]

Religion	%
Orthodox	70·8
Greek Catholic	8·6
Roman Catholic	7·5
Calvinist	4·1
Lutheran	2·3
Unitarian	0·5
Other Protestant	0·5
Armenian	0·1
Moslems	1·1
Jews	4·1
Others	0·4
	100·0

[1] *Breviariul statistic al României* (Bucharest, 1939), pp. 61–8.

Some statistics on East European agriculture

Table 11 shows the high percentage of the population dependent on agriculture in most of Eastern Europe. It also shows the relative backwardness of the agriculture of the area as compared to Western Europe. Table 12 shows one reason for this, the very small number of tractors in the area. The high percentage of peasant proprietors everywhere except in Hungary is shown in Table 13.

Table 11   *Population dependent on agriculture*[1]

Country (date)	Population (000s)	Population dependent on agriculture (000s)	%	Agricultural output (in crop units) per capita of those living from agriculture	Production per hectare of sown area (in crop units)
Albania (1930)	1,003	800	80	10	17
Yugoslavia (1931)	13,934	10,629	76	17	17
Bulgaria (1926)	5,479	4,088	75	20	19
Rumania (1930)	18,057	13,069	72	21	17
Lithuania (1930)	2,367	1,657	70	31	17
Poland (1931)	32,107	19,347	60	21	18
Finland (1930)	3,562	2,015	57	28	22
Estonia (1934)	1,126	626	56	43	17
Latvia (1930)	1,900	1,036	55	48	19
Hungary (1930)	8,688	4,472	51	33	21
Greece (1928)	6,205	2,829	46	21	18
Czechoslovakia (1930)	14,730	4,812	33	45	31
Austria (1934)	6,760	1,772	26	58	37
Germany (1933)	66,029	13,297	20	84	44
France (1931)	41,228	11,890	29	75	26
England and Wales (1931)	39,952	2,117	5	137	46

[1] Based on W. E. Moore, *Economic Demography of Eastern and Southern Europe* (Geneva, 1945), pp. 26, 35.

Table 12   *Tractors in use in Europe in 1939*[1]

Country	Number (000s)	Hectares of arable land per tractor
Finland	4	625
Austria	2	900
Czechoslovakia	6	920
Hungary	7	829
Poland	2	8,400
Rumania	2	4,650
Yugoslavia	2	3,435
Bulgaria	3	1,433
Greece	1	2,200
Great Britain	55	135
Germany	60	227
France	30	700

[1] Based on I. Svennilson, *Growth and Stagnation in the European Economy* (Geneva, 1954), table A.19, p. 250.

Table 13   *Peasant proprietors and agricultural labourers as a percentage of the agricultural population*[1]

Country	Peasant proprietors[2]	Hired labourers[2]
Estonia	87·4	12·6
Latvia	83·7	16·3
Lithuania	84·5	15·5
Poland	85·2	14·8
Czechoslovakia	85·4	14·6
Hungary	60·91	39·09
Yugoslavia	90·60	9·40
Bulgaria	98·94	1·06

[1] Based on W. E. Moore, *Economic Demography of Eastern and Southern Europe* (Geneva, 1945), p. 217.
[2] Data which can be classified under these headings is unsatisfactory for Rumania, Albania and Greece.

Distribution of farms by size in various East European countries

The following tables give some idea of the structure of agriculture in Eastern Europe. One should note the high percentage of large estates in Poland, Hungary and Greece. The relatively healthy agrarian structure of the Baltic states emerges clearly, as does the small size of the average holding in most of the area.

Table 14   *Distribution of farms by size in Poland in 1921*[1]

Size (in hectares)	Percentage of holdings		Percentage of size area	
	Census	Correction	Census	Correction
0–2	33·9	29·0	3·5	2·8
2–5	30·7	32·6	11·3	11·2
5–10	22·5	24·7	17·0	17·3
10–20	9·6	10·3	13·8	13·7
20–50	2·4	2·5	7·1	6·9
over 50	0·9	0·9	47·3	48·1

[1] Based on the census of 1921, and the corrections suggested by M. Mieszczánkowski, *Struktura rolna Polski międzywojennej* (Warsaw, 1960).

Table 15   *Distribution of farms by size in Hungary in 1935*[1]

Size (in holds[2])	Percentage of farms	Percentage of area
0–1[3]	41·0	1·9
1–5	35·1	10·1
5–10	10·8	9·2
10–20	7·6	12·6
20–50	3·9	13·5
50–100	0·8	6·3
100–500	0·6	14·0
500–1000	0·1	7·9
1000–3000	0·1	12·7
Over 3000		11·8

[1] Based on A. Eckstein, 'Land reform and the transformation of agriculture in Hungary', *Journal of Farm Economics*, XXXI, p. 458.

[2] 1 hold = 0·57 hectare.

[3] This percentage is somewhat exaggerated because some of these small holdings were in the possession of industrial workers or farm labourers who used them to supplement their income.

Table 16   *Distribution of farms by size in Czechoslovakia in 1927*[1]

Size (in hectares)	Number of holdings %	Area of cultivated land %
0–1	29·4	2·1
1–5	43·3	21·3
5–10	14·3	18·3
10–30	10·9	30·3
30–100	1·8	14·5
Over 100	0·3	13·5

[1] *Aperçu statistique de la République tchécoslovaque* (Prague, 1931).

Table 17   *Distribution of farms by size in Yugoslavia according to the census of 31 March 1931*[1]

Size (in hectares)	Percentage of holdings	Percentage of area
Under ½	8·0	0·4
½–1	8·8	1·3
1–2	17·0	4·8
2–5	34·0	21·5
5–10	20·5	27·0
10–20	8·8	22·3
20–50	2·5	13·0
50–100	0·3	3·2
100–200	0·1	1·4
200–500	0·0	1·4
Over 500	0·0	3·7
	100·0	100·0

[1] Based on Yugoslavia, *Annuaire statistique, 1936* (Belgrade, 1937), pp. 88–9.

Table 18   *Distribution of farms by size in Rumania, 1930 census*[1]

Size (in hectares)	Holdings (%)	Total area (%)	Cultivated area (%)
0–1	18·6	1·6	2·1
1–3	33·5	11·1	14·4
3–5	22·9	15·3	19·3
5–10	17·1	20·0	24·2
10–20	5·5	12·0	13·3
20–50	1·7	7·8	7·9
50–100	0·4	4·5	4·2
100–500	0·3	10·6	7·2
Over 500	0·1	17·1	7·4
	100·1[2]	100·0	100·0

[1] H. L. Roberts, *Rumania: Political Problems of an Agrarian State* (New Haven, 1951), p. 370.
[2] Rounded upwards.

Table 19   *Distribution of farms by size in Bulgaria and Greece around 1930*[1]

Size (in hectares)	Percentage of holdings		Percentage of land	
	Bulgaria	Greece	Bulgaria	Greece
1–5	57·4	79·3	29·1	16·9
5–10	30·3	14·3	37·3	11·7
10–50	12·2	5·9	32·0	21·6
Over 50	0·1	0·5	1·6	49·8

[1] Based on W. E. Moore, *Economic Demography of Southern and Eastern Europe* (Geneva, 1945), p. 82. Albania is omitted in the absence of data allowing even an estimate.

Table 20   *Distribution of farms by size in the Baltic states around 1930*[1]

Size (in hectares)	Percentage of holdings			Percentage of land		
	Lithuania	Latvia	Estonia	Lithuania	Latvia	Estonia
1–5	18·6	15·7	17·6	3·7	2·3	2·5
5–10	27·2	19·5	16·2	13·9	7·8	6·1
10–50	51·4	57·7	61·0	67·3	64·6	73·3
Over 50	2·8	7·1	5·2	15·1	25·3	18·1

[1] Based on W. E. Moore, *Economic Demography of Eastern and Southern Europe* (Geneva, 1945), p. 82.

Surplus agricultural population

One of the main features of agriculture in Eastern Europe was the fact that there were on the land far more people than was actually required to work it. This inevitably lowered general living standards and impeded the introduction of more advanced agricultural techniques. It is obviously very difficult to estimate, except in the vaguest terms, how much of the agricultural population was superfluous. We provide, here, three alternative ways of estimating this. The first compares the level of agricultural production with the general European level, the second compares the level of agricultural production with French agricultural productivity and the third relates agricultural production to land resources (for this, there are figures only for Yugoslavia, Bulgaria and Rumania). In spite of their defects, these tables do give some idea of the nature of the problem.

Table 21   *'Standard' and 'surplus' agricultural populations, Eastern and Southern Europe, around 1930, assuming existing production and European average per capita level*[1]

Country	Population dependent on agriculture (000s)	Agricultural net production[1] (in crop units) (000s)	Standard[2] population, assuming European per capita level (000s)	'Surplus' population[3] (%)
Albania	800	7,646	178	77·7
Bulgaria	4,088	82,394	1,921	53·0
Czechoslovakia[4]	4,812	216,125	5,038	−4·7
Estonia	626	26,755	624	0·4
Greece	2,829	60,265	1,405	50·3
Hungary	4,472	148,898	3,471	22·4
Latvia	1,036	49,825	1,149	−10·9
Lithuania	1,657	51,713	1,205	27·3
Poland	19,347	404,339	9,425	51·3
Rumania	13,069	272,318	6,348	51·4
Yugoslavia	10,629	175,752	4,097	61·5

[1] Based on W. E. Moore, *Economic Demography of Eastern and Southern Europe* (Geneva, 1945), p. 63.

[2] Column 3 represents column 2 divided by 42·9, the European average *per capita* value of agricultural production expressed in crop units.

[3] Note that lower percentages for agricultural overpopulation would be reached if one takes French agricultural productivity per hectare of arable-equivalent agricultural land (see Table 23).

[4] The contrast between Bohemia and Moravia, on the one hand, and Slovakia and Sub-Carpatho Ruthenia, on the other, should be noted (see Table 22).

Table 22   *'Standard' and 'surplus' agricultural population in Czechoslovakia, around 1930, as contrasted between Bohemia/Moravia and Slovakia/Sub-Carpatho Ruthenia*[1]

Territory	Population dependent on agriculture (000s)	Agricultural net production (in crop units) (000s)	Standard population assuming European per capita level (000s)	'Surplus' population (%)
Bohemia	1,627	107,969	2,517	−54·7
Moravia-Silesia	968	53,734	1,253	−29·4
Slovakia	1,797	46,923	1,094	39·1
Sub-Carpatho Ruthenia	419	7,499	175	58·3

[1] Based on W. E. Moore, *Economic Demography of Eastern and Southern Europe* (Geneva, 1945), p. 63.

Table 23   'Surplus' agricultural population in
Eastern and Southern Europe, around 1930
(see Table 21), as calculated against French
agricultural productivity per hectare[1]

Country	'Surplus' population (%)
Albania	65·3
Bulgaria	35·7
Czechoslovakia	11·7
Estonia	−58·5
Greece	29·3
Hungary	2·9
Latvia	3·0
Lithuania	−15·3
Poland	29·4
Rumania	23·1
Yugoslavia	38·8

[1] Based on W. E. Moore, Economic Demography
of Eastern and Southern Europe (Geneva, 1945).

Table 24   'Surplus' population shown by the
relation of agricultural production to land
resources in 1931[1]

Country	%
Yugoslavia	43
Bulgaria	31
Rumania	15

[1] Based on J. Tomasevich, Peasants, Politics and
Economic Change in Yugoslavia (Stanford, 1955),
pp. 312–14.

Population increase and emigration in Eastern Europe

The rapid rate of population increase in Eastern Europe considerably exacerbated its agrarian problems. This rapid increase is shown in Table 25. Before the war, this increase had, to some extent, been siphoned off by emigration, particularly to the USA. After 1924 this became far less possible. But emigration, above all to France, remained an important safety valve. Tables 26–30 give some details on emigration.

Table 25   *Demographic characteristics of some European states*[1]

Country	Average annual interwar percentage growth	National increase, 1930–31 (per thousand)	Reproduction rates[2] around 1930 Gross	Net
Rumania	1·27	14·1	2·16	1·40
Bulgaria	1·30	13·9	1·70	1·20
Greece	1·93	14·1	1·80	1·26
Yugoslavia	1·43	15·2	2·09	1·45
Hungary	0·76	8·5	1·34	1·01
Poland	1·44	16·0	1·70	1·25
Ukrainian SSR	0·53	23·2	2·49	1·70
Austria	0·36	2·6	0·80	0·66
Czechoslovakia	0·71	7·8	1·22	0·95
England and Wales	0·49	4·2	0·93	0·81

[1] Based on D. Kirk, *Europe's Population in the Interwar Years* (League of Nations, 1946), p. 263.

[2] Reproduction rates are a more accurate way of measuring the direction of population movements. The 'gross reproduction rate' measures the extent to which women of child-bearing age are replacing themselves with girl babies, in the absence of mortality between childbirth and the end of the child-bearing period. The 'net reproduction rate' takes into account the average mortality of females in this period. In both rates, 1·00 equals simple replacement; a rate of 2·00 indicates that the population will double in a generation.

Table 26   *Emigration and repatriation of Polish nationals (yearly average in thousands)*[1]

Migrant group	1919–25	1926–30	1931–5	1936	1937	1938
Total number of emigrants	82·5	192·81	45·9	54·7	102·5	129·1
Emigrants to Europe	32·9	135·8	27·1	29·8	78·6	107·8
Emigrants outside Europe	49·7	57·0	18·8	24·9	23·8	21·3
Repatriates from Europe	4·6	85·3	42·3	41·5	39·0	91·9
Repatriates from outside Europe	23·2	6·6	4·2	2·2	1·8	1·7
Repatriated war refugees	168·8					

[1] Based on E. Kulischer, *Europe on the Move* (New York, 1948), p. 137.

Table 27   *Overseas emigration from South-Eastern Europe (annual average in thousands)*[1]

Period	Hungary Total	Hungary Net	Rumania Total	Rumania Net	Yugoslavia Total	Yugoslavia Net	Bulgaria Total	Bulgaria Net	Greece Total	Greece Net
1920–5	3·8	2·9	8·9[2]	7·3[2]	11·1	3·6			12·9[3]	—
1926–30	5·9	5·4	12·7	9·9	16·4	11·9	2·1[4]	2·0[4]	8·2[3]	2·7[3]
1931–5	0·9	0·0	1·8	0·4	0·4	+1·9[5]	0·3	0·3	11·8	2·6
1936–9	1·4	1·2	1·5	1·1	1·1	1·8	0·5	0·5	8·8	3·6

[1] Based on E. Kulischer, *Europe on the Move* (New York, 1948), p. 152.
[2] 1920–4.
[3] Including tourists.
[4] 1927–30.
[5] Net immigration.

Table 28   *Some population movements in Europe 1918–39*[1]

Period	Direction	Number	Group
1918–39	Poland to France	450,000	Poles
1919–39	Czechoslovakia to France	60,000	Czechoslovaks
1919–39	Various European countries outside the Soviet Union to France	100,000[2]	Workers and others
1919–39	Yugoslavia, Greece, Hungary, Rumania and Turkey to France	150,000	Workers and others

[1] Based on E. Kulischer, *Europe on the Move* (New York, 1948), pp. 248–9.
[2] In so far as not listed elsewhere.

Table 29   *Emigration from Czechoslovakia (in 1,000s)*[1]

Year	European	Overseas	Total
1922	18	21	39
1923	16	16	32
1924	19	35	54
1925	15	5	20
1926	12	14	26
1927	7	16	23
1928	10	15	25
1929	15	16	31
1930	18	8	26
1931	7	3	10
1932	4	1	5
1933	3	2	5
1934	3	2	5
1935	3	3	6
1936	4	3	7

[1] Based on *Aperçu statistique de la République tchécoslovaque* (Prague, 1931), p. 44; *Annuaire statistique de la République tchécoslovaque* (Prague, 1938), p. 33.

Table 30   *Role of France as a country of immigration, 1920–39*[1]

Item	Number (000s)
Alien workers reported arriving	2,473
Alien workers reported leaving	1,446
The numbers were in fact much greater:	
Net immigration	
1919–20	330
1921–30	1,950
Net emigration 1931–6	100
Net immigration 1936–9	120
Total immigration	2,300

[1] Based on E. Kulischer, *Europe on the Move* (New York, 1948), p. 252.

Industry in Eastern Europe

Industry played a relatively small part in the economics of Eastern Europe, outside Czechoslovakia and Austria. This emerges clearly from Tables 31 and 32. The course of manufacturing production between the wars is shown in Table 33. The impact of the depression should be noted, as also the fact that it was only in 1939 that the level of industrial production in Poland in 1913 was surpassed. Foreign capital played a large role everywhere in Eastern Europe. Table 34 shows its significance in Poland.

Table 31   *Percentage of gainfully employed males engaged in manufacturing around 1930*[1]

Country	%
Czechoslovakia	41
Austria[2]	33·4
Hungary	26
Poland	22
Estonia	20
Latvia	19
Greece	18
Finland	18
Yugoslavia	14
Bulgaria	13
Rumania	11
Lithuania	9
Great Britain	50

[1] Based on W. E. Moore, *Economic Demography of Southern and Eastern Europe* (Geneva, 1945), p. 125.

[2] *Breviariul statistic al României* (Bucharest, 1939), p. 170.

Table 32   Apparent consumption of steel in Europe[1] (corrected for indirect trade) 1922–38 (crude steel equivalent in thousand tons)

Year	Great Britain	Germany	Austria	Czecho-slovakia	Hungary	Poland	Rumania	Yugo-slavia	Bulgaria	Greece
1922	3,023	9,853	350	502	285	984	365	238	73	50
1925	5,767	8,773	354	945	213	754	455	242	93	127
1928	6,499	10,047	562	945	380	1,372	477	375	99	183
1929	7,450	11,846	612	1,398	383	1,248	598	366	151	207
1930	6,401	6,488	479	1,094	264	791	470	308	92	222
1931	5,691	4,007	299	779	214	557	309	239	84	167
1932	4,444	3,296	174	504	126	385	213	156	66	137
1933	5,531	5,931	188	502	173	492	302	156	34	126
1934	7,473	10,196	241	640	221	553	389	165	41	153
1935	8,130	12,815	290	770	257	670	419	190	73	176
1936	10,362	14,681	322	1,042	363	861	476	268	94	173
1937	11,287	14,851	431	1,605	454	1,150	501	325	99	196
1938	8,944	18,856	—	1,393	456	1,252	569	380	176	195

[1] Based on I. Svennilson, Growth and Stagnation in the European Economy (Geneva, 1954), table A.42, pp. 278-9.

Table 33   *Annual manufacturing production 1913–1938 (index numbers: 1925–9 = 100)*[1]

Year	Austria	Czecho-slovakia	Hungary	Poland	Rumania	Greece	Finland
1913	94·3	65·9	104·1	135·1	85·7	29·2	55·3
1920	45·3	46·0	50·0	47·4	30·0	65·0	48·4
1921	60·4	65·9	66·6	63·2	40·4	76·0	48·0
1922	71·7	60·5	83·2	99·9	62·7	86·4	57·8
1923	76·4	63·7	58·9	96·2	62·7	80·2	66·2
1924	77·4	85·0	69·3	76·8	76·3	87·5	68·4
1925	89·6	89·9	79·8	85·3	79·0	96·9	84·4
1926	89·6	86·0	86·8	79·6	88·9	91·0	91·1
1927	100·0	101·4	102·7	102·8	101·8	101·6	103·0
1928	109·4	109·4	112·4	116·4	112·9	105·6	112·1
1929	111·3	113·2	118·5	116·1	117·3	104·9	109·4
1930	94·3	102·5	112·5	102·4	113·5	105·9	99·3
1931	77·4	91·3	102·6	87·0	120·5	108·2	87·5
1932	67·9	70·9	95·0	71·2	95·9	99·8	91·1
1933	69·8	66·8	105·2	80·3	116·7	110·1	104·8
1934	77·4	74·8	119·0	92·2	143·8	123·6	126·6
1935	88·7	79·2	128·1	100·3	141·6	139·2	133·4
1936	95·3	91·2	142·1	112·6	150·0	134·6	148·4
1937	117·9	108·6	156·1	131·9	156·7	143·7	166·1
1938	119·8	95·9	149·1	142·2	152·4	156·6	166·1

[1] Based on I. Svennilson, *Growth and Stagnation in the European Economy* (Geneva, 1954), table A.66, pp. 304–5.

Table 34   *Participation of foreign capital in Polish joint-stock companies*[1]

Sector	%
Total	33·3
Mining	51·9
Founding industries	65·4
Machine and electrotechnical	24·3
Chemical industry	40·6
Textile industry	15·9
Gas, water and electric supply	75·6
Private banks	28·0
Communications and telephones	29·3
Other	11·7

[1] *Concise Statistical Year-Book of Poland* (Warsaw, 1931), p. 29, table 4.

The impact of the great depression in Eastern Europe

The great depression was particularly severe in Eastern Europe. Two reasons for this were the heavy dependence of the economies of most of the countries in the area on trade in primary products and their high level of indebtedness. These facts emerge in Tables 35 and 36. One result of the depression was to place agricultural producers at a further disadvantage, since agricultural prices fell much further than those of industrial goods. Tables 37 and 38 show the impact of this 'price scissors' in Poland and Rumania. Another effect of the depression was to increase the dependence of the economies of most of the area on Germany, since the Reich, whose currency ceased to be convertible, was prepared to barter industrial goods for agricultural produce (Table 39). This dependence did not proceed so far in Poland and Czechoslovakia (Tables 40 and 41) primarily for political reasons, although the fact that the economies of Germany and Czechoslovakia were not really complementary was also significant.

Table 35　*Composition of foreign trade in Eastern Europe: average 1929–38 percentage of exports and imports*[1]

Country	Foodstuffs		Raw materials and semi-manufactures		Finished goods	
	Exports	Imports	Exports	Imports	Exports	Imports
Poland	32·3	12·0	44·3	41·3	18·9	40·4
Czechoslovakia	9·0	19·3	19·0	48·1	70·9	30·9
Hungary	57·7	8·5	13·6	46·5	24·4	40·4
Rumania	35·3	7·1	63·8	13·1	0·9	73·9
Bulgaria	42·5	4·7	53·6	24·7	3·8	70·9
Yugoslavia	46·1	9·1	45·8	19·9	7·1	69·7

[1] Based on League of Nations, *Statistics of Foreign Trade 1932–38.*

Table 36   *Indebtedness of East European countries*[1]

Country	Percentage of foreign capital in stock companies	Debts to creditors, 1932 (million gold francs)	Interest payments as a percentage of exports in 1931
Austria		2,423(731)[2]	
Bulgaria	48·4 (1932)	715(34)	16
Rumania	80·0 (1931)	5,226	28
Yugoslavia	35·3 (1936)	3,269	29
Hungary	16·7 (1936)	3,774(1,408)	48
Czechoslovakia	—	2,037(138)	5
Poland	45·4 (1933)	4,457(1,782)	24
Greece	—	2,418(71)	49

[1] Based on J. Marczewski, *Planification et croissance économique des démocraties populaires* (Paris, 1956), vol. 1, p. 58; Royal Institute of International Affairs, *The Problem of International Investment* (London, 1937), p. 246.
[2] Short-term debts in brackets.

Table 37   *Price scissors in Poland (1928 = 100)*[1]

Year	Industrial articles bought by farmers	Articles sold directly by farmers
1929	101	76
1930	99	49
1931	91	55
1932	81	49
1933	73	40
1934	71	34
1935	66	33
1936	65	35
1937	66	52
1938	65	44
1939	65	37

[1] Based on M. Mieszczánkowski, *Struktura agrarna Polski międzywojennej* (Warsaw, 1960).

Table 38   *Price scissors in Rumania (1929 = 100)*[1]

Year	Wholesale agriculture prices	Industrial products required by agriculture
1930	68·2	98·0
1931	50·8	86·6
1932	47·7	80·9
1933	44·9	81·1
1934	44·1	82·6
1935	48·4	90·2

[1] Based on H. L. Roberts, *Rumania: Political Problems of an Agrarian State* (New Haven, 1951), p. 71.

Table 39   *Percentage of trade with Germany in South-Eastern Europe, 1929–38*[1]

Country	1929	1930	1931	1932	1933	1934	1935	1936	1937	1938
Hungary										
Imports	20·0	21·0	24·4	22·5	19·7	18·3	22·7	26·0	25·9	40·9
Exports	11·7	10·2	12·7	15·2	11·2	22·2	23·9	22·8	24·0	40·0
Rumania										
Imports	24·1	25·1	29·1	23·6	18·6	15·5	23·8	36·1	28·9	40·0
Exports	27·6	18·8	11·4	12·5	10·6	16·6	16·7	17·8	22·3	26·5
Yugoslavia										
Imports	15·6	17·6	19·3	17·7	13·2	13·9	16·2	26·7	32·4	39·4
Exports	8·5	11·7	11·3	11·3	13·9	15·4	18·6	23·7	21·7	42·0
Bulgaria										
Imports	22·2	23·2	23·3	25·9	38·2	40·2	53·5	61·0	54·8	52·0
Exports	29·9	26·2	29·5	26·0	36·0	42·8	38·0	47·6	43·1	59·0
Greece										
Imports	9·4	10·4	12·2	9·6	10·1	14·7	18·7	22·4	27·2	29·5
Exports	23·2	23·3	14·0	14·5	17·1	22·5	29·7	36·4	31·0	40·3

[1] Based on C. A. Macartney and A. W. Palmer, *Independent Eastern Europe* (London, 1962), p. 315.

Table 40   *Percentage of Czechoslovak foreign trade with Germany*[1]

Year	Exports	Imports
1931	18·1	26·9
1932	19·6	22·9
1933	19·1	19·5
1934	25·3	16·4
1935	15·4	17·0
1936	15·3	17·3

[1] Based on *Annuaire statistique de la République tchécoslovaque* (Prague, 1933–8).

Table 41   *Poland's trade with Germany*[1]

Category	1928	1932	1934	1938
Import	26·8	20·1	13·6	23·0[2]
Export	34·2	16·2	16·6	24·1[2]

[1] Based on W. Markert (ed.), *Osteuropa-Handbuch Polen* (Cologne, 1959), p. 95.
[2] Includes Austria.

Some statistics on the Jewish problem

Three countries in Eastern Europe where the Jewish problem was particularly acute were Poland, Hungary and Rumania. Tables 42–60 show the distribution and occupational structure of the Jews in these three countries.

Table 42   *Where the Jews lived in Poland in 1931*[1]

Area	Percentage of Jewish population	Percentage of total population
Towns with more than 20,000 inhabitants	46·5	26·4
Towns with less than 20,000 inhabitants	29·9	28·8
In villages and in the country	23·6	3·2
	100·0	10·5

[1] F. Beranek, 'Das Judentum in Polen', in W. Markert (ed.), *Osteuropa-Handbuch Polen* (Cologne, 1959), p. 120.

Table 43   *Distribution of Jews in Poland in 1921*[1]

Areas	Number (000s)	Percentage of population
Former German areas	21	0·67
Former Austrian areas	607	10·00
Former Russian areas	2,217	12·00

[1] Based on J. Parkes, *The Emergence of the Jewish Problem* (Oxford, 1946), p. 131.

Table 44   *Language of the Jews in Poland according to the census of 1931*[1]

Language	%
Yiddish	79·9
Hebrew	7·8
Polish	11·9
Other	0·4
	100·0

[1] Based on *Statystyka Polska*, ser. CIVa, table 4.

Table 45   *Occupation of the Jews in Poland according to the census of 1921*[1]

Occupation	Number of Jews employed	Percentage of all employed Jews	Percentage of Jews to non-Jews
Agriculture	89,987	*9·5*	0·9
Mining and industry[2]		*31·7*	
Iron, steel, etc.	14,420	1·5	15·7
Textiles	24,408	2·6	14·8
Fur and tanning	11,043	1·2	43·6
Timber	19,728	2·1	16·8
Food	45,783	4·9	30·0
Clothing	138,747	14·8	41·7
Building	13,277	1·4	12·7
Miscellaneous	30,011	3·2	10·8
Commerce and insurance		*34·5*	
General commerce	288,685	30·7	73·8
Hotel industry	17,124	1·8	23·1
Accessory trades to commerce	14,781	1·6	81·4
Miscellaneous	4,025	0·4	11·5
Communications and transport		*2·6*	
Post office	457	0·0	1·7
Railways and tramways	1,479	0·1	0·8
Other transport	11,789	1·3	42·5
Accessory trades	11,802	1·2	67·8
Public employment, liberal professions, etc.		*2·2*	
Public services, magistrature and bar	5,618	0·6	0·2
Health	7,278	0·8	17·6
Public institutions	1,779	0·2	11·9
Religion	5,245	0·6	17·1
Education	17,969	*1·9*	19·4
Science, literature, art	370	*0·0*	12·3
Entertainment, sport	2,261	*0·2*	24·4
Army, navy, air force	15,393	*1·6*	4·4
Domestic service	46,121	*4·9*	16·7
Unemployed, etc.	15,734	*1·7*	8·4
Independent	51,472	*5·5*	22·2
Uncertain	33,419	*3·5*	13·6

[1] Based on J. Parkes, *The Emergence of the Jewish Problem* (Oxford, 1946), p. 239.

[2] One should also note that, according to A. Tartakower, 'Zawodowa i społeczna struktura żydów w Polsce odrodzonej', *Żydzi w Polsce Odrodzonej* (Warsaw, 1931), 11, pp. 469–70, Jews constituted 39·7 per cent of all artisans in Poland.

Table 46   *Jewish population of Hungary*[1]

Year	Number (000s)	%
1920	473	5·9

[1] From R. L. Braham (ed.), *Hungarian–Jewish Studies*, (New York, 1966), vol. I, p. 142.

Table 47   *Jews as percentage of urban population*[1]

Sátoraljaujhely	30·2
Kisvárda	30·2
Budapest	23·2
Balassagyarmat	21·1
Ujpest	19·7

[1] From R. L. Braham (ed.), *Hungarian-Jewish Studies* (New York, 1966), vol. I, p. 144.

Table 48   *Percentage of Jews in Hungary living in Budapest*[1]

Jews living in Budapest	45·5
Jews living elsewhere	54·5

[1] Based on R. L. Braham (ed.), *Hungarian-Jewish Studies* (New York, 1966), vol. I, p. 142.

Table 49   *Distribution of the Jews by main categories of occupation in Hungary in 1920*[1]

Main occupational category	Number of Jews employed	National percentage within the given occupation	
Agriculture			*0·4*
Owners of large estates	117	19·6	
Owners of medium-size estates	738	11·1	
Tenants renting large and medium-size farms	891	34·2	
Owners and tenants of small farms	4,665	26·4	
Owners of extremely small farms and farm labourers	2,244	0·1	
Mining			*1·4*
Owners of mines	11	12·1	
White- and blue-collar workers	466	1·3	
Trade and industry			*10·3*
Owners of large and medium-size industrial enterprises	1,109	40·5	
Self-employed tradesmen	26,981	12·0	
White-collar industrial workers	10,097	39·0	
Blue-collar industrial workers	33,010	7·5	
Commerce and banking			*45·1*
Self-employed merchants	40,275	53·8	
White-collar workers in commerce	22,097	46·5	
Blue-collar workers in commerce	18,891	32·6	
Transportation			
White- and blue-collar workers in transportation	6,516		*5·7*
Civil service			
Members of parliament	15	5·7	
Justices, district attorneys	53	12·1	
Civil servants	3,846	5·1	
Education			
University professors	52	5·0	
'High-school' teachers	702	9·0	
'Grade-school' teachers	1,042	5·3	
Kindergarten teachers	31	1·8	
Professionals			
Physicians	2,153	46·3	
Self-employed pharmacists	250	21·4	
Employed pharmacists	377	25·5	
Veterinarians	286	41·3	

[1] Based on R. L. Braham (ed.), *Hungarian-Jewish Studies*, New York, 1969, vol. II, pp. 146–8.

Table 49—*contd.*

Main occupational category	Number of Jews employed	National percentage within the given occupation	
Engineers, chemists (self-employed)	381	39·1	
Lawyers	2,306	50·6	
Lawyer-candidates	322	42·1	
Art, literature, press			
Writers, journalists	365	34·3	
Painters, sculptors	176	16·8	
Singers and musicians	145	24·5	
Actors	521	22·7	
Rentiers			
Capitalists and pensioners	10,482		10·6
Various occupations			
Other white-collar workers	4,452	16·1	
Other auxiliary personnel	1,468	3·1	
Various other self-employed persons	53	12·1	
Midwives	264	5·2	
Armed forces			
Officers, military employees	148	1·6	
Non-commissioned officers	823	3·9	
Rank and file personnel	1,464	2·9	
Day-labourers, domestics	3,607		1·7
Other	2,575		5·2

Table 50   *Distribution of Jewish-owned industrial plants 1920*[1]

Category	All plants	Owned by Jews
Total	2,739	1,109 (40·5%)
Iron and metal industry		89
Manufacture of machinery, means of transportation, electric appliances, musical instruments, scientific instruments and appliances and educational aids		60
Public power stations for the generation of electric energy		15
Stone, earthenware, clay, asbestos and glass		183
Lumber and glue		119
Leather, bristle, fur, feather, oil, cloth and rubber		55
Textiles		90
Clothing		65
Paper		26
Manufacture of food, beverages, tobacco, etc.		268
Chemicals		92
Mimeographing and copying		47

[1] Based on R. L. Braham (ed.), *Hungarian-Jewish Studies* (New York, 1969), vol. II, p. 79.

Table 51   *Occupations of gainfully employed Jews in Hungary in 1920 compared to those of non-Jews*[1]

Occupation	Percentage of Jews	Percentage of non-Jews
Agricultural and non-agricultural pursuits		
Agricultural pursuits	4·42	56·39
Non-agricultural pursuits	95·58	43·61
	100·00	100·00
Non-agricultural pursuits		
Industry	35·7	50·2
Commerce	44·1	11·4
Public service and liberal professions	9·0	10·3
Communications and transport	4·0	10·3
Other	7·2	17·8
	100·0	100·0

[1] Based on *Statistics of Jews 1931* (New York, 1931), pp. 52–4.

Table 52   *Number of Jews in Rumania in 1924*[1]

Region	000s	%
Total	780	5
Regat	230	
Bessarabia	230	
Bukovina	120	
Transylvania	200	

[1] Based on 'Rumania', *Encyclopedia Judaica* (Jerusalem, 1971), vol. XIV, p. 397.

Table 53   *Jews as percentage of population in different parts of Rumania*[1]

Region	%
Oltenia (Wallachia)	2·31
Muntenia (Wallachia)	7·54
Moldavia	15·65
Dobrudja	4·10
Bessarabia	16·03
Bukovina	20·48
Transylvania	7·21
Banat	13·41

[1] H. Shuster, *Die Judenfrage in Rumanien* (Leipzig, 1939), pp. 125–8. These figures are almost certainly too high, but give a general indication of areas of Jewish concentration.

Table 54   *Jews as a percentage of the urban population in certain Rumanian provinces according to the census of 1930 (percentage of Mosaic persuasion)*[1]

Muntenia	8·4
Moldavia	23·6
Banat	7·2
Crişana-Maramureş	19·3

[1] H. Shuster, *Die Judenfrage in Rumanien* (Leipzig, 1939), p. 121.

Table 55   *Where the Jews lived in Regatine Rumania: location of Jewish population according to the census of 1899*[1]

Area	Percentage of Jews	Percentage of Jews to non-Jews
Towns	79·73	32·10
Countryside	20·27	1·10

[1] Based on 'Rumania', *Encyclopedia Judaica*, vol. XIV, p. 397.

Table 56   *Percentage of Jews in certain Moldavian towns in 1889*[1]

Falticeni	57
Dorohoiu	53·6
Botoșani	51·8
Jassy	50·8

[1] Based on 'Rumania', *Encyclopedia Judaica*, vol. XIV, p. 397.

Table 57   *Occupational structure of Jews in Regatine Rumania in 1899* (%)[1]

Agriculture	2·5
Industry and crafts	42·6
Trade and banking	37·9
Liberal professions	3·2
Other	13·8
	100·0

[1] Based on 'Rumania', *Encyclopedia Judaica*, vol. XIV, p. 398.

Table 58   *Jewish participation in certain occupations in Regatine Rumania in 1904* (%)[1]

Merchants		*21·7*
Artisans		*20·07*
Engraving	81·3	
Tinsmiths	76	
Watchmakers	75·9	
Bookbinders	74·6	
Hatmakers	64·9	
Upholsterers	64·3	
Officials and workers in industrial enterprises		*5·3*
Doctors		*3·8*

[1] Based on 'Rumania', *Encyclopedia Judaica*, vol. XIV, p. 398.

Table 59   *Jewish factory owners in Rumania*
$(\%)^1$

Total (625 firms)		19·5
Of which:		
Glass industry	52·8	
Wood and furniture	32·4	
Clothing	32·4	
Textiles	26·5	

[1] Based on 'Rumania', *Encyclopedia Judaica*,
vol. XIV, p. 398.

Table 60   *Occupational distribution of Jews in Bessarabia in 1930*[1]

Industry and crafts	24·8
Trade and banking	51·5
Liberal professions	2·9
Miscellaneous	8·2

[1] Based on 'Rumania', *Encyclopedia Judaica*,
vol. XIV, p. 398.

Suggestions
for further reading

This list does not in any sense pretend to completeness. What I have attempted to do is to list a number of books on the various countries dealt with in this book to enable students to follow up some of the themes I have discussed. I have limited myself to books in English, except where there were obvious gaps. Where this is the case, I have given references in western languages (French and German). I have omitted books in East European languages.

General books

Of the general studies of Eastern Europe between the wars, the most detailed is C. A. Macartney and A. W. Palmer, *Independent Eastern Europe* (London, 1962). It is particularly strong on foreign policy and has an excellent bibliography. H. Seton-Watson's *Eastern Europe between the Wars* (Cambridge, 1945) gives a vivid picture, written shortly after the events it describes, of the functioning of political life. The relevant sections in L. S. Stavrianos, *The Balkans since 1453* (New York, 1958), are very useful, and much interesting information is compactly presented in A. W. Palmer, *The Lands Between. A History of East-Central Europe since the Congress of Vienna* (London, 1970). G. D. Jackson, *Comintern and Peasant in Eastern Europe 1919–1930* (New York, 1966) has a good deal to say on the character of peasant politics. Useful journalistic accounts are provided by G. E. R. Gedye, *Heir to the Habsburgs* (London, 1932) and E. Wiskemann, *Undeclared War* (London, 1939).

The foreign policies of the great powers impinged continuously on the states of Eastern Europe. Considerations of space, however, make it impossible to mention more than a few books on this subject. On the

collapse of the Habsburg monarchy, useful accounts are provided by
Z. A. B. Zeman, *The Break-up of the Habsburg Empire 1914–1918*
(Oxford, 1961) and A. J. May, *The Passing of the Habsburg Monarchy*
(2 vols, London and Philadelphia, 1966). Sir Lewis Namier's essay
'The Downfall of the Habsburg Monarchy', which contains many
valuable insights, is reprinted in *Vanished Supremacies* (London,
1958). The most valuable book on the Peace Conference is still
Harold Nicolson's *Peacemaking* (London, 1933, and New York, 1966),
while much material relevant to Eastern Europe is included in
A. J. Mayer, *The Politics and Diplomacy of Peacemaking* (London
and New York, 1968). Three other useful books are I. Lederer,
Yugoslavia at the Paris Peace Conference (London and New Haven,
1963), S. D. Spector, *Roumania at the Paris Peace Conference* (New
York, 1962) and F. Deák, *Hungary at the Paris Peace Conference*
(New York, 1942). Deák's account should be compared with that of
H. W. V. Temperley, 'How the Hungarian frontiers were drawn',
Foreign Affairs, vol. VI, April 1928. A rather partisan account of
the re-emergence of Poland is provided by T. Komarnicki in *The
Rebirth of the Polish Republic* (London, 1957).

On French policy in the 1920s, much useful information is contained in D. S. Wandycz, *France and her Eastern Allies, 1919–1925*
(Minneapolis, 1962). Less satisfactory are two rather dated books by
R. Machray, *The Little Entente* (London, 1929) and *The Struggle for
the Danube and the Little Entente, 1929–1938* (London, 1938).

For the general background of German policy, H. C. Meyer,
Mitteleuropa in German Thought and Action, 1815–1945 (The
Hague, 1955) is interesting. German policy in the 1920s is described
by H. W. Gatzke, *Stresemann and the Rearmament of Germany*
(Baltimore, 1954), H. L. Bretton, *Stresemann and the Revision of
Versailles* (Stanford, 1953) and H. A. Turner, *Stresemann and the
Politics of the Weimar Republic* (Princeton, 1963). On the German
policy towards Poland, see H. von Riekhoff, *German-Polish Relations,
1918–1933* (Baltimore and London, 1972), C. H. Kimmich, *The Free
City: Danzig in German Foreign Policy, 1918–34* (New Haven and
London, 1968) and J. Korbel, *Poland between East and West. Soviet
and German Diplomacy towards Poland 1919–1933* (Princeton, 1963).
The two articles by Z. Gąsiorowski, 'Stresemann and Poland before
Locarno', *Journal of Central European Affairs*, vol. XVIII (1958),
no. 1, and 'Stresemann and Poland after Locarno', *Journal of
Central European Affairs*, vol. XVIII (1958), no. 3 are also significant.
On Soviet–German relations, there is much material, particularly on
the 1920s, in G. Freund, *Unholy Alliance* (London, 1957) and E. H.
Carr, *German–Soviet Relations between the Two World Wars, 1919–
1939* (Baltimore, 1951). For the late 1930s, R. J. Sontag and J. S.
Beddie (eds) *Nazi–Soviet Relations, 1939–1941; Documents from the*

Archives of the German Foreign Office (Washington, 1948) and G. L. Weinberg, *Germany and the Soviet Union* (Leiden, 1954). For Soviet policy, in general, the best account is unquestionably that of A. Ulam, *Expansionism and Coexistence. Soviet Foreign Policy, 1917–1967* (New York, 1968). M. Beloff, *The Foreign Policy of Soviet Russia* (2 vols, Oxford, 1947–9) still has much value.

There is an enormous literature on the crises of the 1930s, of which only a few items can be mentioned here. The period from 1934 onwards is comprehensively described in T. A. Lukacs, *The Great Powers and Eastern Europe* (New York, 1953), while the first years of Hitler's foreign policy are admirably dealt with in G. L. Weinberg, *The Foreign Policy of Hitler's Germany: Diplomatic Revolution in Europe, 1933–1936* (Chicago and London, 1970). For Italo–German relations, E. Wiskemann, *The Rome–Berlin Axis* (London, 1949) and M. Toscano, *The Origins of the Pact of Steel* (3rd rev. ed. Baltimore, 1967) are useful.

On Italy generally, M. H. H. Macartney and P. Cremona, *Italy's Foreign and Colonial Policy 1914–1937* (Oxford, 1938), though somewhat dated, is still valuable. Keith Robbin's account of *Munich, 1938* (London, 1968), is the most recent study to appear, while British policy and public opinion is surveyed in M. Gilbert and R. Gott, *The Appeasers* (London and New York, 1963). The view that Hitler did not deliberately plan war in September 1939 was expounded in a stimulating, though not entirely convincing, manner by A. J. P. Taylor in *The Origins of the Second World War* (London, 1961). Some of the more valuable products of the controversy which this thesis gave rise to are collected in E. M. Robertson, *The Origins of the Second World War, Historical Interpretations* (London, 1971).

A good deal of useful material exists on the economic problems of Eastern Europe. The general character of the economies of Eastern Europe is described in O. S. Morgan (ed.), *Agricultural Systems of Middle Europe: A Symposium* (New York, 1933), and W. E. Moore, *Economic Demography of Southern and Eastern Europe* (Geneva, 1945). The problems posed by the creation of independent states are discussed in S. Pasvolsky, *Economic Nationalism of the Danubian States* (New York, 1928), F. Hertz, *The Economic Problems of the Danubian States* (London, 1947) and the article by I. J. Berend, 'Economic Problems of the Danube Region after the Break-up of the Austro–Hungarian Monarchy', *Journal of Contemporary History*, vol. IV, no. 4. For the depression, useful works are the two League of Nations publications, *The League of Nations' Reconstruction Schemes of the Interwar Period* (Geneva, 1945) and *The Course and Phases of the World Economic Depression* (Geneva, 1945), as well as two articles, C. H. Lee, 'The Effects of the depression on primary producing countries', and H. Raupach, 'The impact of the Great Depression on

Eastern Europe', both in the *Journal of Contemporary History*, vol. IV, no. 4. German economic penetration is described in A. Basch, *The Danube Basin and the German Economic Sphere* (New York, 1944) and G. Schacher, *Central Europe and the Western World* (English ed., London, 1936).

The literature dealing with national minorities will mostly be dealt with under individual countries. But there are a number of books dealing with the subject which transcend national boundaries. Two valuable surveys are C. A. Macartney, *National States and National Minorities* (Oxford, 1934) and J. Robinson *et. al.*, *Were the Minorities Treaties a Failure?* (New York, 1943). On the Jewish question, probably the most acute of all minority problems in the area, there is useful material in O. Janowsky, *People at Bay: The Jewish Problem in East-Central Europe* (London, 1938), and A. Margolin, *The Jews of Eastern Europe* (New York, 1926).

Poland

Two useful introductory handbooks are B. Schmitt (ed.), *Poland* (Berkeley, 1945) and W. Markert (ed.), *Osteuropa–Handbuch Polen* (Cologne, 1959). W. F. Reddaway (ed.), *The Cambridge History of Poland*, vol. 2 (Cambridge, 1941) and A. Gieysztor *et. al.*, *History of Poland* (Warsaw, 1968) contain general accounts, both of the pre-independence years and of the interwar period. A useful short history of Poland in the twentieth century is H. Roos, *A History of Modern Poland* (London, 1966, translated from the German edition, Stuttgart, 1961) while a more detailed account of the interwar years is provided by A. Polonsky, *Politics in Independent Poland 1921–1939* (Oxford, 1972). A brief, but still valuable, account is that of F. Zweig, *Poland between Two Wars* (London, 1944). The perceptive observations of an acute American journalist are summarized in R. L. Buell, *Poland: Key to Europe* (London, 1939). A. Bromke makes some penetrating remarks on the character of Polish history in his *Poland's Politics: Idealism vs. Realism* (Cambridge, Mass., 1967). Older general accounts, now looking rather dated, are W. J. Rose's two books *The Rise of Polish Democracy* (London, 1944) and *Poland's Political Parties* (London, 1947). R. Machray's, *Poland 1914–31* (London, 1932) and *The Poland of Piłsudski* (London, 1936) are little more than chronicles, while W. F. Reddaway's biography *Marshal Piłsudski* (London, 1939) is rather uncritical. A selection of Piłsudski's own writings was translated, with an introduction by D. R. Gillie, as *Memories of a Polish Revolutionary and Soldier* (London, 1931).

On the crucial period of 1918–21, there are three new valuable books, M. K. Dziewanowski, *Joseph Piłsudski: A European Federalist*,

1918–1922, (Stanford, 1968), P. S. Wandycz, *Soviet–Polish Relations 1917–1921* (Cambridge, Mass., 1969) and N. Davies, *White Eagle, Red Star: The Polish–Soviet War*, 1919–1920 (London, 1972). Two other important monographs are M. K. Dziewanowski, *The Communist Party of Poland* (Cambridge, Mass., 1967) and J. Rothschild, *Piłsudski's Coup d'Etat* (New York, 1966). The chapter 'Poland' by S. Andreski in S. J. Woolf (ed.), *European Fascism* (London, 1968) is interesting on the Right-radical movements of the 1930s.

There is no satisfactory work in a western language on the Polish economy in the interwar years, though S. Taylor, *The Economic Development of Poland 1919–1950* (New York, 1952) will serve as an introduction, and there is some useful documentation in L. Wellisz, *Foreign Capital in Poland* (London, 1938). Important material on the social background of Polish politics is contained in W. Thomas and F. Znaniecki, *The Polish Peasants in Europe and America*, 5 vols (Boston, 1918) and in F. Gross, *The Polish Worker* (New York, 1946). On the Polish intelligentsia, there are useful articles by A. Hertz, 'The case of an East European Intelligentsia', *Journal of Central European Affairs*, vol. XI (1951), no. 1 and J. Szczepánski, 'The Polish intelligentsia: past and present', *World Politics* (1962), no. 3. The impact of the social structure on political life is discussed in A. Hertz, 'The social background of the pre-war Polish political structure', *Journal of Central European Affairs*, vol. II (1942), no. 2, and G. Kagan, 'Agrarian regime of pre-war Poland', *Journal of Central European Affairs*, vol. III (1943), no. 3.

On the minorities, a strongly anti-Polish account is given by S. Horak, *Poland and Her National Minorities* (New York, 1961). Useful material on the Germans is contained in I. F. D. Morrow, *The Peace Settlement in the German–Polish Borderlands* (Oxford, 1936), G. Kaeckenbeeck, *The International Experiment of Upper Silesia* (Oxford, 1942) and W. J. Rose, *The Drama of Upper Silesia* (London, 1936). A. Żółtowski, *Border of Europe*, (London, 1950) expounds the Polish point of view on Eastern Poland generally. For the Ukrainians, S. Vyvytsky and S. Baran, 'Western Ukraine under Poland', *Encyclopedia of the Ukraine;* for the Byelorussians, N. Vakar, *Belorussia: The Making of a Nation* (Cambridge, Mass., 1956), are useful. Two important works on the Jews are S. Segal, *The New Poland and the Jews*, (New York, 1950) and J. Gliksman, *L'Aspect économique de la question juive en Pologne* (Paris, 1929). A more recent article on this subject is E. Wynot's ' "A necessary cruelty". The emergence of official anti-Semitism in Poland 1936–39', *American Historical Review*, vol. 176 (1971), no. 4.

On foreign policy, in addition to the works by Korbel, von Riekhoff and Kimmich mentioned above, one should note R. Dębicki, *The Foreign Policy of Poland, 1919–1939* (New York, 1962) which provides a straightforward apologia for Polish policy. Z. Gąsiorowski has written two useful articles, 'Polish–Czechoslovak relations 1918–1922', *Slavonic and East European Review*, XXXV (December 1956) and 'Polish–Czechoslovak relations 1922–26', *Slavonic and East European Review*, XXXV (June 1957). His two subsequent articles, 'Did Piłsudski Attempt to Initiate a Preventive War in 1933?' *Journal of Modern History*, XXXVII (June 1955) and 'The Polish–German Non-aggression Pact of 1934', *Journal of Central European Affairs*, vol. XV (1955), no. 1, are indispensable for any understanding of Polish foreign policy in the thirties. B. Budurowycz provides a clear account in his *Polish–Soviet Relations, 1932–1939* (London and New York, 1963), while A. Cienciata defends Beck's policy in *Poland and the Western Powers, 1938–1939* (Toronto, 1968). Beck gave his own version of events in *Dernier Rapport: Politique Polonaise 1926–1939* (Neuchâtel, 1951). Other memoirs are those by two French ambassadors in Poland, J. Laroche, *La Pologne de Piłsudski; Souvenirs d'une ambassade, 1926–1935* (Paris, 1953) and L. Noel, *L'Aggression allemande contre la Pologne* (Paris, 1946), by the Permanent Under-Secretary in the Polish Foreign Office, Jan Szembek in *Journal 1933–39* (Paris, 1952) and by the Polish ambassadors in Berlin and Paris: J. Lipski, *Diplomat in Berlin, 1933–39* (New York, 1968) and J. Łukasiewicz, *Diplomat in Paris, 1936–1939* (New York, 1970).

Hungary

The outstanding work on interwar Hungary is C. A. Macartney's *October Fifteenth*, 2 vols (Edinburgh, 2nd ed., 1961). It is enormously detailed and, though its general right-wing bias should be noted, it draws a picture of striking vividness and authenticity. Shorter accounts are those by C. A. Macartney, *Hungary, a Short History* (Edinburgh, 1962) and D. Sinor, *History of Hungary* (London, 1959). On the nineteenth-century background, R. W. Seton-Watson, *Racial Problems in Hungary* (London, 1908) and O. Jászi, *The Dissolution of the Habsburg Monarchy* (Chicago, 1929) take a critical view of Hungarian policy. A more favourable account is contained in C. A. Macartney, *The Habsburg Empire, 1790–1918* (London, 1969). One final work of Macartney's should be noted, *Hungary and her Successors* (Oxford, 1937). Two useful brief introductions to the main problems of Hungary between the wars are J. Erös, 'Hungary' in S. J. Woolf, (ed.) *European Fascism*, (London, 1968) and I. Deák, 'Hungary' in E. Weber and H. Rogger (eds), *The European Right* (London, 1965).

For the Soviet period, there are two important recent works, R. Tökes, *Bela Kun and the Hungarian–Soviet Republic* (New York,

1967) and A. D. Low, *The Soviet Hungarian Republic and the Paris Peace Conference* (*Transactions of the American Philosophical Society* (Philadelphia), new ser., vol. 33, pt 10, December 1963). Two older books, still of some value, are O. Jászi, *Revolution and Counter-Revolution in Hungary* (London, 1924) and A. Kaas and F. de Lazarovics, *Bolshevism in Hungary* (London, 1931). The article by F. T. Zsuppan, 'The early activities of the Hungarian Communist Party, 1918–1919', *Slavonic and East European Review*, XLIII (June 1965), should also be noted. Károlyi gave his own version in *Fighting the World* (London, 1925) and *Faith with Illusion* (London, 1956).

Horthy's *Memoirs* (London, 1956) have little political content, but much more is included in M. Szinai and L. Szücs (eds), *The Confidential Papers of Admiral Horthy* (Budapest, 1966). The biography by O. Ruther, *Regent of Hungary* (London, 1939) is quite uncritical. N. Kállay, prime minister during the war, published an interesting memoir, *Hungarian Premier* (New York, 1954). On the Left between the wars, two useful articles have appeared, P. Ignotus, 'Radical writers in Hungary', *Journal of Contemporary History*, vol. 1, no. 2, and R. R. Tökes, 'Popular Front in Hungary', *Journal of Contemporary History*, vol. V, no. 3. On the important Jewish community see R. L. Braham, 'Hungarian Jewry: an historical retrospect', *Journal of Central European Affairs*, vol. XX (April 1960), no. 1.

Hungarian foreign policy in the 1930s is described in J. F. Montgomery, *Hungary, the Unwilling Satellite* (New York, 1947) and S. D. Kertesz, *Diplomacy in a Whirlpool: Hungary between Nazi Germany and Soviet Russia* (Notre Dame, Ind., 1953). Interesting information is also contained in the article by I. Berend and Y. Ranki, 'German–Hungarian relations following Hitler's rise to power', *Acta Historica*, VIII (Budapest, 1961). On the war years, J. Czebe and T. Pethi, *Hungary in World War II: A Military History of the Years of War* (Budapest, 1946) is useful, but needs to be used with caution. I. Boldizsar, *The Other Hungary* (Budapest, 1946) describes the anti-German resistance and A. Rozsnyoi, 'October Fifteenth 1944 (History of Szalasi's Putsch)', *Acta Historica*, VIII (Budapest, 1961) gives an account of the fall of Horthy. A recent book on Hungarian foreign policy during the war is M. D. Fenyo, *Hitler, Horthy and Hungary: German–Hungarian Relations, 1941–44* (New Haven and London, 1972).

Austria

The best short introduction is that by K. R. Stadler, *Austria* (London, 1971), while there is much of value in H. Benedikt (ed.), *Geschichte der Republik Österreich* (Munich, 1954). Briefer treatments are provided by A. G. Whiteside, 'Austria', in E. Weber and H. Rogger (eds) *The European Right* (London, 1965), and K. R. Stadler, 'Austria' in S. J. Woolf (ed.), *European Fascism* (London, 1968). On the pre-1914 background of Austrian Right-radicalism, see A. G. Whiteside, *Austrian National Socialism before 1918* (The Hague, 1962) and P. C. J. Pulzer, *The Rise of Political Anti-Semitism in Germany and Austria* (New York, 1964). The first years of the republic are described in K. R. Stadler, *The Birth of the Austrian Republic, 1918–1921* (Leiden, 1966). C. A. Gulick, *Austria: From Habsburg to Hitler*, 2 vols (Berkeley and Los Angeles, 1948) is a mammoth history of the republic from a Social Democrat viewpoint. Two other works written from a similar position are J. Braunthal, *The Tragedy of Austria* (London, 1948) and J. Buttinger, *In the Twilight of Socialism* (New York, 1953). More recently, interesting material on the Left has been presented in the articles by N. Leser, 'Austro-Marxism: A Reappraisal', *Journal of Contemporary History*, vol. 1, no. 2, and W. J. McGrath, 'Student Radicalism in Vienna', *Journal of Contemporary History*, vol. 2, no. 3.

On the Right, A. Diamant, *Austrian Catholics and the First Republic: Democracy, Capitalism and the Social Order, 1918–1934* (Princeton, 1960) deals with the period to the collapse of democracy. The Heimwehr is discussed by L. Jedlicka, 'The Austrian Heimwehr', *Journal of Contemporary History*, vol. I, no. 1, and C. A. Macartney, 'The Armed Formations in Austria', *International Affairs*, vol. 8, no. 6, November 1929, the biography of *Dollfuss* (London, 1961) by G. Brook-Shepherd is rather uncritical. The background to the Anschluss is described by Brook-Shepherd in *Anschluss: The Rape of Austria* (London, 1963) and, with more criticism of Austrian actions, by J. R. Gehl, in *Austria, Germany and the Anschluss, 1931–1938* (London, 1963).

The economic problems of Austria are described in K. W. Rothschild, *Austria's Economic Development between Two Wars* (London, 1947) and also in C. A. Macartney, *The Social Revolution in Austria* (Cambridge, 1926). A vivid account of Austria in the 1930s is provided by the veteran journalist, G. E. R. Gedye in *Fallen Bastions* (London, 1939). Two of the main figures of this period have given their own version of events, K. von Schuschnigg, *Farewell, Austria* (London, 1938) and *Austrian Requiem* (London, 1947) and E. R. Starhemberg, *Between Hitler and Mussolini* (London, 1942).

Rumania

H. L. Roberts, *Rumania: Political Problems of an Agrarian State* (New Haven, 1951) is an account of Rumanian politics set against a

200 Suggestions for further reading

detailed discussion of the state's economic problems. R. W. Seton-Watson's *A History of the Roumanians* (Cambridge, 1934) does not really go beyond 1920. J. S. Roucek, *Contemporary Roumania and her problems* (Palo Alto, 1932) does not go past the 1920s, while G. C. Logio, *Rumania* (Manchester, 1932) is a colourful journalistic account. Useful discussions of the agrarian problems of the country are I. L. Evans, *The Agrarian Revolution in Roumania* (Cambridge, 1924) and D. Mitrany, *The Land and the Peasant in Rumania* (London, 1930).

There are a number of useful articles on Right-radicalism in Rumania and on the Iron Guard: E. Weber, 'The men of the archangel', *Journal of Contemporary History*, vol. 1, no. 1; E. Weber, 'Romania' in E. Weber and H. Rogger (eds), *The European Right* (London, 1965), and Z. Barbu, 'Rumania' in S. J. Woolf (ed.), *European Fascism* (London, 1968). The Left is discussed in G. Ionescu, *Communism in Rumania, 1944–1962* (Oxford and New York, 1964) and B. Vago, 'Popular Front in Rumania and Hungary: a comparison', *Journal of Contemporary History*, vol. 5, no. 3.

Pro-Rumanian accounts of the situation in Transylvania are given by R. W. Seton-Watson, *Transylvania, a Key Problem* (London, 1943) and J. Dragomir, *La Transylvanie roumaine et ses minorités ethniques* (Bucharest, 1934). For pro-Hungarian views, see Z. de Szasz, *The Minorities in Roumanian Transylvania* (London 1927) and C. A. Macartney's *Hungary and her Successors* (Oxford, 1937). G. Castellan, 'The Germans of Rumania', *Journal of Contemporary History*, vol. VI, no. 1 is useful, while much material on Jews is contained in M. Broszat, *Das Dritte Reich und die Rumänische Judenpolitik* (Munich, 1958).

A. L. Easterman provides an account of Rumanian foreign policy favourable to the king in *King Carol, Hitler and Lupescu* (London, 1942). A more objective account is that of A. Hillgruber, *Hitler, König Carol und Marschall Antonescu* (Wiesbaden, 1954). Much interesting information is contained in the memoirs of the Rumanian Foreign Minister, G. Gafencu, *Prelude to the Russian Campaign* (London, 1945) and *Last Days of Europe* (London, 1947), and those of the Rumanian diplomat, A. Cretzianu, *The Lost Opportunity* (London, 1957).

Yugoslavia

Two useful introductory works are S. Clissold (ed.), *A Short History of Yugoslavia* (Cambridge, 1966) and R. J. Kerner (ed.), *Yugoslavia* (Berkeley, 1949). *Osteuropa-Handbuch Yugoslawien* (Cologne and Graz, 1954) edited by W. Markert has much of value, while an older but still interesting account is that by G. C. A. Beard and by G.

Radin, *The Balkan Pivot: Yugoslavia* (New York, 1929). On the
Serbs, H. W. V. Temperley's *History of Serbia* (London, 1917) is now
rather dated. *Serbia between East and West, 1903–8* (Stanford, 1954)
by W. Vucinich has much of interest outside its narrow chronological
limits. The wild atmosphere of Montenegro is well captured by
M. Djilas in his *Land without Justice* (New York, 1958).

On the South Slavs in Austria–Hungary, R. W. Seton-Watson's
Habsburg Monarchy (London, 1911) is still worth consulting. Two
histories of Croatia, both rather critical of Yugoslavia, are R. Kiszling,
Die Kroaten; der Schicksalsweg eines Sudslawenvolkes (Cologne and
Graz, 1956) and F. H. Eterovich (ed.), *Croatia; Land, People, Culture*
(Toronto, 1964). The history of the Slovenes down to 1910 is des-
cribed in D. Loncar, *The Slovenes, a Social History* (Cleveland,
1939), and in the interwar period as well in J. A. Arnez, *Slovenia in
European Affairs* (New York, 1958). Two valuable articles on the
emergence of Yugoslavia are C. Jelavich, 'Nicola P. Pasic: Greater
Serbia or Yugoslavia?', *Journal of Central European Affairs*, vol.
XVI (1956), no. 2, and D. Sepić, 'The Question of Yugoslav Union in
1918', *Journal of Contemporary History*, vol. III, no. 4.

The favourable account by S. Graham in his *Alexander of Yugoslavia* (London, 1938) should be set alongside the more critical work
of S. Pribicevic, *La Dictature du roi Alexandre* (Paris, 1933). Useful
articles on the royal dictatorship are those of R. W. Seton-Watson,
'The background of the Yugoslav dictatorship', *Slavonic and East
European Review*, X (December 1931), and 'The Yugoslav dictatorship', *International Affairs*, vol. II, January 1932 and those of H. Fish
Armstrong, 'The royal dictatorship in Yugoslavia', *Foreign Affairs*,
vol. 7, July and 'After the assassination of King Alexander', *Foreign
Affairs*, vol. 13, January 1935. J. B. Hoptner's *Yugoslavia in Crisis,
1934–41* (London and New York, 1962) is an excellent account of the
Regency. The revolution which brought King Peter to the throne is
described in D. Ristić, *Yugoslavia's Revolution of 1941* (University
Park, Pa., 1966; London, 1967). There is also some material in King
Peter's autobiography, *A King's Heritage* (London, 1955). On the
Left, much information is contained in I. Avakumovic, *History of the
Communist Party of Yugoslavia*, vol. I (Aberdeen, 1964) and D. A.
Tomasić, *National Communism and Soviet Strategy* (Washington,
1957). P. Auty, 'Popular Front in Yugoslavia', *Journal of Contem-
porary History*, vol. V, no. 3, is also useful.

For the Croat problem, the memoirs of the Croat leader, V. Maček,
In the Struggle for Freedom (New York, 1957) has large gaps, which
should be supplemented from Kiszling. L. Hory and M. Broszat,
Der Kroatische Ustascha-Staat, 1941–1945 (Stuttgart, 1964) is also
valuable. The agrarian problems of the state are analysed in J.
Tomasevich, *Peasants, Politics and Economic Change in Yugoslavia*

(Stanford, 1955), R. Trouton, *Peasant Renaissance in Yugoslavia, 1900–1950* (London, 1952) and R. M. Brashich, *Land Reform and Ownership in Yugoslavia, 1919–1953* (New York, 1954).

Foreign policy is described in J. B. Hoptner, 'Yugoslavia as neutralist, 1937', *Journal of Central European Affairs*, vol. XVI (1956), no. 2, and in R. L. Kneyevitch and D. Tsvetkovich, 'Prince Paul, Hitler and Salonika', *International Affairs*, vol. 27, January, October 1951. Also useful are St K. Pawlowitch, 'Yugoslavia and Rumania, 1941', *Journal of Central European Affairs*, vol. XXII (1964), no. 4, and the memoirs of Neville Henderson, who was British Ambassador in Belgrade, *Water under the Bridges* (London, 1945).

Czechoslovakia

R. W. Seton-Watson's *A History of the Czechs and Slovaks* (London, 1943) is still the best introduction. A good deal of useful information is contained in R. J. Kerner (ed.), *Czechoslovakia: Twenty Years of Independence* (Berkeley and Los Angeles, 1940) and S. H. Thomson, *Czechoslovakia in European History* (Princeton, 1943). S. Taborsky, *Czechoslovak Democracy at Work* (London, 1945), is rather uncritical, while V. Olivova, *The Doomed Democracy* (London, 1972), is somewhat thin on domestic politics.

Masaryk's memoirs, *The Making of a State* (London, 1927) are full on the achievement of independence, but do not say much on politics after 1918. The same is true of Beneš's *My War Memoirs* (London, 1928), while his *Memoirs* (London, 1954) describe the period after Munich. The book by M. Hodza, prime minister at the time of Munich, *Federation in Central Europe: Reflections and Reminiscences* (London, 1942), is basically an autobiography. A useful article on Masaryk is that by R. Szporluk, 'Masaryk's idea of democracy', *Slavonic and East European Review*, XLI, no. 96, (1962). Sir Compton MacKenzie's *Dr. Benes* (London, 1946) is in effect an official biography.

The standard account of the problem of the German minority is E. Wiskemann, *Czechs and Germans* (London, 1938, New York, 1967). On Slovakia, R. W. Seton-Watson, *Slovakia Then and Now* (London, 1931) is uncritical, while there is much useful material in Y. Jelinek, 'Storm-troopers in Slovakia: The Rodobrana and the Hlinka Guard', *Journal of Contemporary History*, vol. VI. no. 3. J. K. Hoensch, *Die Slowakei und Hitler's Ostopolitik: Hlinkas Slowakische Volkspartei zwischen Autonomie und Separation, 1938–1939* (Cologne, 1966) is a valuable account. On Sub-Carpatho Ruthenia material is hard to come by. Some information is contained in M. Yuhasz, *Wilson's Principles in Czechoslovakian Practice* (Homestead, Pa., 1929) and M. Winch, *Republic for a Day* (London, 1939).

A straightforward account of Czechoslovak policy is provided by F. J. Vondraček, *The Foreign Policy of Czechoslovakia, 1918–1935* (New York, 1937). Useful articles on this subject are P. E. Zinner, 'Czechoslovakia: the diplomacy of Edward Beneš' in G. A. Craig and F. Gilbert (eds), *The Diplomats, 1919–1939* (Princeton, 1953), G. L. Weinberg, 'Secret Hitler-Beneš negotiations in 1936–37', *Journal of Central European Affairs*, vol. XIX (1960), no. 4 and J. W. Bruegel, 'German diplomacy and the Sudeten question before 1938', *International Affairs*, vol. 37, no. 3, July 1961. D. Vital gives an interesting, if not entirely convincing, account of the Czech dilemma in 1938 in 'Czechoslovakia and the Powers, September 1938', *Journal of Contemporary History*, vol. I, no. 4. On the period after Munich, one should consult G. J. Kennan, *From Prague after Munich: Diplomatic Papers, 1938–1940* (Princeton, 1968), S. Grant Duff, *A German Protectorate: The Czechs under Nazi Rule* (London, 1942) and V. Mastny, *The Czechs under Nazi Rule* (New York and London, 1971).

Bulgaria

There is no history of Bulgaria in the interwar period in a Western language. G. C. Logio, *Bulgaria, Past and Present* (Manchester, 1936) is an interesting journalistic account. J. Rothschild, *The Communist Party of Bulgaria: Origins and Development, 1883–1936* (London, 1959) is particularly useful on the Stamboliisky period. On the IMRO, see J. Swire, *Bulgarian Conspiracy* (London, 1939) while on Macedonia, generally, E. Barker, *Macedonia. Its Place in Balkan Power Politics* (Oxford, 1950), is valuable. For the Left, see also N. Oren, 'Popular Front in Bulgaria', *Journal of Contemporary History*, vol. V, no. 3.

Greece

There are general accounts by J. Mavrogordato, *Modern Greece: A Chronicle and a Survey, 1800–1931* (London, 1931) and E. S. Forster, *A Short History of Modern Greece, 1821–1940* (London, 1941). On the attempt to create a Greek empire in Asia Minor, A. A. Dallas, *Greece's Anatolian Venture and After* (London, 1937) and D. Alastos, *Venezilos* (London, 1942).

Albania

For a general account of Albanian politics, see S. Skendi, *The Political Evolution of Albania, 1912–1944* (New York, 1944). Two books on the historical background are C. A. Chekrezi, *Albania Past and Present* (New York, 1919) and J. Swire, *Albania, The Rise of a Kingdom* (London, 1927).

Baltic states

Useful introductions are the Royal Institute of International Relations publications, *The Baltic States* (London, 1938) and the relevant sections in M. V. Graham, *New Governments in Eastern Europe* (London, 1928). On Soviet policy, see A. N. Tarulis, *Soviet Policy towards the Baltic States, 1918–1940* (Notre Dame, Ind., 1959). The loss of independence is described in A. Oras, *Baltic Eclipse* (London, 1948).

   J. Hampden Jackson's *Estonia* (London, 1941) is useful and there is much information in H. de Chambon, *La République d'Estonie* (Paris, 1936). A. Balmanis gives a general account in *A History of Latvia* (Princeton, 1951). Rather more is available on Lithuania. For more general works, see H. de Chambon, *La Lithuania moderne* (Paris, 1933) and B. V. Maciuka (ed.), *Lithuania in the Last Thirty Years* (New Haven, 1955). More specialized topics are discussed in A. E. Senn, *The Emergence of Modern Lithuania* (New York, 1959) and *The Great Powers, Lithuania and the Vilna Question* (Leiden, 1966), and in L. Sabaliunas *Lithuania in Crisis, Nationalism to Communism 1939–1940* (Bloomington, 1972).

Finland

A brief introduction which still has much of value is J. Hampden Jackson, *Finland* (London, 1938), while an enormous amount of useful information is contained in M. Rintala, *Three Generations: The Extreme Right Wing in Finnish Politics* (Bloomington, 1952). Interwar developments are well summarized by M. Rintala, 'Finland' in E. Weber and H. Rogger, *The European Right* (London, 1965), and A. F. Upton, 'Finland' in S. J. Woolf (ed.), *European Fascism* (London, 1968).

   M. Rintala has written several other important articles on the Right: 'An image of the European politics: the People's Patriotic Movement', *Journal of Central European Affairs*, vol. XXII (1962), no. 3, 'The politics of Gustaf Mannerheim', *Journal of Central European Affairs*, vol. XXI (1961), no. 1, and 'Vaino Tanner in Finnish politics', *American Slavonic and East European Review*, February 1961, while an older but still interesting work is S. H. Wuorinnen, *Nationalism in Modern Finland* (New York, 1931).

   J. H. Hodgson has described 'Finland's position in the Russian Empire 1905–1910' in *Journal of Central European Affairs*, vol. XX

(1960), no. 2. The civil war is dealt with by C. Jay Smith in *Finland and the Russian Revolution 1917–1922* (Athens, 1958) and by V. Rasila in 'The Finnish Civil War', *Scandinavian Economic History Review*, 1969. For the Left, there are J. H. Hodgson, *Communism in Finland: A History and an Interpretation* (Princeton, 1967), M. Rintala, 'The problem of generations in Finnish communism', *American Slavonic and East European Review*, April 1958 and D. Kirby, 'The Finnish Social Democratic Party and the Bolsheviks', *Journal of Contemporary History*, vol. VII, nos 1–2. L. C. Lundin's book, *Finland in the Second World War* (Bloomington, 1957) is also worth consulting.

Index